Tourist Behaviour and the Contemporary World

MIX
Paper from
responsible sources
FSC® C014540
www.fsc.org

ASPECTS OF TOURISM
Series Editors: Chris Cooper, *Oxford Brookes University, UK,* C. Michael Hall, *University of Canterbury, New Zealand* and Dallen J. Timothy *Arizona State University, USA*

Aspects of Tourism is an innovative, multifaceted series, which comprises authoritative reference handbooks on global tourism regions, research volumes, texts and monographs. It is designed to provide readers with the latest thinking on tourism worldwide and push back the frontiers of tourism knowledge. The volumes are authoritative, readable and user-friendly, providing accessible sources for further research. Books in the series are commissioned to probe the relationship between tourism and cognate subject areas such as strategy, development, retailing, sport and environmental studies.

Full details of all the books in this series and of all our other publications can be found on http://www.channelviewpublications.com, or by writing to Channel View Publications, St Nicholas House, 31–34 High Street, Bristol BS1 2AW, UK.

ASPECTS OF TOURISM
Series Editors: Chris Cooper, *Oxford Brookes University, UK,* C. Michael Hall, *University of Canterbury, New Zealand* and Dallen J. Timothy *Arizona State University, USA*

Tourist Behaviour and the Contemporary World

Philip L. Pearce

CHANNEL VIEW PUBLICATIONS
Bristol • Buffalo • Toronto

Library of Congress Cataloging in Publication Data
A catalog record for this book is available from the Library of Congress.
Pearce, Philip L.
Tourist Behaviour and the Contemporary World/Philip L. Pearce.
Aspects of Tourism: 51
Includes bibliographical references and index.
1. Travelers--Psychology. 2. Tourism--Psychological aspects. 3. Tourism--Social spects.
I. Title. II. Series.
G155.A1P36218 2011
306.4'819–dc23 2011027892

British Library Cataloguing in Publication Data
A catalogue entry for this book is available from the British Library.

ISBN-13: 978-1-84541-222-7 (hbk)
ISBN-13: 978-1-84541-221-0 (pbk)

Channel View Publications
UK: St Nicholas House, 31–34 High Street, Bristol BS1 2AW, UK.
USA: UTP, 2250 Military Road, Tonawanda, NY 14150, USA.
Canada: UTP, 5201 Dufferin Street, North York, Ontario M3H 5T8, Canada.

The policy of Multilingual Matters/Channel View Publications is to use papers that are
natural, renewable and recyclable products, made from wood grown in sustainable forests. In the manufacturing process of our books, and to further support our policy, preference is given to printers that have FSC and PEFC Chain of Custody certification. The FSC
and/or PEFC logos will appear on those books where full certification has been granted
to the printer concerned.

Typeset by Techset Composition Ltd., Salisbury, UK.
Printed and bound in Great Britain by Short Run Press Ltd.

Contents

Preface

The core aim of this book is to review and stimulate interest in a number of emerging and fresh topics in contemporary tourist behaviour and experience. In the existing tourism literature there are already many detailed and valuable contributions informing major issues such as tourists' destination selection and consumer satisfaction. Additionally, there are strong sets of studies in tourists' impacts, interpretation for tourists and tourist–local interaction. The topics covered in this volume are less developed. The work to be reviewed includes the effects of newer technologies on tourists' behaviour and experience, tourists' experience of safety and the responsibility they bear for their own well being, individual perspectives on sustainability, and some dimensions of tourists' personal development and connections to others.

The choice of these topics is inevitably personal and reflects the selections of one researcher. A key link among the relatively fresh topics chosen is that at the broad scale they represent powerful contemporary issues shaping the world of tourism today. Some of the key concerns of this volume are blossoming rapidly into substantial research fields in tourism analysis. Others are just emerging as new areas of interest.

In this book the topic areas are linked by pursuing a behavioural and experiential perspective which argues that studies of tourists' experience may be likened to attending to the work of a full orchestra. From this perspective there are multiple contributions to the ensemble of tourist experience. In the tourists' experiential world the contributing components to a holistic or orchestrated sense of experience are the sensory inputs, the affective reactions, the cognitive mechanisms used to think about and understand the setting, the actions undertaken and the relevant relationships which define the participants' world. These component parts of the experiential orchestra all provide different influences over time and situations to achieve the full effect. Researchers may isolate the components of the experience for analysis, but when doing so, need to be aware that the full experiential array may be richer than that described in one focused study. Behaviour and experience can be studied in an immediate or ongoing sense but more usually by later recall and analysis. In this book there will be a special emphasis on tourists' stories and accounts as a pathway to access the nature of the travel experience and tourists' behaviour.

For those who have already read similar volumes – examples might include my own earlier work in this area, Pearce (2005); the British perspectives on contemporary tourist behaviour offered by Bowen and Clarke (2009); the edited volumes by Pizam and Mansfeld (2000), Kozak and DeCrop (2009) or Morgan *et al.* (2010) – an incentive might be needed to undertake another tourist behaviour journey and traverse a similar landscape. In addition to the emphasis on the contemporary topics, three minor but hopefully appealing features can be promised.

The first somewhat novel feature is the inclusion of some tourists' tales. These accounts are extracted from previous research studies, tourists' websites and travel writing and will be used to enhance the readability of the text. Typically, they will be short pieces and provide a mix of personal and colourful accounts of the themes of the section. It will be argued that travel stories are not a minor entertainment in thinking about tourist experience – they are in fact at the very core of the analysis and provide insights of substance (cf. Moscardo, 2010a; Noy, 2005).

The second feature will be the inclusion of select visual material. The intention of using organising diagrams and select images is of course to enliven the text and to illustrate key points in the academic analysis. Again this approach, which appears to be simple, is deceptively complex. The perspective offered by diagrams and images as illustrations of research effort constitutes a different kind of language, accessed and recalled more clearly than pages of text. Readers are encouraged to linger over such material so that the possibilities for understanding sub sections of tourists' behaviour can be enhanced. While the format provided here is entirely about illustrating research-related issues in the main text, it is possible to envisage that researchers and readers who are also educators in tourism and allied courses could use this kind of format as a student exercise. The task for researchers and students alike is to see in the contexts depicted the ongoing operation of the ideas and conceptual schemes presented in the academic literature.

A final but recurring feature to encourage readers lies in the identification of research opportunities; that is prompts and suggestions for what can be done rather than just documenting what we know. These sections are identified at the end of each chapter under the heading 'Directions' but potential lines of further inquiry are also sometimes noted in the body of each chapter.

A volume in this rich and complex field by one author has some advantages. One author does have the opportunity to develop ideas across chapters and this practice has been adopted on this occasion. Such efforts are, however, never truly solo affairs. I would like to thank many colleagues and graduate students whose work influences my perspectives. In particular for this specific work I would like to thank those who provided immediate support; Robyn Yesberg, Huan (Ella) Lu, Tingzhen (Jane) Chen, Maoying Wu and John Pearce.

Philip L. Pearce
Townsville, James Cook University
Australia, 2011

1   Pathways to Understanding

Introduction

Smart tourists everywhere plan carefully for a successful holiday. They develop a clear sense of their destination and take with them only the luggage needed for the pursuit of their focused purposes. Astute preparation is also required to enjoy the benefits of this volume. Readers, in common with the tourists they study, need to know what locations will be visited and how the time spent at these destinations will be used. Where will we travel in the following pages? The major academic destinations in this volume include a consideration of technology and its influence on tourist behaviour; tourists' experience of safety and the responsibility they have for their own well being, individual perspectives on sustainability, and aspects of tourists' personal development. Tourists' concern for connecting to others through volunteering, their perceptions of poverty and the uses of humour will also be considered. In the final chapter a small set of supplementary topics will be noted including the experiences tourists have in the area of slow tourism and patterns of tipping and bargaining. This concluding section will also provide an overview of the linkages among the topics reviewed.

This chapter offers a gentle guide to this journey by outlining key foundation concepts pertinent to researching tourist behaviour and experience. The terms behaviour and experience will be considered and their close alignment in this volume explained. It will then be suggested that it is desirable for students and scholars of tourism to think about what constitutes theory in tourism studies and how researchers in this area approach the topic of relevance. These concerns will also be reviewed in this chapter together with an overview of the guiding schemes or paradigms in which research is conducted. Further, it is valuable for all researchers to build a familiarity with key organising concepts that illuminate much observed tourist behaviour and experience. Some of the key conceptual schemes used in the book will be briefly noted in this chapter.

Throughout this volume, key and solid references for many conceptual schemes of interest will be provided but we will attempt to avoid inundating the pages with exhaustive citations available in other locations. It is our aim to travel efficiently but not superficially. In earlier reviews of the psychology of tourist behaviour it was almost possible to catalogue the full array of pertinent studies to the many themes. That is no longer possible. The surge of publications and their availability reflects one key aspect of the world with which we will be concerned – the new levels of information access which shape how so many people now think and interact in the contemporary world. By adopting a light luggage approach to the journey it is hoped that readers will find space for their own souvenirs and emerge with fresh ideas from their reading.

Behaviour and Experience

The title of this volume refers to tourist behaviour and throughout the volume there is also a consistent concern with the topic of tourist experiences. What if any are the distinctions between these terms? To answer this question requires a short excursion into the history of psychology and the more recent rise of tourism studies. When psychology was established as a separate area of inquiry from philosophy in the late 19th century the new discipline was built on forging a scientific approach to the study of behaviour (Boring, 1950). Here the term behaviour included all external actions of human beings as well as all internal mental processes and reactions to the world – thus effectively embracing and including the concept of experiences. The term behaviour was therefore the inclusive or umbrella expression. For the decades from the 1880s to the 1930s it was unambiguous that the study of behaviour included the study of experience.

Behaviourism as an approach to the study of psychology commenced in the 1930s and persisted as a powerful influence until the 1970s. This style of work, which is most closely associated with the founding figures of Watson and Skinner, placed its emphasis on studying only externally visible and readily observed acts. Behaviourists did not disavow the existence of experience but for them it had no place in a scientific dialogue. Their efforts muddied the use of the terms behaviour and experience as the approach they advocated disassociated behaviour from experience.

The study of tourism emerged as a significant area of academic interest in the 1970s. For the geographers, sociologists, anthropologists, marketers and economists who first wrote about tourists and who were largely interested in the mental world of the tourist, there was wariness about using the term behaviour because of its restrictive use by some branches of psychology. While not fully conversant with the changing uses of the term in psychology they certainly did not want to limit their interests to observable actions. The concept of experiences became the preferred expression and was reinforced at the end of the century by the business authors Pine and Gilmore (1999) writing about the experience economy. This adoption of the new term of experience was particularly powerful in some parts of Europe. As studies of tourists' experience became more popular, some authors stressed that experience was also embodied, that is there is a need to consider the physical dimensions of human acts and actions (Morgan *et al.*, 2010; Uriely, 2005). In many ways those who had adopted the term experience recognised that behaviour mattered as well.

In the last two decades of the 20th century and in contemporary times the power of the behaviourist movement in psychology has diminished, some would say all but vanished. In the broad discipline of psychology the term behaviour has been consistently redeployed in the original way to mean both observable actions and the internal cognitive and affective world of individuals. The use of the term behaviour in the title of this volume is in line with its inclusive meaning. More specifically, the use of the term behaviour in this work asserts that we need to look at what people do and how their bodies function in time and space but we also need to link this examination with how they think, feel and react to tourism settings. Behaviour then in this volume will embrace observable actions as well as both the ongoing and reflective but less observable psychological reactions to all the contexts and stimuli which tourists may encounter.

Much recent tourism writing uses the term experience as the core expression to embrace these same areas of interest (Morgan *et al.*, 2010). While our brief historical review sees this use as redundant if behaviour is used in its fullest sense, it is the intent of this volume to communicate with all those interested in tourists' mental lives and travels so both expressions will be deployed in subsequent work. In summary, the compass of our interest thus includes tourists' sensory systems and emotions, their attitudes and their understanding as well as how they interact with others and move in space and time.

As a theme to help readers grasp the approach to experience adopted in this book the nature of experience may be likened to the music produced by an orchestra. There are multiple contributing sections, each of which has its own elements. These sources of influence contribute different component parts at different times to achieve the full musical effect. In the tourists' experiential world the contributing components are the sensory inputs, the affective reactions, the cognitive abilities to react to and understand the setting, the actions undertaken and the relevant relationships which define the participants' world. The component parts of these elements are sometimes more powerful than others such as when smell rather than sight dominates a food experience. Nevertheless, the totality of the food experience will also include affective, behavioural, cognitive and relationship contributions. Behaviour and experience can be studied as they occur or more usually by later recall and analysis. In the following chapters, the way experiences are presented in tourists' stories and accounts will be stressed. This approach expands upon and provides an alternate and sometimes richer and more holistic pathway to review how tourists think about their encounters and settings than relying solely on attitudinal studies (Pearce, 2010). The component parts of experience are itemised in Figure 1.1. The sources of this way of thinking about experience are derived from the work of Ryan (1997),

Key defining feature	Supportive elements and components	Major conceptual schemes employed in this volume
Sensory elements	Visual Hearing Smell Touch Taste Orienting responses	Urry's Gaze approach Panksepp's behavioural responses to stimuli
Affective components	A broad range of states including but not limited to the basic emotional categories (happiness, surprise, fear, joy, anxiety) Additional specific affective states include excitement, exhilaration, love, sympathy, indifference	Panksepp's core emotional responses Frederickson's broaden and build theory Pearce and Lee's travel career pattern approach Ruch's approach to humour
Cognitive elements	Perceiving Thinking Choosing Learning Character strengths	Goffman's frame analysis Langer's mindfulness Moscovici's social representations Zimbardo's time perception Attribution theory Positive psychology approaches Mundane and existential authenticity
Behavioural components	Technology linked behaviours Movement in space Movement over time Specific behaviours Sustainable behaviours	Social identity theory, Pro-social behaviour Bitgood's general value principle Crott's hotspot theory Ryan's routine activities perspective Crowding norms Ecological footprints Specific sustainability enhancing behaviours
Relationships	Intimate relationships Developing relationships Tourist local relationships	Equity theory Identity and social identity theory Social support

Figure 1.1 Linkages among key, supportive and conceptual elements in the orchestra of tourist experience

Ashcroft (2000), Schmitt (2003), Baerenholdt *et al.* (2004), Peters (2005), Pearce (2005) and some of the work of Cutler and Carmichael (2010).

Tourists: The Focus of Our Concern

One reasonably clear and initially satisfying approach to defining tourists, or at least international tourists, is to follow the criteria adopted by the United Nations World Tourism Organisation. This approach requires an individual to have crossed an international boundary for non-remuneration purposes and to have stayed for 24 hours but less than one year in that new setting. Certain exclusion principles add complexity to the definition (nomads, refugees and army personnel are not included as tourists nor are those who are involved in the diplomatic service, those who work across borders or those who are forced to resettle due to disaster or famine). The resulting statistics which are collected globally on the basis of this definition will tend to exaggerate the sheer numbers of tourists in countries which have many borders and through which many pass en route to other locations. Consequently tourists' lengths of stay and expenditure patterns become more compelling statistics when examining the scale of the tourist presence in any location (cf. Morrison, 2010).

Domestic tourists are somewhat harder to define. The approach appears to depend on the purpose of the tourism analyst. Ambiguities revolving around how far an individual has to travel, their trip purpose and their length of stay in the visited destination appear to be interpreted differently in diverse countries (cf. Masberg, 1998). The problem is simplified with an example. Are the father and the son travelling to another city 100 km away for the son to play junior sport domestic tourists? What if they stayed for the weekend? Does this make them more like tourists? And what if they were visiting a festival and not playing sport – would that also make them more 'tourist-like'? The questions raise more questions. Is there really something out there called a tourist – a species we will all recognise? The answer takes us into the territory of the nature of what is real (ontology) and how do we know and study what is real (epistemology) and beyond that to the paradigms of research which might usefully be employed to study the intricacies of tourists' experiences (cf. Tribe, 2009: 6). These are all concepts which must be considered further in the forthcoming phases of this chapter.

These difficulties have led one group of tourism researchers, and particularly those with a background in sociology or geography, to adopt what has been termed the new mobilities paradigm (Hall, 2005; Urry, 2000). At core this approach emphasises the commonalities amongst many travel behaviours and sees positive synergy, for example, in researching everyday commuting, weekend leisure travel and domestic tourism. It is congruent with the mobilities paradigm that residents sometimes report feeling like a tourist in less familiar or intensely structured recreational settings in their own

home towns. These local experiential realizations are additional considerations which will be considered at times as we review tourist behaviour.

More will be made of the use of the term paradigm later in this chapter,
but the value of grouping diverse travel categories together remains uncertain. Aramberri (2010) for example suggests that it is difficult to see that the
mobilities approach adds any value. It is perhaps an example of what has
been rather inelegantly labelled the difference between 'lumpers' and 'splitters' (Gold, 2002). The terms were initially used to describe differences in the
approach to taxonomic work in classifying species but have become more
widely used to describe approaches to identifying similarities or differences
amongst terms within other disciplines. The mobilities paradigm like other
lumping approaches consistently tries to create coherent patterns from much
diversity while splitters, by way of contrast, emphasise differences and prefer
to emphasise context and complexity.

For the purposes of this volume, a constructivist approach to defining
domestic tourists will be pursued. In this linguistic and ontological sense, we
create tourists with our definitions rather than set out to describe a fixed
entity. In particular it can be argued that we impose our definitional boundaries on the behaviours of people who travel. In this way we can firstly
identify prototypical tourists; those we see as sharing some but maybe not
all of the behaviours necessary for a meaningful, socially useful category to
exist. Pivotal considerations include being somewhere different, not being
paid for the experience, seeking to fulfil a pattern of predominantly leisure-
related motives and participating in the experience for shorter time periods.
Next, there are also travellers whom we can describe as exhibiting several of
the characteristics of our core domestic tourists. Here the travel to the different place may be shorter and the motives more a hybrid of work and leisure purposes. Finally there are some travellers who at times resemble the
first group of tourists' motives, on-site activities and outcomes. In such
instances, recurring and repetitive travel to a destination may differentiate
the individuals from those who frequent a destination only occasionally (cf.
Cohen, 1974).

This approach can be conceived as a set of onion rings or concentric circles with the innermost core comprised of sets of people exhibiting behaviours who most would label as typical of tourists whereas the outer rings
describe activities and experiences less commonly seen as warranting the
tourist label. In the more formal mathematical terms of fuzzy set theory,
there are people with high degrees of core membership and others where the
overlap with the core behaviours are tangential and fractional as befits the
notion of graded membership of a group (cf. Smithson & Verkuilen, 2006;
Zadeh, 1998).

Whether or not they acknowledge these conceptual roots, the definitional studies of tourists and tourists' roles which have been in the academic
literature for some time implicitly depend on these themes of either variation

from a central core or variations in the approach to lumping and splitting on select variables which produces alternate tourist forms (Cohen, 1974, 1979, 1984; Foo *et al.*, 2004; Gibson & Yiannakis, 2002; Wickens, 2002; Yiannakis & Gibson, 1992). The fuzzy set theory approach, in particular, offers rich views of the contrasting meanings of group membership and has been adopted in some recent as well as some formative tourism research (Cohen, 1974; Pearce, 1982; Woodside & Ahn, 2008).

In brief, the resolution to our fundamental definitional dilemma about domestic tourists can be seen as simple, if somewhat trite. Within certain constraints imposed by a sense of linguistic consensus, domestic tourists are those we want them to be. Certainly for the pragmatic purposes of tourism industry bodies there appears to be a political agenda to include as many visitors to a region as possible. In this approach all who are in the core, as well as all who surround such a symbolic centre, are counted as domestic tourists. Counting more people as domestic tourists can form stronger arguments for funding and power. For the management of people at tourist sites, whether this be in developed or developing countries, domestic tourists can be all those who visit, irrespective of the length and duration of their travels (Ghimire, 2001). And in our academic analyses the ways in which we construct a view of domestic tourists again depends on the sense of purpose for the studies and our inclination to assign tourists to full or partial set membership or pursue a lumping or splitting approach.

A particular consequence of the definitional variability which follows these choices is that the groups researched in separate studies may be quite different. For those seeking to understand contradictions in study findings, the very basis of sampling due to definitional differences is one source of variation among studies. A second and often overlooked source of difference across studies, the context of the tourism itself, will be considered in a subsequent section.

Since the term tourist is so central to the purpose of this volume there are further reasons to be very concerned about how we use the construct. As McCabe (2009) asserts, the concept of the tourist cannot be used without recognising that it is commonly associated with pejorative overtones both in public life and in academic circles. In this context several descriptive phrases, similes and metaphors creep into the research literature with notions that tourists swarm, flock to and invade destinations. At a more micro level of analysis the concept of the intelligent tourist is often viewed as an oxymoron despite attempts by some authors to advocate responsible and thoughtful travel behaviours (Horne, 1992; Swarbrooke, 1999). There are also unflattering descriptions of the physical appearance of many tourist groups. Most of the common jokes about tourists play on the notion that the tourist is foolish, awkward and opportunistic (refer to Table 1.1).

TABLE 1.1 JOKES ABOUT TOURISTS: THE COMIC VALUE OF THE ROLE

Novel requests

'Is that room service? Could you please send up a larger room?'

An American, travelling in Europe (asks the driver):

- Where are we?
- In Paris, sir.
- I don't need details, I mean what country?

Complaints made by holidaymakers to travel agents

On my holiday to Goa in India, I was disgusted to find that almost every restaurant served curry. I don't like spicy food at all.

The beach was too sandy.

We bought 'Ray-Ban' sunglasses for five Euros [£3.50. $5 USD] from a street trader, only to find out they were fake.

The brochure stated: 'No hairdressers at the accommodation'. We're trainee hairdressers – will we be OK staying here?

We had to queue outside with no air conditioning.

Queries to guides

On the Grand Canyon National Park

Was this man-made?

What time does the two o'clock bus leave?

On Mesa Verde National Park

Did people build this, or did Indians?

Why did they build the ruins so close to the road?

Do you know of any undiscovered ruins?

Why did the Indians decide to live in Colorado?

Questions to travel agents

Q: In coming to Australia from the USA, will I be able to see kangaroos in the street?

A: Depends how much you've been drinking.

Q: I am from the UK; can I wear high heels in Australia?

A: You are a British politician, right?

Q: I was in Australia in 1969 on R + R, and I want to contact the girl I dated while I was staying in Kings Cross. Can you help?

A: Yes, and you will still have to pay her by the hour.

Tourist interaction and experience

Westerners are met by some traditional looking primitive tribesmen in a rainforest setting. One says to his companion I think I will use some sign language to explain our needs. Just then a cell phone rings; an older tribesman pulls it from his side and says 'Ah Sting. How are you? About the conference ... the dates are looking difficult.'

(continued)

TABLE 1.1 CONTINUED

The aggressive western tourist in China had been complaining a great deal about the food. He summons the waitress holding out a piece of meat for inspection, "do you call that pig?' 'Which end of the fork, sir?' the waitress asks sweetly.

A young male tourist was flying across Europe. Next to him a very attractive girl sat reading a thick textbook. Seizing a chance to speak to her he asked: 'What are you studying?' I'm finishing my thesis about which group of men gives a woman the most sexual pleasure.' 'And what is the conclusion?' 'The two groups are Australians and Indians.' 'Nice to meet you, my name is Bruce Gandhi'

Novel requests http://www.shortjokes.com.au/jokes_Travel-and-tourist-jokes.html

Holiday complaints http://www.guy-sports.com/humor/jokes/jokes_travel_agent.htm

Queries to guides http://www.jokebuddha.com/web/5cx/Tourist

Questions to travel agents http://www.jokesphotos.com/2008/05/australian-tourist-jokes.html

Tourist interaction and experience http://www.awordinyoureye.com/jokes5thset.html; Cohen (2010)

The seeds of these ideas about tourists were planted a long time ago. Adam Smith, the defining figure in the construction of economic rationalism, had this to say about returning tourists in 1770. There is nothing:

> More conceited, more unprincipled, more dissipated and more incapable of serious application to either study or business. (in Hibbert, 1969: 224)

It is perhaps a short step from deriding tourists to adopting a superior tone to those who study them. This is familiar ground for those who explain academic status in terms of hierarchies of competing tribes and territories (Becher, 1989). McCabe highlights that these rhetorical uses of the term tourist, and by implication attitudes to tourism study, are phenomena to be explored in their own right. A particular implication for this volume and our immediate concern with the topic of defining tourists lies in being alert to the intrusion of judgemental and ideological perspectives when the term tourist is used. Our goal is to study tourists in all their complexity rather than prejudge behaviours and experiences through lenses shaped by self-serving status biases. There is of course the possibility of gaining other psychological insights by studying the views of those who hold such strong perspectives on tourists.

Whose Perspective?

Being alert to ideological and status-driven commentary on tourists is a useful item to include in our preparation for studying their behaviour and experiences. The challenge of defining what kinds of researcher perspectives can be employed in studies about tourists requires further elaboration. Wiseman (2007) suggests undertaking a small personal test. The task can be conceived as a brief act of reader involvement. Using the tip of your finger, trace the capital letter Q on your forehead. Now you have done that; which way did the tail of the Q face? Was it over your right eye or over your left eye?

It is suggested that this is a quick test as to how you are oriented to others. If the tail is over your right eye you have effectively drawn it so you can read it – possibly indicative of putting your own feelings and needs first. If you have drawn the tail of the Q facing over your left eye you are already sensitive to how others see you and perhaps you are thinking about their perspective. The Q test serves to introduce the fundamental emic and etic distinction in social science research. The emic view means to adopt the perspective of the participant, to see the world not from your point of view but from the point of view of the other. The etic perspective by way of contrast consists of imposing your perspective, your definition of reality on the observed phenomenon. The Q test analogy here is that the emic approach corresponds to drawing the letter Q so others can read it, while the etic view is to see the world only through your own eyes.

An emic approach to research, as opposed to an etic approach, was first suggested in 1967 by Pike, an anthropologist and linguist. The foundation idea is that emic research should be carried out so insider's perspectives, beliefs, thoughts and attitudes can be fully articulated. Pike's concept was further elaborated by Berry (1999), Feleppa (1986), Niblo and Jackson (2004), Walle (1997), Warner (1999) and other researchers in a wide range of areas. Such work has had a particular impact in observational methods in cross-cultural psychology and psychological anthropology (Flaherty et al., 1988). Some scholars have suggested that the emic approach is useful in all cross-cultural studies, as well as for many studies that deal with human relationships including tourism (Berry, 1999; Niblo & Jackson, 2004).

Cohen was the first researcher in tourism to advocate the emic approach (Cohen, 1979). He argued that it is not sufficient to study the touristic process from the outside, and the emic perspective of the different parties participating in the tourism process should hence be given explicit recognition in research design (Cohen, 1993). In the following years, this research approach has been supported and incorporated in many research efforts in the field. Evans-Pritchard (1989) emphasised hosts' perspectives to explore how 'they' (Native American) see 'us' (tourists and tourism in their communities). Pearce et al. (1996) reviewed literature in tourism community relationships research and reported the domination of survey studies which were etic in nature. They responded to Cohen's appeal and, using social representation theory, designed several emic studies assessing community reactions to tourism in regional Australia. For example respondents were asked to rate a list of impacts generated initially from assessing community views. They further developed the emic character of their work by asking respondents to assess the relative importance of the impacts.

Walle (1997) systematically introduced and compared emic and etic approaches, and advocated greater adoption of the former. The applicability of the emic approach to cross cultural research is especially marked. Tao (2006), in her study of tourism in indigenous communities in Taiwan, notes that contemporary tourism is primarily a western phenomenon, but it is imperative that researchers do not make assumptions for other cultures. Similarly, when examining the construction of post-modern tourist categories, Maoz and Bekerman (2010) adopted an emic approach to learn about tourists' views and self-perception. They argued that contemporary researchers using an emic approach should now revisit the previous claims made in earlier eras from etic perspectives (Maoz & Bekerman, 2010). The emic–etic distinction neatly addresses whose perspective we are considering as we approach the study of tourist behaviour. Other questions about our intentions and purposes in seeking to examine tourist behaviour also need to be addressed (Figure 1.2).

Theory and Relevance

Discussions about theory and relevance raise very fundamental questions; what do we think we are doing in tourism research and for whom are we doing it? Several forces shape the answers researchers are likely to give to these questions. First, there are cultural expectations about what an academic life should be about. This is not the same in every location and Galtung (1981) characterizes some of the differences as follows. In his view British and United States social scientists differ. Neither group, he asserts, is very strong on theory. Both groups have traditions of being helpful to industry, with the United States scholars strongly supporting the role of academic studies as one of informing better management (cf. Gunn, 1994; O'Leary, 2011; Pizam, 2011). Further he suggests British researchers are very concerned with scholarly documentation while United States social scientists tend to be more impressed with statistically based models. He suggests that German, or more broadly Teutonic researchers, seek purely deductive theory and use relevance principally as a touchstone for assessing their theoretical success (cf. Mazanec, 2011). French or Gallic researchers and those influenced by them are more concerned with grand perspectives. For the so-called Gallic researchers (and the expression might be extended to Spanish and Italian counterparts) theory matters, and the development and production of

Figure 1.2 Contrasting perspectives I:
This photograph was taken on Kuta beach, Bali, Indonesia. Together with its companion image it represents both in dress and intent the different perspectives of tourists and local workers. The women improving their suntan are from the Netherlands and the contrast between life in Amsterdam in November and beach life in Bali is considerable. In countries where having a suntan is still seen as healthy and an occasional opportunity, then basking until brown is an ongoing mark of status and a visible demonstration of holiday good times.
Contrasting perspectives II:
In common with local people in other sunny settings such as the Mediterranean, local Balinese cover up from the sun. This image of a massage worker who plies her trade on the beach as an approved and registered tourism employee is an outward demonstration of the emic–etic distinction. Establishing what the same physical setting means to different people and how they use and see it depends on spending time assessing their insider (emic) view of their circumstances rather than imposing an etic (external) perspective

theories is a primary academic task. Galtung's assertions are consistent with the view that critical and interpretive approaches for instance seem to have a stronger hold in European work, while essentially pragmatic studies concerned with the operations of tourism businesses are commonly found in North American countries as well as deriving from scholars in Asia influenced by US links (Pearce, 2004; Tribe, 2008; Zhang, 2003).

These observations force a direct questioning of what is seen as theory. Smith and Lee (2010) provide an overarching category scheme by itemising seven ways in which the term theory is used in tourism studies. Their scheme includes theories of the type found in the natural sciences; theory synonymous with an empirical model; theory equated with statistical analysis; theory as a verbal or graphic model; epistemology as theory; grounded theory, and the use of the term as an adjective or descriptor. In assessing these uses, Smith and Lee propose that only the first two categories should really be considered as theories and suggest that researchers in tourism sharpen their language in relation to the other five uses to avoid miscommunication.

The two elite categories they identify have the following core components; capable of providing an integrated understanding, potentially linked to other theories, desirably cast as set of propositions (possibly in mathematical language), and giving rise to specific predictions which may be reasonably tested by the collection of empirical evidence. These required elements of a sound theory are consistent with observations about theories from outside of the field of tourism with the noted biologist Richard Dawkins (2009) dismissing criticism that evolution is only a theory with a trenchant defence of its power. He builds his case on the definition that a theory is: 'a scheme or system of ideas or statements held as an explanation or account of a group of facts or phenomena; a hypothesis that has been confirmed or established by observation or experiment, and is propounded as accounting for the known facts' (Dawkins, 2009: 9).

In addition to these broad cultural expectations about what researchers should be doing and views about what constitutes theory, there are arguably four forces which are important in determining the work which emerges within academic tourism research settings. These forces define what we do and what we think is important. The proposed four points of the academic compass are the value placed on the relevance of research, the status of tourism research in the academic life of the country, the freedom permitted to individuals to work in innovative ways and the machinery available in the country to foster knowledge management. All of these forces work in cooperation to shape the kinds of studies in tourist behaviour which inform this volume but the two of most interest in this context are relevance and the transfer of knowledge.

Tourism researchers, like many other social science academics, often have to confront the issue of relevance. The relevance push derives from industry practitioners and persons in government who require that their scholarly community provides useful or relevant insights into their world (Fuchs, 1992). Additionally, it can be proposed that many tourism academics have internalised this drive for relevance and seek to justify their work to others in their institution and beyond by outlining its commercial contribution and sometimes by its direct value to the host community. Relevance can be seen as having six dimensions. These can be identified as follows.

Time: There is potentially an immediate, mid-term, long term or even generational relevance for tourism studies.

Sector: There is sector and sub-sector relevance with the different applicability of work to the components of the total tourism phenomenon such as the hotel/accommodation sector, the transport sector and the attractions sector.

Spatial scale: There is relevance of spatial scale with some work being of local applicability some of regional consequence and other analyses of concern at a national or international scale.

Focus: As well as the relevance of scale there may be the focus or level of concentration which is concerned either with single units of operation or broader aggregations (such as one hotel or a hotel chain).

Domain: The content area of interest may be drawn from an economic, socio-cultural or environmental perspective – the three recognised tenets of the triple bottom line (Elkington, 1997). Recent writing on sustainability tends to add an administrative or managerial dimension to sustainability discussions as this dimension identifies capacity in a location to manage sustainability.

Style: Finally there is the relevance of style where either the approach to the topic (a way of conceptualising and assessing problems) or the immediacy and pragmatism of the data and results are the chief contributions.

Relevance has been interpreted in tourism as closely aligned to work which is short term, local, sector biased, unit oriented, economic and results driven. These are not inherently poor criteria; it is simply that other criteria also matter. Work in other styles can be relevant and valuable and, as the sophistication of the research community and its users grow, it can be anticipated that these wider frames of relevance will be better appreciated.

The limited ways in which relevance has been viewed is also connected to a simplistic view of knowledge transfer and knowledge management. This is a large discussion in contemporary tourism studies. Cooper (2006), among others, considers the transfer of tourism research to be a long-standing challenge 'with few advances so far' (Cooper, 2006: 48). One key to understanding the use of tourism research is to recognise that the pathways to its use are varied. Occasionally a direct application can be seen from one study. More often an iterative and then cumulative program of work is required and this program should give solid and reliable findings rather than scattered and idiosyncratic information. Even then, there may be circuitous pathways to the adoption of the research with multiple intermediaries between the researcher and the user. In this context an insightful guide is provided by the work of Flyvbjerg (2001) in his book *Making Social Science Matter*. The argument employed by Flyvberg and of use to tourism study is that in addition to their academic voices, researchers who want to make a difference have to develop alternative or parallel public and rhetorical voices. This is not quite the concept of the old-fashioned public intellectual but it is a view that the way to significant influence lies in engagement in the media, participation in public debates, submissions to hearings and policy processes as well as active membership of organisations. Additionally, identifying and influencing transmitters, those individuals who in turn influence others, is critical to knowledge transfer and ultimately uptake. As Crompton (2005) reports, it is arrogant for academics to simply believe that busy professionals will be able to find, read and sort through the implications of the necessarily formal and refereed academic work.

Key concepts from the expanding knowledge management literature have the specific potential to alter the directions and future trajectories of tourism research. The concepts which may provide a new way forward supplement Flyvberg's views and include knowledge capture, knowledge codification and knowledge diffusion (Cooper, 2006; see also Cooper & Sheldon, 2010). In essence, these terms describe a sequence of consultative and clear communication processes which can build better use of tourism and tourist behaviour studies.

Clearly discussions of theory and relevance in tourist behaviour study are complex. They may also evoke strong emotions. Mazanec (2011) restates the relevance divisions in tourism as the evolution of two poles, one of which serves industry and one which develops academic ideas. For younger researchers he recommends a deliberate choice 'Cling to one pole or get torn apart' (Mazanec, 2011: 92). He also identifies another schism; on this occasion he focuses on the style of research rather than its usefulness. He comments 'study mathematics and computer science first, before specializing in anything else. If this is (not) done, one has only two alternatives: muddling through as a lifelong dilettante in advanced methods, or becoming a narrative scientist confined by the ambiguity and fuzziness of natural language' (Mazanec, 2011: 92). Aramberri (2010) provides similar views noting the unsustainable separation within tourism research between 'the rants of cultural critics' and those from 'business schools who shirk from every possible theoretical confrontation' (Aramberri, 2010: 17–19).

These kinds of comments lead to two considerations which are essential to understanding tourist behaviour research. First, as has been argued elsewhere, conceptual schemes rather than attempts at large scale theories have much to offer tourism study (Pearce, 2005: 12–15). Such schemes can be depicted as sets of interrelated ideas and variables which illuminate specific areas of interest and while they may be similar to mini-theories they are more modest in their range and less likely to have a full base of propositions and implications. Second, the concern with theories and discussions of relevance exist within the broad sweep of paradigms of research and it is valuable to review these larger frames shaping academic inquiry before setting forth on the further investigation of contemporary tourist behaviour.

Paradigms

Changes in the meaning and use of the term paradigm have been underway for some time. Whereas the expression was once used to refer rather exclusively to describe a shared meaning about and agreed on ways to undertake research held by a community of scholarly practitioners, it is now often used to mean little more than a system or practice. We now hear football coaches talk about 'changing the paradigm' and politicians use expressions such as a 'new paradigm' in policy discussion. The elements of the term they are using are essentially about shifting from one approach or system to another. Kuhn (1962) the first to develop and write about scientific paradigms also had this element of meaning (approach to a topic) but the original use of the term had additional meanings. For Kuhn a paradigm was a 'policed' approach to research. In the original view, paradigms were 'enforced' in the sense that they were policed by grant authorities, journal editors, and panels responsible for academic promotion. Research paradigms, as Kuhn portrayed them, were underpinned by a specific ontology, an epistemological position, well-defined methodologies, plus commonly used methods and agreed-on criteria for good research. People practising outside of the shared and agreed on way of researching either had their work rejected or helped create a paradigm shift.

The number of paradigms which exist in the sense described by Kuhn and pertinent to tourism research is limited to five, possibly six, main groupings of academic communities. There are several valuable contemporary accounts of the differences and underpinning philosophies driving these ways of seeing and behaving as researchers (Tribe, 2009; Jennings, 2010). It is tempting to draw neat boxes around these paradigms and specify absolute characteristics, but the behaviour of researchers is not quite so rigidly organised in the tourism research field. Not only are there shades of meaning and some different labels and subtleties of interpretation by researchers, but tourism researchers appear also to be participants in different paradigms in different studies. Additionally discussions about paradigm membership are not a daily occurrence. Researchers can work within a tradition, that is within a framework of similar research and not even realise that they are making key assumptions and behaving according to a shared system of understanding until either someone verbally challenges them or their work gets rejected as 'not proper X'. Detailed discussions about these paradigms are available in many sources and in our endeavour to 'pack lightly' for our examination of tourist behaviour these core paradigms will be presented succinctly here. (For corroborating views and accounts see Harris, 2004; Jennings, 2010; Tribe, 2009.)

Positivism is the mainstream approach used in physical and natural sciences – also known as the 'hypothetico-deductive' approach – that is theory driven and built on hypotheses which are tested by data most often analysed with statistics (Outhwaite, 2000). For some this is the only paradigm which is true or proper science. An important link here can be established with the type 1 and 2 theories highlighted by Smith and Lee (2010). Such formal theories are almost exclusively likely to be located in a positivist paradigm. Post-positivism is a slightly adapted form of positivism somewhat more suitable to the interactive and complex nature of social science research where the influence of the observer and the observed on each other is rather more striking than in the physical world of natural science. The criteria for good research which drive the post-positivists – validity, reliability generalisability – are shared with the positivists. There is though a greater emphasis on checking the meaning of the situation to participants, with some sensitivity to the balance between etic (researcher-derived measures and categories) and emic (participant-derived views). Post-positivists think generalisations about behaviour and social issues are attainable only probabilistically and tentatively – they are never certain – but scholars can agree and draw closer to a workable consensus.

The constructivist or interpretive paradigm (both names are used with little variation in their meaning) has as its criteria for good research the careful articulation of the question, in particular not accepting power-laden questions; a respectful mode of inquiry concerning human dignity and well-being; an awareness of researchers' choices, and a presentation of those choices in the writing up of the study. There is also the distinctive ontological position held by interpretivists that reality as we know it is constructed among people only through agreed-on meanings and understandings. This approach also confers the perspective that multiple realities exist and can be presented in academic writing. The approach does not neglect evidence and it is characteristic of constructivist research that the cases for and against interpretations are delivered through detailed sourcing of interview material, text pages or relevant sources.

In the 1990s, the interpretive or constructivist position developed many adherents and it became somewhat fashionable for some sociologists, cultural studies commentators and philosophers of science to criticise science and the positivists. Sometimes these criticisms were not well informed – a bit like the earlier separation of science and the humanities in C.P. Snow's 1960 book *The Two Cultures*; a book which arguably exaggerated the differences by sampling extreme cases. The interchanges between scientists writing about what they do and sociologists of knowledge commenting on the nature of research became known as the 'science wars'. Alan Sokal, Professor of Physics at New York University, wrote a parody, a full comic send up of the social science critics of science, which was readily accepted as a serious critique in the journal *Social Text* (Gould, 2004). The event has become known as the Sokal hoax and was used as demonstrable evidence that the constructivist paradigm can be easily lampooned and that the critics of science are foolish. The episode can be seen as a reminder for all sides to be careful writing in this field so that superficial caricatures of complex and graded positions are not taken as the norm (Gould, 2004).

The critical realist paradigm offers something of a compromise position. In terms of ontology it adopts a realist view – there is a real world outside of the observer although our ability to know it is imperfect and there must be a wide examination to get to our best understanding. As an approach to epistemology, critical realists have a modified subjectivist epistemology; that is they suggest it is hard to separate ourselves from what we know but we can check the trustworthiness or credibility of our own or other people's positions through seeing what the studied community thinks of our account or how other researchers respond to our views. Good research for the critical realist resembles most closely the criteria held in high esteem by the post-positivists, although there are components of the critical realist position about which the constructivist adherents would feel reasonably comfortable. That is, critical realists seek objectivity in the research process and strive towards this goal even if it is difficult. They value thoughtful, purposive or theoretical sampling, prolonged engagement with respondents, standardised field notes, good records and transcripts, triangulation, peer review or debriefing of perspectives taken, inclusion of negative or opposing cases and a consideration and reasonable approach to alternative explanations.

One further paradigm known as critical theory also requires consideration. It is not a 'last is least issue' because the rise of this approach has been the subject of several substantial tourism conferences and publications. These approaches were initially developed in Europe but there are now contemporary adherents and special interest groups formed on several continents. Critical theory is known in some writing as the 'critical turn' – a view that researchers are coming to question the power and political underpinnings of what they do and to ask whose interests are served by their labours. Critical theorists depend on the insights of Wittgenstein and other analysts of language to understand that the way we use language perpetuates power and privilege. As an example, the notion that physical sciences are objective and social sciences subjective is a linguistic device – a classification that privileges one group (see also Gould, 2004).

Critical theorists are often actually trying to change situations not just understand them. The approach can be linked to a paradigm or approach identified in the 1980s as emancipatory with which it is similar. It is also allied to some of the intentions of feminist theory and more recently to queer theory (Swain & Momsen, 2002) – a position which questions the roles and labels for women and men and directs attention to the construction of power. If these approaches are seen as consistently different to critical theory views we will count six or so paradigms; if we choose to integrate them as specialist versions of critical theory then we have five major positions.

Critical theory with its emphasis on change is also potentially linked to action research which can be described as an iterative approach of participating in change through cycles of research influencing immediate action (McTaggart, 1991). Good research for critical theorists requires close attention to the meanings and implications of core concepts and an explicitly recorded transparency outlining the researcher's position in relation to controversial issues. Critical theorists usefully report the emic views of marginalised group (indigenous, disabled, front-line workers) and the value of the research is judged partly on its social import and its stimulus and role in expanding people's discourses or ways of seeing.

In reviewing studies of tourist behaviour in this volume, material published within the paradigmatic styles of all of main systems will be considered. Clearly the different approaches demand different skills from researchers and to some extent serve different purposes. For example, the relevance issues which were described previously are met in different ways and for different stakeholders by the efforts of critical theorists and positivists. The value of an eclectic approach to considering tourist behaviour studies lies in benefiting from the strengths of the varied approaches. At times this will require willingness to state a position or perspective about one's research intentions, even as a reviewer and author integrating other studies, while on other occasions the logic of the paradigm work being reviewed will demand a more formal approach to examining weaknesses and insights. The paradigm discussion like our consideration of emic and etic research and our examination of theories and preference for conceptual schemes assists in mapping out the territory to be traversed in this book. As many of the studies to be considered in later sections use different approaches and perspectives, readers will be referred repeatedly to the style of work being considered in the terms reviewed in this chapter. Other related ideas lie in wait to help plan our reading journey.

Levels of Analysis

A related construct worthy of attention as we prepare to examine tourist behaviour is known as the level of analysis. This can be conceived in two ways – either the choice of a disciplinary approach or the scale at which we contemplate public behaviour (Hofstede, 1995; Pearce & Coghlan, 2008). We can view tourists from different disciplinary perspectives – physiology, individual psychology, social psychology, micro or macro sociology or anthropology as well as some other hybrid disciplinary lenses or choices germane to tourism analysis. This volume will favour the narrower end of this spectrum as we focus on behaviour and experience rather than larger social processes and generalities. There is necessarily a close relationship between the disciplinary frameworks and the paradigms which dominate those disciplines so many of the comments previously developed about paradigmatic issues in tourism study will reappear when studies from disciplines allied to tourism research are employed in this volume.

Tourists may also be seen on different physical as opposed to disciplinary scales such as when we contemplate mass movements, rather than small groups or isolated individuals. Some of these diverse levels will be pursued when particular content themes such as safety issues, panic and sustainability are considered in subsequent chapters. These preliminary observations about levels of analysis serve to remind researchers and tourist analysts that there are diverse contexts to be considered in approaching the study of contemporary tourist behaviour and experience. As the focus of our interest in tourist behaviour develops it becomes more imperative both to define exactly the kinds of tourism research contexts in which we are especially interested and how to deal with differences in these settings.

Phenomenon Sampling

The discussion about paradigms and levels of analysis assists in the understanding of the diversity of phenomenon to be considered in tourist behaviour studies. In a positivist paradigm and physical science research world, the phenomena to be studied, for example interactions amongst chemical substances, are relatively invariant. Research in laboratories in Paris and New York are dealing with the same materials. For studies of tourists and tourism the contexts and locations are inevitably subtly different. Visitor centres for example, which are some of the few buildings globally built exclusively for tourist use, are subtly different according to their country of location and their purpose (cf. Pearce, 2004). It follows that the use of the centres and their influence on those who use them may not be invariant in the way that the physical scientist can guarantee when assessing standard combinations of chemical compounds.

Much attention is given in statistical texts to the topic of sampling. The application of most of this information to tourist research has been in the selection of individuals who are involved in survey or interview studies. Much less attention has been given to the way researchers sample the phenomenon in which the tourist behaviour is embedded. Often the consideration of this issue is minimal and limited to a few lines of descriptive text. If the purposes or goals of the research are to describe only that setting, then the issue of phenomenon sampling does not matter very much. It does, however, become a concern when researchers try to compare findings from apparently 'similar' settings but are unable to reconcile the results. The desirable goal of phenomenon sampling is to be able to categorise, or provide a pattern identifying the key dimensions creating variability within the phenomenon of interest.

Several illustrations may assist with the explanation of the approach. A researcher interested in family satisfaction with cruise ship holidays may only have the resources to study one location – that of Caribbean cruises. If the goal of the work is to produce findings which reach beyond the specific context, then a pre-investigation typology or map of the phenomenon of family cruises would be an additional achievement in the research. Such a map of the family cruise market might differentiate cruises on price, ship size, location, entertainment variety and so on. Multidimensional scaling is suited to the depiction of the similarity of entities in this approach and has been used to provide an overview of research for different kinds of tourist highways, visitor centres and tropical island tourism settings (Pearce & Fenton, 1994).

Sometimes the mapping of the differences in the phenomenon under consideration can be usefully achieved with a nested or hierarchically organised category scheme. As an example of this approach, Moscardo et al. (2000) presented a typology of the visiting friends and relatives market paying attention initially to the differences between those whose VFR visit was a major motive and those who contact known others as an incidental activity supplementing their overall trip purpose. As illustrated in Figure 1.3 other phenomenon defining variables were employed and included a consideration of whether the visiting parties were domestic or international visitors involved in long or short haul trips and staying with the visited parties or accommodating themselves elsewhere. A further distinction was noted between whether the visit consisted of visiting friends, visiting relatives or a mixture of both types of visitors. Subsequent research using the scheme has been able to detect and explain differences within parts of the VFR market segment (Pennington-Gray et al., 2003).

The issue of variability in tourism contexts helps explain why the kinds of grand theories preferred in the Gallic tradition and to a lesser extent in the Type 1 and Type 2 approaches to theory building as defined by Smith and Lee (2010) are somewhat unlikely in tourism studies. Context matters and the differences amongst contexts mean that broad cross situational generalizations are frequently going to fail due to the inherent variability in the phenomenon. For example we can consider, as many tourist researchers have done before us, the original work of MacCannell (1973, 1976). At core this account argues that tourists seek authenticity. The phenomenon sampling perspective on this assertion would be that some tourists may do so in some places, and possibly at some points in their travel life span. To these phenomenon-related considerations one can also add that the time at which the ideas about tourist behaviour and experience are formulated are also influential. The elucidation of when and how and why authenticity matters is a subtle route for inquiry which may augment and help specify the overall appropriateness of the proposal (cf. Aramberri, 2010). The approach may be likened to recommendations for big business. It has been suggested that a model for

Sector	Scope	Effort	Accommodation used	Focus of visit
Visiting Friends & Relatives As 1. Major Motive or Trip type, or 2. As one activity	Domestic	Short Haul	AFR (Accommodated solely with friends &/or relatives)	VF, VR, VFVR
			NAFR (Accommodated at least one night in commercial property)	VF, VR, VFVR
		Long Haul	AFR	VF, VR, VFVR
			NAFR	VF, VR, VFVR
	International	Short Haul	AFR	VF, VR, VFVR
			NAFR	VF, VR, VFVR
		Long Haul	AFR	VF, VR, VFVR
			NAFR	VF, VR, VFVR

Figure 1.3 An initial typology of VFR travel
Note:
VFR = visiting friends and relatives;
VF = visiting friends;
VR = visiting relatives;
VFVR = visiting both friends and relatives.
Source: Moscardo, G., Pearce, P., Morrison, A., Green, D., and O'Leary, J.T. (2000) Developing a typology for understanding visiting friends and relatives markets. *Journal of Travel Research* 38, 253.

large enterprises is to construct within their corridors fleet footed, nimble mini organisations capable of responding to specific context-dependent opportunities (Moss Kanter, 1989). Entitled when *Giants Learn to Dance* the work provides an analogy for the efforts of tourism researchers who can be seen as using a set of flexible conceptual schemes to address and attack clearly contextualised tourist behaviour issues rather than pursuing a monolithic goal of building overarching theory. In a more recent rendition of this same theme, Peters (2005: 48–66) stresses that the design of experiences and the delivery of ideas are likely to work best with contextually relevant approaches where the systems are elegant and focused.

Key Conceptual Schemes

A succinct guide to the key routes and pathways used to explain tourist behaviour represents the final preparation for the reader to make the most sense out of the coming chapters. There are 12 such items. Each approach is identified in the following paragraphs with indicative references. This documentation serves simply to highlight initial sources for those who wish to undertake further investigation of each approach. In this preparation chapter these conceptual schemes are being presented as advanced organisers; that is helpful guides to exploring the topic areas which follow in subsequent chapters.

The first conceptual scheme is a view of tourist motivation through (1) the travel career pattern model which is multimotive, dynamic and emphasises a tapestry of push forces (Pearce, 2005; Pearce & Lee, 2005). As a consequence of this approach to tourist motivation the view of tourist markets adopted in this volume emphasises (2) the specialisation to general interest gradient; that is degrees of interest in visited destinations (Prentice, 2003). Another conceptual approach of recurring interest is (3) role theory and this set of descriptive phrases pays attention to the roles in which tourists wish to be cast as well as those they may be forced to play (Goffman, 1959; Simmel, 1950). There is also an ongoing awareness that tourist experience is (4) an embodied process involving the physical world and the human body (Ashcroft, 2000). A central notion for understanding how visitors react to other people and settings lies in the application of the (5) mindfulness model which may also be cast as emphasising the psychology of possibility (Langer, 2009; Moscardo, 1999). A somewhat neglected factor in assessing how tourists behave is a consideration of the perception of time. The notion of (6) a positive past-focused present-modest future orientation to time also provides some understanding of tourists' responses to their world (Zimbardo & Boyd, 2008). The centrality of tourists' relationships, both their connections to the people they visit and those with whom they travel are also pivotal to tourists' good and bad times. The conceptual schemes of (7) equity theory and the (8) coordinated management of meaning help clarify, respectively, the balancing of rewards among interacting parties and the features of close cross national social interaction (Cronen & Shuter, 1983; Walster et al., 1973). In assessing the outcomes of tourist behaviour and experience for the tourists themselves (9) benchmarking and importance – performance approaches to satisfaction will be employed (Pearce, 2005). For the outcomes focused on learning and personal change some appraisals of (10) character strengths, emotions and human potential will be considered (Fredrickson, 2002;

Seligman, 2000). Allied to these assessments of the outcomes of travel will be the prevailing view that tourists' experiences may be viewed as post-experience attitudes which are traded in the form of (11) narratives with others (Noy, 2005). An overall integration of tourist values and knowledge in relation to any major topic is usefully integrated through considering the power of (12) social representations which are organising everyday theories shared with others on how aspects of the world do and should work (Moscovici, 1984). It is the interpretations of their experiences to themselves and the framing of these experiences as they report them to others which make travel such a social activity, not only in its production but through its extended consumption and reporting.

Topics to be Explored

As the specific topics in this volume are visited and the interesting components of these specific content areas revealed, other locally applicable conceptual schemes and insights will be highlighted. The topics which will capture our attention on this contemporary journey are the role of technology in the world of 21st century travel (Chapter 2), the difficulty of being a tourist in an at times dangerous and hostile world (Chapter 3), the pressure to develop sustainable tourist behaviours (Chapter 4), the learning and personal growth achieved through tourist experiences and relationships (Chapter 5) and the study of tourists linking to the needs of others (Chapter 6). The final component of the book (Chapter 7) will provide some further notes and integrative views of the journey. It is time to undertake these investigations of people who cross the borders and who seek new destinations in the complex contemporary world.

2 The Digital Tourist

Introduction

At all points in human history the prevailing nature and availability of technology has strongly shaped social life. Diamond (2005: 504–507) points out that advances in technology increase our ability to do many things – to move further and faster, to communicate with more people more often, to eat food sourced from distant locations, and to live longer and on the whole more comfortably. But technology bites back as well (Tenner, 1997). Using new technologies we are able to extract more from the world's resources and consume more but we also pollute the planet more making our world less rather than more liveable (Watts, 2010). New technology and media may connect special interest groups and like-minded communities but also expand the North–South split in human well being (Blainey, 2004: 447–449). Similarly, within privileged communities those individuals with access to the technologies underpinning the good life may be greatly advantaged compared to those who are unable to afford or know how to use the connections available to them (Grayling, 2005: 8–20). Both the positive benefits and unintended consequences of technology are also played out in the world of tourism and in particular in the ways today's technology influences the experiences of tourists.

This chapter pursues the duality of technology's influence – its promise and its pitfalls – on tourist behaviour. It is not the purpose of the chapter to be judgemental but rather to examine the way the paradigms of research have been active in this area and, further, to see what has not been studied and where more questions can be raised.

Such a vast topic as technology, which is effectively the delivery and application of the knowledge of the age to its society, needs to be considered in manageable units. The interest in this chapter is on technology's role in shaping key components of current rather than futuristic tourist experiences. The concern is not directly about the way tourism-related businesses use technology in their workplaces although some authors have pointed out that if technology does not ultimately enhance the customers' experiences then it may be serving the wrong organisational goals (Schmitt, 2003). In particular, the core units for consideration will be information use, and on-site applications of technology. Contemporary technologies are also used heavily in the recording of tourists' experiences most notably in the form of tourists reporting feedback on products and in recording travel blogs about their experiences. These narratives and reports will feature heavily in several other chapters of this volume. There is though a circularity of influence with these records of experiences. Since they are posted in a public domain, not only are they records about the travel but they act as resources for others to use to plan and shape travel choices and itineraries. This resource component of the recording of travel events and business appraisals will be explored in this chapter but more detailed appraisal of the meaning of the records and what they imply about tourist experience are contained in later parts of the volume.

Technology and Tourist Information

It is a brave act to cite any statistics about the overall use of technology-assisted access to tourism information. The access exists in multiple forms. Mobile phones, websites, Facebook and multiple media are key but not exhaustive components (Buhalis & Law, 2008; Lincoln, 2009). The uses of such technologies grow daily and are not easily monitored in any comprehensive way. Linear predictions of growth from earlier reports are unreliable because the technology evolves. Sheldon (1997: 88) one of the first tourism authors to write in detail about the links between tourism and technology cites 40 million users of the web in 1996. She noted that access to the information was provided by predominantly North American companies but was growing in Europe and would be available to all in the 21st century. More recently it has been suggested that internet use in developed countries is now stabilising at about 70% of the adult population (European Travel Commission, 2009). Irrespective of the precise figures used, it is clear that the power and the uses of the internet are having major global influences on tourists' access to pre-travel knowledge. China alone, for example, has 400 million users of the internet as the second decade of the 21st century unfolds (Watts, 2010). It appears to be clear that the citing of any specific number is likely to date rapidly but what is commonly agreed is that the transformative power of new technologies for tourism and tourist behaviour are considerable (Buhalis & Law, 2010; Wang et al., 2010).

A first consideration about technology provided information and the tourist experience can be identified as changes in the sources providing the material. In 20th century models of tourist information flow, suppliers provided information to potential customers in many forms but brochures, commercial advertising and information centre facilities played key roles. All of this material offered one view; that of the business to the customer. The models that were built in tourism studies of tourists' destination images and decision making were constructed by paying attention to the role of dominant information sources such as the media, travel agents, tour operators, and travel writers, as well as the depiction of destinations on film and through news stories (Gartner, 1993; Gunn, 1972). In these models it was also recognised that word of mouth was powerful and that travellers either by inquiring directly or simply by picking up information in conversation might also receive key tips from their contacts. It was of course an unstated component of these models that such direct word of mouth information was supplied by just a few people; those with whom the potential tourist could communicate.

The newer technologies have enabled the sharing of information about tourism destinations by a much wider network of contacts. Some of these contacts are known to the traveller, such as when friends and relatives record and report their travel experiences on line. Additionally there is also a vast new group of tourism information providers – the customers of the global tourism businesses who convey electronically their experiences of tourist destinations and products. One kind of information recorded by these tourists is illustrated in Table 2.1. The material in the table is a succinct revision of actual comments reported about accommodation in the commentary system entitled TripAdvisor. The comments raise a host of questions about the value and role of this kind of material in tourist information provision and the analyses of such remarks offer multiple research opportunities.

TABLE 2.1 TOURIST COMMENTARY ON ACCOMMODATION AS INFORMATION PROVISION

Property: Somewhere on the Beach, Queensland, Australia

'Great location for a beachy holiday'

Provided by Cathy who has made a total of 13 contributions
From Rockhampton, Queensland, Australia
October 2010 Trip type: couple on holiday
It is right on the beach precinct within walking distance to heaps of restaurants, and actually right across the road from the beach. We went and saw the footy when we stayed here, so it was great coz the bus stopped right out the front of the motel. We stayed in what was meant to be an 'Executive Deluxe' room. The room itself was great. Possibly newly renovated, but quite small. The TV was a good size, and there was a nice little kitchenette. The bathroom also looked new. Some of the furniture however was worn. There was a little balcony. There was only one chair at the table. The only view we had was overlooking the roof of the motel, the road, and the trees blocking the beach. But we could hear the water. That is my biggest gripe about this place. We spent a lot of money, thinking we would get a nice view, only to look at the road. Bit sad. The bed was

(Continued)

TABLE 2.1 CONTINUED

comfy. We didn't hear a lot of noise, so it was nice and relaxing. The service was okay. We had to check in late, so the key was left in a secure, accessible location. We didn't have a lot to do with reception, but on the morning we left, they called the maid to check the room before letting us leave. Found this a little odd. We also had to pay a deposit despite having fully paid for the room before staying there. Wasn't aware of these practices. Anyway, it was pretty good, but I don't think I'll go for an 'executive' room next time I stay. Maybe if I go for something cheaper, we will end up on a better level.

- My ratings for this hotel (out of 5)
  - Value 2
  - Rooms 4
  - Location 5
  - Cleanliness 4
  - Service 4
- Date of stay September 2010
- Visit was for leisure

'O.K. for 1 night'

Provided by mexicanbutterfly who has made a total of 11 contributions. From San Francisco, California USA

Nov 20, 2009 | Trip type: Friends getaway

There were 3 of us travelling we only planned to spend 1 night in the city. we got a cheap deal online and given that the hotel is advertised as 3 stars, we decided to go for it. I agree that the building itself is quite ugly and feels out of place but we thought that the beach strip was lovely and were glad we didn't stay downtown (i loved hanging out next door) as far as the room is concerned, it was quite small and very run down, frayed carpet and rusty bathroom, certainly NOT luxury. Since we were there for just 1 night, we didn't care too much. However, I just happened to sneak a peak at a refurbished room while the maid was cleaning and i must say, it was much nicer & comfy (tiled floors & new furniture) bottom line is this: location is great but if you book a cheap room, it'll be quite crummy and you'll get something decent if you're willing to upgrade.

- My ratings for this hotel
  - Value 2
  - Rooms 2
  - Location 4
  - Cleanliness 3
  - Service 3
- Date of stay November 2009
- Visit was for Leisure

(Continued)

TABLE 2.1 CONTINUED

'Adequete Only'

Provided by CuteEmmawho has made a total of 9 contributions. Brisbane
Oct 28, 2009 | Trip type: Business, Solo travel

I stayed here recently and booked through a 'last minute' hotel website. It
was advertised as being an 11–13 floor room – I got put on the 1st floor.
I didn't bother complaining because I was there for business and got in at
7 and was checking out the next day. Both people I talked to on Reception
were ok – but it seemed like everything was a chore and that they had
better things to do. My toilet did not flush properly and I woke up to ants
in my bed, even though I consumed no food in my room. The bathroom
was not very clean. It was advertised that there was a cafe in the hotel –
but I never saw it. The price was ok – within my business budget ... but
I have stayed at a lot nicer places for similar or less money. I would not
stay here again for a holiday.

- My ratings for this hotel
  - Value 3
  - Rooms 2
  - Location 5
  - Cleanliness 2
  - Service 2
- Date of stay October 2009
- Visit was for Business

'Brilliant View'

Provided by Faithwho has made a total of 5 contributions. Brisbane
July 2010 Trip type: Family travel

We stayed in July and absolutely loved it! I felt compelled to add a review
when I read the other review. Our experience was very positive. We stayed
in an end room on the 12th floor, so it was a bit roomier with a separate
kitchen area. This unit/room was beautifully renovated with comfy bed,
LCD TV, small sofa and nicely renovated bathroom. But above all was the
VIEW – absolutely spectacular – at any time of the day – the colours
changed with different light! There is a small balcony and I could sit
there forever! There are good options for dinner, coffee and wonderful
gelato just a short walk away. The beach area across the road is one of the
best water's edge developments I have seen – great playgrounds, water
park, walking area, ocean pool etc. As for the actual rooms/units which
are individually owned the standard can vary as I think some are not yet
renovated – so be sure and ask for one that has been and I'm sure you'll be
happy. By the way they don't have full cooking facilities – just microwave,
fridge, sink – enough for brekkie etc.

(Continued)

TABLE 2.1 CONTINUED

- My ratings for this hotel
  - Rooms 4
  - Location 5
  - Cleanliness 3
  - Service 4
- Date of stay July 2010
- Visit was for leisure

Adapted from TripAdvisor
Overall information:
The same site where these reviews are available had a total of 32 reviews
The property was ranked 3rd out of 21 in its city context.
The average of the rankings and assessments fell into the following categories:
Excellent = 4, very good = 11, Average = 7, Poor = 5, Terrible = 5

There are challenges in considering the power and the influence of the comments embodied in Table 2.1. Firstly, who writes and then who reads these sorts of the comments? How are they read? Is it by glancing at the first two or three or is it by searching for a really negative comment which overpowers all the others. Yet again, perhaps it is one positive attribute that matters to the potential tourist. It may be a comment on this issue – perhaps it is access, perhaps a component of cleanliness, perhaps the attitudes of staff – which is all important and the decision to use or avoid the business is dependent on this specific dimension. The important constructs of trust and similarity of the commentator to the tourist can also be suggested. Do the inspectors of these advisory notes trust the comments, bearing in mind that there are possibilities that businesses may pose as covert consumers and write flattering remarks? Or is there a diligent searching of the features of the people who post the comments to identify those closest to the tourist in age, gender, nationality, and travel experience or further still, is it the tone of the post in terms of word use and style? These are all questions where some research is underway but more studies are needed.

Technology Insights

A more detailed breakdown of some of the questions raised reveals some specific information of interest. The specific consideration of who contributes to online tourism communities has been underway for some time (Casalo *et al.*, 2010; Wang & Fesenmaier, 2003, 2004; Yoo & Gretzel, 2008). In an early study in the United States, Wang and Fesenmaier (2003) based their analysis of contributor motivation on ideas from social identity theory, pro-social behaviour (especially related to gift giving) and concepts from social capital. Using these ideas as well as recognising the role of individual personality factors and the importance of the ease of use of the technology to affect the likelihood of making online contributions, they built a model with online contribution as the dependent variable. The factors they considered explained 47% of the variance. The motives of the online contributors which were prominent in contributing to the successful model were labelled instrumental (predominantly a relationship building set of items), efficacy (a willingness to satisfy others and give advice) and expectancy (anticipating reciprocity from others). Both ease of communication components as well as 'helpful' personality characteristics were also contributors to the overall power of the model to explain the contributions. The respondents on whom the model was built were arguably a special group in that they were 'double contributors'-willing not only to contribute online comments but additionally willing to respond to a research survey about giving online advice and evaluations. A second study by the same authors explored more closely the factors affecting the level of involvement in the same online community. This variation on the first study revealed the strong positive link between high levels of involvement (amount and detail of the actual contributions) and the likelihood of making a further contribution (Wang & Fesenmaier, 2004).

Yoo and Gretzel (2008), again working in the United States, developed some slightly different motivational items with a stronger focus on motives previously reported as relevant to communicating in an internet environment (Hennig-Thurau et al., 2004). Using respondents from a TripAdvisor panel of site users they identified four factors; enjoyment and positive enhancement, venting negative feelings, concern for other consumers and helping the company. Only the venting negative feelings motive received a low importance rating with the other three motives being rated as highly important forces driving contributors' reasons for posting comments about tourism products.

Studies of the intentions to contribute to online communities are not confined to North America. The Spanish researchers Casalo et al. (2010) used ideas from a technology acceptance model combined with social identity theory and attitude theory to demonstrate that intention to again use the firm's products boosted the likelihood of making an online contribution. The construct of identification considered in their study provides an interesting link to one of our previous questions about the influence of online community information. In the Spanish study it was found that the degree to which individuals felt themselves to be a part of the group affected their eagerness to provide comments. The link to the earlier questions lies in suggesting that the degree to which the readers of the posts also feel themselves to be part of the community may affect their effort in searching and using the information.

Who then uses online services for travel information? Clearly many people do so and studies have focused on both the larger framework of asking how internet searching fits in with other modes of information hunting as well as investigating what kinds of tourists use the services. Lee et al. (2007), working in Australia, offer a rich view of these information search processes by comparing how potential tourists from six countries (United States, United Kingdom, New Zealand, Germany, South Korea and China) use internet sources, interpersonal sources, expert sources and media sources for different kinds of information. The varied information under investigation included destination details, pricing advice, accommodation options and flight schedules. They presented their findings using correspondence analysis which enabled them to depict the pattern of information searching for each country. The results highlighted some solid differences both for the type of information sought and the way in which tourists from different countries approached the task. For example, Chinese tourists as compared to all others did not use the internet as frequently for pricing, accommodation and flight information but they did use the web to the same extent for collecting destination-related material. The reliance on travel agents in China and New Zealand was the highest for all information sources while the United States and United Kingdom tourists were higher users of interpersonal information when considering the choice of destination. Travel and guide book information was used by over 50% of all tourist samples for destination information but was used with much lower frequencies for pricing and flight information. The subdivision of levels of use within the internet sources revealed internet travel sites to be regularly used (at least 40% by all countries for all information sources) with slightly lower rates of use for online newsletters/email updates and airline sites (at least 20% by all countries for all information sources). The study was conducted in reference to sourcing information for travel to Australia and consistent with the ideas about phenomenon sampling discussed in Chapter 1, this choice of destination may have affected the use of some sources. United Kingdom visitors, for example, are more likely to have had friends and contacts to question about the destination than are South Korean and Chinese tourists.

The widespread and frequent use of the internet for sourcing information for all types of travel relevant activities is confirmed in many other studies. Law et al. (2008) studied international visitors at the Hong Kong airport departure lounges and compared the satisfaction with internet information sources between mainland Chinese and United States tourists. The Chinese respondents were somewhat younger and less affluent in terms of annual income. There were significant differences in the reported evaluations with the Chinese travellers being less satisfied, more inclined to distrust the website information and slightly less likely to make repeat purchases from the sites than the United States tourists. As with all individual studies some cautionary remarks about these comparisons are needed. Not only are the two samples different in age and income levels but it is likely that shopping behaviours dominate the mainland Chinese travellers' use of time in Hong Kong (Yeung et al., 2004). For these shopping enthusiasts the quality of information about pricing on the internet may have been a particular concern.

A bigger issue also exists in reading this study. It is always important to focus on the absolute level of the measures in comparative studies. It is statistically accurate to report that the United States tourists were more satisfied but their mean score on the 7-point scale hovered around the 6.0 mark whereas the Chinese mean score on the specific items were of the order of 5.4. The latter score still indicates satisfaction and it is important not to confuse a difference in the scores with the absolute or substantive value of the responses. The Chinese tourists in effect were still satisfied with their internet inquiries.

There are other characteristics of the tourists who go searching for internet information which might make a difference to the way the task is approached and the sources used. Some of these variables such as the demographic factors of age and gender, as well as value orientations (liking or disliking technology) are undoubtedly influential. Rather than pursuing a host of minor variations on this theme, it is more inclusive to segment the tourist users according to innovation theory (Kah *et al.*, 2008). Several terms have been developed to capture the phases of technology adoption. Some of the first users of a new approach are referred to as innovators and these individuals are seen as those who are able to cope with high levels of uncertainty about the performance of the new process or product (Rogers, 2003). The groups who follow the innovators are given a set of self-explanatory labels; that is early adopters, early majority, late majority and laggards. One category apparently missing from this listing is those who choose never to adopt the technology.

The ideas proposed by Rogers were generic and intended to describe all kinds of innovations and new processes and products. In the tourism and technology applications of these ideas Kah *et al.* (2008), using reports from Canadian tourists' travel diaries, were able to show that those with existing high internet use and those who owned comparatively more technology-based items were more likely to adopt other newer technologies. Experience in one technology domain seems to foster confidence in tackling the use of other new product innovations resulting in a spiralling process of adoption. The groups were distinguished in some important business-related senses with late adopters being more likely to still use travel agents for purchasing many categories of products while the innovators, early and middle adopters were quite willing to buy online.

The studies of the use of internet sites in tourist information collecting and differences among the individuals undertaking the process do not directly address the issue of how the sites are being used. A potentially overwhelming issue in this context is the amount of information available. One can speculate, for example, that if a Google search for the destination 'London' provides over 100 pages of related websites, then not very many visits will be made to sites listed after the first five pages. The information overload issue introduces the topic of search heuristics which can be described as the rules of thumb or simple rules used by those who search sites. In reconsidering the TripAdvisor sites provided earlier in this chapter the question was raised do individuals synthesise the data or do they seek a specific attribute. More generally the question is simply one of how do they manage the process? Zhang et al. (2008: 163) suggest the following three decision heuristics. A single criterion stopping rule can be identified and this approach describes tourists searching for adequate amounts of information to make a decision on this key factor. Credibility heuristics are also described in Zhang et al.'s scheme. On this occasion the credibility of the message is based on the communicator's credibility. The third approach they identify is labelled consensus heuristics where the aggregate of the recommendations is given priority in the decision-making process.

Additional Dimensions in Information Search

There are further influential components of some of the online information systems. In particular, there are ratings and evaluations of products which some businesses would want to avoid as well as some which provide highly desirable ticks of approval. As an example of the least preferred designation TripAdvisor provides a listing of the top 10 worst accommodation products in every continent and often provides such ratings at the level of individual countries. Of more value to an accommodation business is the elite positive ranking system (cf. America's best 25 hotels) which the same travel online service provides. Further, even the impact of being rated highly (such as number one, two or three out of a large city's accommodation options) is presumably not only effective for attracting tourist bookings but financially beneficial and valuable for staff morale.

Summaries of approval (and disapproval) ratings represent the contemporary equivalents for tourist behaviour of the recommendations provided in earlier times by the Baedeker guides with their system of recommending the elite attractions. There is also a parallel with the substantial influence of being recommended in popular guidebooks such as Lonely Planet. Again research opportunities abound in this area. Tourist researchers have not considered the comparative power of recommendation systems in much detail. Do the comments of a prestigious guidebook matter more than the positive ratings on TripAdvisor website? How might one set about measuring this effect? There would appear to be both issues to be addressed from the point of view of the supplier (such as the number of people influenced) and the customer (the strength of the influence) and the possibility that the influences are changing over time. These kinds of questions are extensions to the work initiated by Lee et al. (2007) who really examined frequency of use rather than power or the notice taken of the material.

It is likely that an important dimension of particular interest affecting the influence of the newer technologies is the timeliness and currency of the information. For example, a key component of the timeliness of the information lies in whether the material reported on a website or information service is truly up to date. Websites may or may not be superior to guidebooks on this dimension but personal service from a well informed local in a visitor centre may be superior to all non-personal techniques. The immediacy of knowing whether or not a hotel room is available through such sites as 'Find a room' or 'Wotif' relieves adventurous tourists of the kinds of anguished wandering around a destination in search of accommodation which prevailed just a few decades ago. Similarly, the troubles of many travellers occur because advice about key facilities can be inaccurate or outdated.

An Africa travel story

http://www.travelblog.org¿Print¿Blog/74850/306690.html (retrieved July 2010).

Yesterday afternoon I left the guest house on a wander around Cape Town, carrying my shoulder bag which contained WAY more important stuff than I should have been toting around (including my passport, driver's license, credit and debit cards, all my cash camera, cell phone, medicines and journal). I found an internet café several blocks away and sat down for a quick check of my email. I decided I wanted a coffee so I stood up and turned around to order my coffee. And left my bag at the computer console just a few feet away. When I returned with my coffee, my bag was gone without a trace. The security guards and café monitor hadn't seen anything, so that was that, my stuff had been stolen.

I looked up the address of the American consul in Cape Town and walked there, only to discover that they'd moved to a suburban location several months ago and were closed for the rest of the day (THANKS (not) for keeping the website up to date guys). Having no money, no ID, nothing. I had to walk the several miles back to the guest house but better news the next day I was issued with an emergency passport usable for all upcoming travels I called my brother he's going to wire me money to get me through until my debit and credit cards can be reissued. So I was let down by people and technology one day saved by good people and technology the next.

A further dimension of tourist information searching and technology which has received little attention is the issue of privacy (Brown *et al.*, 2007). There are two dimensions to this topic. On the one hand contact with a travel agent, for example, requires an individual to discuss and expose their interests, motives and financial capacity to undertake their holiday. The contact is direct, personal and in public. For many tourists revealing these kinds of personal interests and capacities are not troubling. For others it may be disconcerting to expose one's insecurities, financial status and relationship complexities as well as one's secret motives in a direct and personal encounter. Using the internet by way of contrast the tourist can arguably make all sorts of inquiries anonymously. It is of course well known that many organisations track the nature of inquiries made on the internet to build consumer profiles and this area of the ethics of tourism business practice and research is just emerging as a concern (Moscardo, 2010b). Nevertheless it is likely that tourists' access to practices where there is the potential for moral concerns and challenges to one's identity may be pursued almost entirely within the domain of technology dominated information searching. Further consideration of the privacy issues as well as other comments on the information and tourism technology studies reviewed to date will be considered in later chapters of this book.

On-Site Uses of Technology

A second and substantial use of technology affecting tourist behaviour lies in its applications to the on-site experience of tourists. Some of these uses may be identified under the label of social communication. There are also technologies which provide tourists with localised on-site information while others relate to experience enhancement serving entertainment and interpretive goals. These topics will be pursued in sequence in this section but initially it is valuable to preview some of the features of technology which help describe its on-site uses (Figure 2.1).

Facets of Technology

The facets of any technology which influence its use can be highlighted by considered one item possessed by nearly all tourists: the wristwatch. These dimensions of interest include frequency of use, access and ease of use, cultural and social meanings and the continuing evolution of the approach. For the wristwatch the frequency of use is very high, so high in fact that it would be very difficult to meet the schedules of transport and travel without a personal timepiece. As the commonest item of technology and the only one strapped to the human body on a daily basis, the wristwatch provides immediate access to its time telling function and using the instrument is a widely dispersed skill. The cultural meanings which make the wearing of a wristwatch so functional are considerable. The systems of numbers we use to tell the time is a complex amalgam of base number systems which include a Sumerian derived base 60, an Egyptian and Roman derived base 12 and a Julian derived calendar where we have agreed to count the year as consisting of 364 and a quarter days (Waugh, 1999). Additionally the globe operates on a Greenwich Time base so there are international regularities in deciding on time across the planet. In the sense of agreed technology this is something of a remarkable achievement – we have not managed to be so consistent with many other technology systems.

Figure 2.1 On-site technology use
This photograph of two tourists listening to audiotapes was taken at the Forum in Rome, Italy. On-site technologies may powerfully supplement tourists' experience but individuals and their companions must deal with issues of convenience and the physical need to carry equipment. Some forms of technology enhance social interaction while other forms isolate the individual tourist. The public use of such devices also identifies individuals as tourists which in some circumstances may make them visible targets for criminal activity.

The wristwatch like other items of technology is also richly imbued with images of social status with subtle shades of power and privilege indicated by brands and styles (cf. de Botton, 2004). As many Western tourists know when visiting developing countries the selling of imitation and counterfeit watches is a almost a defining item in tourist shopping (van Egmond, 2007). While arguably the oldest of the technology items of interest, the wristwatch is still an evolving product. Digital displays compete with more conventional time displays while watches which function underwater, and those which can be used as stopwatches and alarms, those can resist shock damage and those powered by thermal or solar inputs are quite common. Like other tourist relevant technology in which we are interested there are often many underused functions, in this particular case the capacity to tell time in other locations, to set multiple alarms and to vary those signals. Most of all, as Waugh (1999) highlights, the function of telling time to the nearest second is far more precise than we really use in everyday interaction. Does the ubiquitous watch have competition? Arguably the mobile phone is gaining some ground as an alternative time piece but the visible role of the watch in the conspicuous consumption stakes is likely to ensure its future.

The facets of technology, illustrated with the wristwatch, can be applied to the many devices which shape the world of the contemporary tourist. Our review of on-site tourism technologies will include similar facets of technology use; specifically use levels, access and ease of use, cultural and social effects and evolution of the approaches. Like the watch, many of the technologies have not been created just for the tourist behaviour context but are now widely adopted when people travel.

Social Communication

As with the issues in reporting statistical data about information searching and the internet, so too the reliability of information about tourists' social communication uses of technology while travelling is subject to much measurement error and the fluctuations of context. One indication of tourists using social communication technologies is reported in work on young international travellers; 1555 of them travelling around Australia for an extended period (Pearce *et al.*, 2009). The sample consisted of travellers from over 25 countries with larger numbers coming from the United Kingdom, Ireland, Scandinavia, Germany and the United States. The data are presented in Table 2.2.

As reported in Table 2.2 there are some high use levels of some items and lower reported involvement with some of the more expensive technologies less relevant to the style of these young travellers. The tourists in the Pearce *et al.* study were often staying in Australia for extended periods of time

TABLE 2.2 YOUNG TRAVELLERS AND THE USE OF TECHNOLOGIES FREQUENCY OF TECHNOLOGY ITEMS USED WHILE TRAVELLING

Item used	Often	Sometimes	Never
Camera	88%	9%	3%
Video camera	11%	27%	61%
Internet access at café/ accommodation	60%	30%	10%
Own laptop	23%	11%	66%
MP3/iPpod for music	58%	23%	19%
MP3/iPpod for other media	16%	14%	70%
Blackberry/ PDA	3%	3%	94%
GPS Navigation device	4%	9%	87%
Mobile phone	64%	27%	9%

Source: Pearce *et al.* (2009)

TABLE 2.3   YOUNG TOURISTS' USE OF SOCIAL NETWORKS WHILE TRAVELLING
FOR EXTENDED PERIODS IN AUSTRALIA

	Facebook	MySpace	Bebo	Twitter	YouTube	Other
Stay in touch with other travellers	64%	4%	6%	0.5%	3.6%	15%
Stay in touch with home	58%	6%	7%	0.6%	4%	25%
Join or contribute to backpacker group	18%	1%	1%	0.5%	1.6%	9%
Upload photos	59%	4%	6%	0.4%	6%	18%

Source: Pearce *et al.* (2009)

(mean length of stay was 26 weeks) so their social communication requirements were arguably quite prominent. The uses of the mobile phones
reported by the international sample included the following varied activities:
text messages 74%, phone calls 70%, taking photos 31%, taking videos 17%,
sending and receiving email 17%, sending picture or video messages 13%,
accessing Facebook 7%, mobile searching 7%, browsing for news weather
and sports 6%, seeking maps 6%, SMS competitions 6% and GPS navigation
5%. Questions directed at the kinds of social platforms they used to stay in
touch with others were determined and are reported in Table 2.3.

The high use of the category of other sites in Table 2.3 is explained by the
German, Chinese, Korean and Swedish young travellers using country-
specific social networking sites. Additionally a percentage of all respondents
from across the varied nationality groups used Photobucket, Flickr and Picasa
as sites to upload photos.

Like our defining example of the wristwatch the social communication
technologies considered in the survey of younger travellers can be considered
and understood in terms of more than frequency of use. In particular, access,
cultural meaning, social identity value, continuing evolution and competition are worth considering for some of the dominant technologies in use.
The initial focus will be on two specific communication and social connection technologies – the mobile phone and the internet. The special functions
of the camera or the video camera will be considered separately though of
course many mobile phones now contain quite sophisticated capacities for
the recording and communicating of visual material.

The Mobile Phone and the Internet

Accessing the internet through using mobile phones, carrying laptop
computers or by visiting internet cafes brings both positive possibilities and
pitfalls. In the example of carrying one's own laptop, additional baggage is
always unwelcome and proceeding through multiple airports and security

screenings can be frustrating. For the internet café user there can be charges and time limitations but also the need to locate suitable facilities particularly in developing destinations. For the mobile phone users there is the ever present threat of loss or theft as well as some inconvenience in dealing with the cross national compatibilities of systems. Nevertheless in general terms the mobile phone using tourists in particular have the capacity to be connected to their social circles on a 24-hour basis.

As White and White (2007) observe the issues of remaining wired to the home world are often more problematic in a social and cultural sense than the immediate stress of accessing or caretaking one's connection tools. The regular access to significant others in the tourists' home world changes some of the fundamental dimensions of the tourist experience. Three points can be made to distinguish contemporary tourists on this issue from their predecessors. By maintaining regular contact with others the tourist is not really crossing the sharp kind of threshold, the entry into a liminoid state of an uncertain world which applied in previous eras (Graburn, 1989; Ryan, 1997; Turner & Turner, 1978). In addition to celebrating and sharing travel successes, the technologies provide a reassuring set of contacts during times of self-doubt, stress and anxiety. Previously, the links to the tourists' home world were episodic and infrequent. Secondly by having contact at or close to the high points of the tourist experience through sharing photographs and using mobile phones, White and White argue that there can be a co-creation of the travel moments. Urry has termed the effects of this technological link to one's social world as occasional co-presence, imagined co-presence and virtual co-presence (Urry, 2002: 256–257). This co-presence can make tourists appreciate an experience not just for themselves but with and on behalf of others. It is perhaps also notable that the prospect of a key figure contacting you at any point of your travels may also act as a controlling or social conscience force militating against indulging in illicit behaviours.

A third issue distinguishing contemporary travellers from their earlier counterparts lies in the way the more continuous link to the home world can also generate disquiet for the tourist. Some of this doubt and sense of unease is evident in the following extract from Garland's novel *The Beach*. On this occasion Richard, the principal character questions a fellow backpacker Francoise as to whether she ever thinks about home and her parents.

'"Parents ..." "Francoise frowned as if she were struggling to remember the word." Yes it is strange, but ...'
'When did you last contact them?'
'I do not know ... It was ... That road. The road we met you'
'Khao San'
'I called them from there ...'

> 'Three months ago.'
> 'Three months ... Yes ...'
>
> We both lay back down on the hot sand. I think the mention of the parents was slightly disquieting and neither of us wanted to dwell on the subject." (Garland, 1997: 206)

The disquiet, it appears, stems from the struggle between the tourists' life and experience in the new location compared to their views of their former selves and the obligations in the worlds they have left behind. These reflections can cause individuals to analyse the value of home relationships and sometimes the undesirability of other aspects of their life such as work problems (White & White, 2007: 98–99). In a comment which bears on the very core travel career pattern concept that nearly all travel motivation involves a sense of escape (cf. Pearce, 2005: 79) one of the older tourists studied by White and White remarks;

> People expect too much of traveling because they think that the farther you go away the more you forget your problems that are waiting for you at home. This is not true. You are traveling with your problems. You carry them with you ... The regular contact. It reduces the feeling of being away. Because you get involved in (family members') problems you are aware of the fact you still belong to them and that you will go back to them. (White & White, 2007: 99)

The social communication opportunities which newer technologies offer tourists arguably require a different metaphor to characterize the tourist experience. Crossing thresholds and moving between distant worlds needs to be replaced with a notion of digital elasticity – tourists remain electronically linked to their home worlds as they stretch and explore their identity and the worlds of others. The image of the prodigal son (or daughter or other relative) lost in another world and suddenly returning is outdated. Now the same tourists have been in touch frequently; their relationships stretched by the distance and change but held together by the technologies of contact.

Photography

Digital cameras and highly portable video cameras, either as separate devices or incorporated into the more expensive Blackberry and iPod phones, also assist social communication. As with the other technologies we are considering there are issues of frequency of use, access, social identity and cultural dimensions as well as the ongoing evolution of and competition in the technology forms. While there are some travellers who never take photographs, presumably an inaction which they see as useful in distancing themselves from the core role of being a tourist, nearly 90% of the backpackers in the Pearce *et al.* (2009) study were frequent users of cameras. A further 38% used videos often or sometimes. The close identification of camera use with the tourist role has been used by Berger *et al.* (2007), amongst others, to segment tourists into different market types. In that study the larger market segments of sun seekers, explorers and educational tourists, in particular, were shown to be the most active in compiling photo albums generated by their tourist experiences (Figure 2.2).

The access issues for taking tourist photographs can involve a number of subtle dimensions. The taking of photographs and the composition of those photographs is research topic in its own right (for reviews see Albers & James,

Figure 2.2 Photography as core behaviour
A common image of Asian tourists is that they like to take photographs. While this behaviour is not confined to tourists from these communities, photography can be seen as a core interpretation and a tangible observable behaviour of the tourist role. The image of the photographers is taken near Shanghai China. At this site Chinese tourists are almost as curious about their history as the international visitors. Photography fosters mutual gaze as both parties frame the other.

1988; Chalfen, 1979; Crang, 1997; Garrod, 2009; Sontag, 1979). The capacity to take multiple images quickly and inexpensively is a particular feature of the digital camera. This can produce many repeated images with only the best retained for later use. The power of even inexpensive cameras to use the zoom function to capture distant points of interest provides a level of some-times backstage access which is denied to the naked eye. There are also socially and culturally negotiated issues of who can take what sort of photo-graphs which vary from country to country (Cohen *et al.*, 1992; Scales, 2009). One of the author's own travel experiences captures the challenge of photog-raphy in an unpredictable setting:

> Visiting Jerusalem I was on my way to see the oldest part of the city. Accompanied by two friends, a senior professor of Middle Eastern stud-ies and his tourism researcher daughter, we walked past the American Embassy. As a tourist behaviour researcher I sometimes take photo-graphs, often of other tourists. Stretched out for some 100 meters along-side the wall of the Embassy was one of the most colourful queues you can imagine. There were gaudily dressed Americans, Arabs in long flow-ing white robes and Jews of various persuasions with their hair and clothes in customary identity confirming styles. This little line-up of humanity was all neatly obeying the orderly demands of the queue despite the heat and possibly their personally stressful circumstances. I took a photo and then another.
>
> Two uniformed soldiers, carrying weapons and looking very serious, appeared from nowhere. Embarrassed and realizing I had done some-thing seen as inappropriate in the tense environment of Israeli life, I apologized. Not good enough. I was asked to come to their office, which I assumed was a military post. Such a visit seemed to me like a very bad idea. My professorial colleague tried to intervene explaining briefly who I was and what I was doing. Not good enough. But my technology saved me. It was a good camera but not a digital one. I opened the back of the camera, ejected the roll of film and tossed it to one of the interrogators. He looked surprised but caught it and we walked off. . . . . very quickly. I am not sure if deleting photographs from a digital camera would have worked so easily.

The lesson of being cautious about what and whom to photograph is an important one, and key aspects of these kinds of encounters will be explored further in Chapter 5. There is also an additional social and cultural implica-tion of the use of photography and videos and to some extent mobile phone and internet use in on-site tourism settings. The acts of using the technology disrupt the gaze behaviour of the tourist and replace the personal gaze with an electronic view. It is a refocusing of attention and in that act there is implicitly a moment of choice requiring mindfulness. This moment of choice has further implications for the flow of the whole tourist experience. In particular engagement in the gaze switch can shape the full recall of the experience. Definitive acts of taking a photograph or making the effort to record a one minute video effectively identify and select moments or chunks of time from the entire holiday timeline. An implication of this behaviour is that it then becomes the prominent memory hook for recalling the holiday and maybe later the only remaining point of access for some of the memories. The digitally recorded traces are selected slices of experience but the gaze switch involved in creating them, and later the memory triggers elicited by re-visiting such images, can dominate the mental souvenirs of travel.

For researchers, there are opportunities associated with the photography linked experiential timeline which have not yet been pursued in this field. Researchers have typically conducted inquiries seeking to understand why tourists take photographs and the technique of giving tourists disposable cameras and seeing what they do capture on film has become a research tool offering some insights (Jennings, 2010; Markwell, 2000). The newer research opportunity lies in asking people to recall what photographs they might have but did not take.

In this kind of study, information might be accessed by prompt questions such as what was too difficult to capture in a photograph, what else did you do that day that was worth remembering or why did you not take a photograph of that encounter? Zimbardo and Boyd (2008) highlight the perspective that our memories are complex and are much more than file drawers of what happened to us. As the work of Loftus (1997) and Braun *et al.* (2002) has shown, we can forget things that actually happened and apparently remember things that did not occur. The photographs that tourists take can be a trap in the sense that repeated viewing of them will give that small slice of the holiday timeline a prominence it may not deserve and richer experiences which are not able to be visually recorded may fade. The 'what else did you do?' or 'what did you not photograph?' lines of inquiry may offer to tourist behaviour researchers some new directions in the analysis of memory in relation to on-site technology use.

Way Finding

Navigation devices, particular in-vehicle satellite technologies which provide car drivers with display screens and offer spoken directions have become a common technology for tourists in the self-drive sector of the travel market. Such devices are one of the topics of interest in the rapidly developing field of study which can be referred to as urban informatics (Foth, 2009). This set of technology, engineering architecture and social science linked studies is concerned with 'the collection, classification, storage, retrieval and dissemination of recorded knowledge of, relating to or characteristic of or constituting a city' (Townsend, 2009: xxiii).

The approaches developed in this transdisciplinary field seek to map and record the living anatomy of cities so that it is not simply the shape of the roads and their interconnections which interest researchers but the way the city functions in terms of flows and the pulses of people's experience. The current technologies available for tourists to use do not meet all the requirements that the urban informatics specialists see as desirable for their information laden real time cities. In line with the facets of technology being considered throughout this chapter urban informatics specialists are also concerned with the frequency of technology use, the access to it and the social and cultural meaning of the products and systems employed. They also consider the interconnections among the unseen systems of information and pay some attention to the issues of evolution and business competition.

Many tourists are most likely to encounter the in-vehicle navigation systems in rental cars, while some will be using the advice systems on longer distance tourist trips in their own vehicle. The information available about in-car navigation systems and its use comes predominantly not from tourist studies but research on regular urban users. The frequency of use of in-vehicle guidance systems can be quite high. For example, over 30% of urban drivers employ the technology in some European settings (Vonk *et al.*, 2007). There are though limitations of the systems in terms of the users' access to exactly what is required. Cooley (2005) commenting on the operation of in-car navigation suggests that they are 'lame' and delivered through lockout technologies that 'insult the user'. A particular problem he identifies is the need to punch in the destination required and then reset it manually if something goes awry. For example, the organic nature of urban life with its traffic accidents, temporal surges of vehicles and adverse weather conditions are not yet adequately incorporated into the systems. Cooley also suggests that drivers are often given clumsy routes that no resident would ever take. There are though apologists for the systems with data from manufacturer sponsored studies showing that in car navigation using drivers have fewer accidents and report less stress, and passengers attending to their driver behaviour report safer actions (SWOV, 2009; TOMTOM, 2008). These are not studies of tourists using the systems but they set the groundwork for comparative research.

The researchers in urban informatics point to several social and cultural issues which continue to trouble the applications and success of in-vehicle wayfinding devices. Firstly cities in particular, but destinations generally, undergo change and evolve like living entities. Road authorities supply information to map producers about changes to the road system but there are literally thousands of changes in a year in large cities. This comment applies not only to European and North American cities but also to rapidly evolving Asian cities which may be seen as living entities undergoing rapid growth phases. Road users have to buy the latest information and their comments indicate that many do not always purchase the regular updates which would make their system more accurate (SWOV, 2009). An additional problem is the subtle but not unimportant issue that specifying a route between points is a trade-off activity. Distance and time are the entities needing to be balanced. If the system simply works on an algorithm which chooses the shortest route, the recommended route may be along the busiest roads, so that distance travelled may be less, but time taken considerably more.

The challenges to the existing in-car technologies come in various forms. First there is ongoing research work on the effectiveness of voice-activated navigation systems. When asked whether they would prefer voice-activated systems to ones which require setting up the requests for directions manually, 80% of respondents preferred the voice-activated approach (Shaw, 2009). The problem persists, however, that there are consistent errors in the voice recognition systems when employed inside moving vehicles with 18% errors being regarded as a typical result (Shaw, 2009; Westphal & Waibal, 1999). Clearly being directed to the wrong location, possibly slowly, at least 18% of the time is a problem. In the future, however, more refined and powerful programs supplemented by commentary when required on features of tourist interest may further advance the systems. Its a challenge for tourism researchers to continue to understand how these provided and directed orientation systems reshape the tourists' experience, not only in cars but in the expanding urban informatics of many locations.

A link to existing tourism research may provide some options for further analysis of wayfinding. The approach to orientation research in tourism has stemmed from the cognitive mapping work of Lynch (1960) and has been concerned with the post visit images of cities. The city oriented studies have been global in their coverage with applications in Libya (Gulick, 1963), Italy (Francescato & Mebane, 1973), the United Kingdom (Eyles, 1988; Oliver, 2001; Pearce, 1977), Australia (Fagence, 1983; Pearce, 1981; Walmsley & Jenkins, 1991, 1992) and Germany (Guy et al., 1990). Much of this work has employed hand-drawn sketch maps as a tool to access visitors' sense of orientation and their evaluations of city experiences. It is noteworthy that the draw a map technique which is at the heart of the method is rarely used in isolation and is just one of several techniques to gain destination experience or route-based information from tourists.

It appears that tourism researchers have not yet used this research method and applied it to the driving experiences generated by the in-car navigation technology. Some questions of interest may be raised. Do tourists remember more or less of their journey with the in-car navigation system? Exactly what differences occur between those using their own navigational prowess and those following the structured advice? What are tourists' specific reactions to the technology in unfamiliar settings? How do the experiences of passengers and drivers differ with the application of the in-vehicle navigation systems? Further, are the impacts of the in-car navigation systems on tourists' overall destination experience affected by the nationality of the visitor, the country visited and the kinds of the environments they traverse? A cumulative body of work possibly involving cross national cooperation is needed to understand the evolving experience-technology interface in these kinds of tourist settings.

Mobile Recommender Systems

A defining feature of the in-vehicle navigation systems is that they retain some characteristic of the older technologies; that is they provide standardised responses which are not sensitive to the users' context and needs. The new mobile recommender systems which may be thought of as electronic guides combining some of the functions of both guidebooks and personal guides offer some more interactive and flexible options. The mobile electronic guides are referred to as context aware mobile applications and can be seen within the broader framework of multiple mobile technologies relevant to tourists' use. It is challenging to appraise the mobile *in situ* advice guides in the terms of frequency of use, ease of use and access and social and cultural meanings because the number of studies and contexts in which these kinds of ideas are fully developed is limited. Nevertheless there is some background work and some early studies which are helpful in addressing our concerns.

Hyun *et al.* (2008) have provided a typology of these mobile communication systems. They include in their appraisal 15 mobile applications and rate these forms along the dimensions of vividness (intensity of presentation to the senses) and interactivity (users' ability to shape the form and content of the information). The highest items on both interactivity and vividness are virtual tours, 3D games and Second Life while voice telephony, text chatting, SMS applications and mobile voice messages are the lowest on both dimensions. Mobile video albums, mobile photo albums, location-based services and video telephony are high on vividness and moderate on interactivity. The remaining mobile applications – multimedia messages are rated as high on vividness but low on interactivity. The authors suggest that the uses of the mobile technologies during on-site phases of the tourist experience can be described as follows:

> When mobile travelers arrive at the destination, LBS (location based services) navigation is a necessity to find roads, attractions or restaurants. Mobile travelers can enjoy the destination through real time videomobile phone calls with their friends. During a break or waiting time they can forget their boredom by playing mobile 3D games. (Hyun *et al.*, 2008: 160)

These mobile applications can be specified in more detail. Tan *et al.* (2009) argue that the successful deployment of mobile tourist applications depends on a rich understanding of the contexts in which they function. Their work extends the analysis offered by Hyun *et al.* (2008) since the generic properties of interactivity and vividness may be modified by the characteristics of the setting and the user demands. In a detailed review of the literature of context defining studies, supplemented by their own focus group work, Tan *et al.* suggest that there are five kinds of contexts which may affect the operation of mobile technologies. They use the acronym TILES to refer to the categories of context they determine as of most influence. The letters represent in turn the Temporal context, requirements varying according to time such as the day, year and season; Identity context, requirements due to user demographics, interests, motives and preferences; Location context, requirements due to the immediate location and movement of the user; Environmental context, requirements due to the weather and physical stressors and Social context, requirements arising from the users' social setting in terms of group and travelling party needs. The researchers argue that these contextual requirements can be the basis for evaluating the adequacy of the performance of mobile recommendation systems.

A number of studies are underway which seek to evaluate the effectiveness of mobile guides. Such studies are usually confined to trials of specific recommender systems in single cities or buildings (Kramer *et al.*, 2007; Modsching *et al.*, 2007). One focus of work in this tradition by a team of authors is based on information relevant to the easternmost city in Germany, that of Gorlitz. The city has attracted some recent global attention with the Quentin Tarantino film *Inglourious Basterds* using the well preserved buildings of the older part of the city as a its core set for the movie. The city's tourist appeal is considerable and since it escaped serious bombing in World War Two there is a rich architectural heritage including Gothic, Renaissance, Baroque and Art Nouveau buildings. The Modsching *et al.* (2007) study compared three groups of tourists who explored the city. One control group carried no mobile devices but were simply monitored for their movement patterns. A second group carried a dynamic tour guide planner which enables tourists to choose attractions and the system then provided a sequence of suggested visits by taking into account the opening hours and distances. A third group, referred to in the study as the explorer mode, used a more flexible recommendation system. The explorer mode provided a constantly updated list of sites within a distance of 100 m. The access devices to receive the information were distributed to tourists during the summer of 2006. Compared to the control group both the explorer mode and the planner mode increased the time spent at sites – in fact the time was doubled – and they paid attention to four times the number of attractions.

In related reporting of the same kind of work in the same city, the researchers found evidence that those using the Planner mode were effectively receiving an organised guided tour from which they were free to deviate (Kramer *et al.*, 2007). This was appreciated as a somewhat easier approach to way finding and interpretation than the advice given to those in the explorer mode who received the more continuous information updates. The findings reinforce the locational and individual context issues raised by Tan *et al.* (2009). Planner mode information empowered the tourists in the locational context; that is they were able to focus on the details of the interpretive material rather than continuously having to monitor their location and route. Additionally, the planner mode also assisted the individual context since the tourists could make choices to alter their route. Such actions can also be seen as supporting the flexibility and interactivity issues identified by Hyun *et al.* (2008).

Other researchers have drawn attention to the possibilities inherent in mobile tourists recommending sites to each other while in the process of travelling (Paganelli & Giuli, 2008). This kind of recommendation is slightly different from the kind of post visit appraisal offered in the TripAdvisor kinds of systems. The mobile recommender systems embrace the notion that there is a community of fellow travellers who might appreciate immediate information from like-minded individuals. In this kind of mobile community interaction tourists communicate with others who are in the same location and within the reach of instant messaging systems or approved links from social media sites such as Facebook (de Spindler *et al.*, 2008). Such immediate advice might offer the possibility of altering the tourist's itinerary within the confines of a day or even an hour if the message comes from a known and trusted source.

There is a recent blossoming of this kind of research work about mobile recommender systems and online communities (Sigala *et al.*, 2007). In terms of the key technology facets being considered in this chapter the frequency of use of the mobile recommender systems are growing and the issues of access have been implicitly considered within the frames of reference outlined by Tan *et al.* (2009) and Hyun *et al.* (2008). The commercial and competitive nature of the technologies and their evolution is very much an ongoing concern as evidenced by the small scale trials of localised city and regional systems (see Sigala *et al.*, 2007). The larger social and cultural meanings which adhere to the new technologies are less clear. Information is not always a neutral commodity, especially when elements of recommending locations and providing interpretation of sights are involved in the communications. It can be noted briefly here, and it is a theme to which we will return at the end of the chapter, that the critical theory paradigm which addresses the issue of power and whose interests are being served by the kinds of information provided is not considered in most of the emerging literature. The focus of the tourist studies in this area has been about the ways and means to provide and communicate the data with a lesser concern for what that data might mean and signify. It does not really matter whether the city is Gorlitz or Gaborone; the way in which the information is presented and what information is presented both shape tourists' experience of the organic nature of contemporary cities.

Entertainment and Interpretation

The notion that there are multiple narratives which can potentially be conveyed by the contemporary technologies forms an effective bridging statement leading us to the topic of entertainment and interpretation. It has already been briefly noted that mobile phone and internet connections provide tourists with the opportunities to play games and select from diverse music, film and entertainment programs (Hyun et al., 2008). In flight entertainment systems also now have the flexibility to put the tourists in charge of the programs they see and hear. In hotels there is access to local television as well as films and specialist channels thus providing through contemporary technologies a near constant availability of both familiar and novel content.

An interesting social and cultural dimension of the capacity of these entertainment systems lies in the extent to which tourists choose to travel in a cultural bubble, that is watch the same kinds of media content when they are in Manila or Bangkok as when they are at home in Manchester or Boston. Those who choose to maintain their home-based interests and entertainment patterns can again be seen as not stretching their personal horizons. In the metaphors discussed earlier, such tourists are not leaping across thresholds but they are better described as gently leveraging themselves across spaces while tied by comforting electronic links. Following the terms used by Hottola to discuss cross cultural interaction they are possibly likely to encounter a little cultural confusion rather the greater trauma of severe culture shock (Hottola, 2004) (Figure 2.3).

These descriptions are not meant to be harshly evaluative, simply observations about the behavioural patterns and experiences which prevail when tourists remain linked to familiar products and people. There appears to be little work plotting the patterns of entertainment use in these systems of consumer choice and the possibility of linking these behaviours to other on-site tourist endeavours can be presented as a topic for further study.

A critical theory approach to any overview of the link between technology and tourist entertainment involves a consideration of who provides what kind of content in what forms and hence to the symbolic topic of Disneyization (Bryman, 2004). Everyday comments and substantial academic discourse indicate that phrases such as 'that is pure Disney' or 'that is turning the setting into Disneyland' have strong connotations of scorn and distaste. Bryman (2004) notes that

Figure 2.3 Cultural confusion
Cultural confusion, which may be seen as a diminished or lesser form of culture shock, is applicable to tourists but is softened by guides and the creation of a tourist bubble of familiar cultural practices. Nevertheless, the tourists who confront new levels of crowding, novel locations, and challenging weather and climate conditions as well as a myriad of minor changes due to different food, sleep disruptions physical activity and language contexts, can experience mood swings and levels of annoyance which can be temporarily exhausting. New mobile technologies can provide a continuity of familiar links to soften the cultural challenges, especially if the mobile recommender systems can assist tourists locate venues and facilities where they feel comfortable.

> the problem for a social scientists confronting a discussion of the wider impact of the Disney company and the emblematic aspects of its operations is that the term with the widest currency – Disneyfication – has become tainted with a largely negative view ... namely that it is mainly to do with sanitization and trivialization. (Bryman, 2004: 9)

This distaste which is widespread in cultural commentary (cf. Giroux, 1999; Harris, 2004; Huxtable, 1997; Ritzer, 2004; Ross, 1999; Zukin, 1991) frequently neglects to recognize the leading technological achievements of Disney entertainment. Irrespective of whether or not one subscribes to the

view that the narratives and theming trivialize complex social and historical issues, the evolution of three dimensional and four dimensional film
experiences, the development of audioanimatrons, the creation of holo-
graphic images and the evolution of the ride and tour format are all Disney
entertainment achievements. There is, though, in the criticism of the cultural commentators an implicit warning about the use of technology in
entertainment offerings. The view echoes a critical comment on Alfred Lord
Tennyson's poetry – 'a beautiful voice with nothing to say.' The theme of
trivialization of content which some see as the result of using Disney
inspired technologies is applicable both to presentations of natural environments and to cultural shows and performances. For tourism researchers
there is a clear message flowing from these discussions. There needs to be
simultaneous research attention and evaluation to both what is being
delivered as well as to the effectiveness of the technology in creating the
experience.

In an example of related work, Ryan and Collins (2008) using the theme
of hybridization drawn from the writing of Bryman and others, identify the
importance of technology in fusing drama, fantasy and spectacle in cultural
shows and performances. In their detailed study of the Japanese cultural
show 'An eastern odyssey' based in the heritage theme park of Huis ten
Bosch near Nagasaki, they report that the synthesis of traditions – some
Japanese, some western – delivered through costume, laser lighting and staging design creates an interpretation of a place which offers spectators their
own individual engagement with what is viewed. The researchers view this
cultural show as symbolic of post modern tourism in the sense that the layered meanings of the performance permit individual interpretations and
varying levels of engagement with the material.

The use of technology to develop staged performances and manage
impressive cultural shows for tourism is internationally widespread and
through combinations of laser lighting, big screen projections, sophisticated
music and sound systems and creative set design, prominent examples of
tourist technology assisted tourism entertainment exist in numerous locations. Interested researchers could usefully undertake many more comparative studies assessing attractions as diverse as Siam Niramit in Thailand, The
Xian Tang Dynasty Music and Dance Show in China with Western performances which adopt cultural heritage themes (c.f. Pearce et al., 2008). Above
all, it is the hybrid nature of these cultural shows delivered to multinational
audiences through contemporary technologies which often shape the appeal
of these performances (Figure 2.4).

The concern with technology in this chapter has been about what is
available to tourists at the present time. There is much speculation about
newer and innovative forms of technology which could powerfully influence
on-site behaviour. Two linked ideas can be briefly mentioned. Buhalis and
O'Connor (2006: 200) describe the concept of an ambient intelligent

Figure 2.4 Hybrid nature of cultural shows
Staged cultural performances are a pastiche of entertainment elements often presenting simple story lines and traditional routines supported by contemporary technologies in sound, lighting and special effects. Contemporary success may be seen to be more about the power to engage and communicate across audience types through sincere and effortful performances rather than being necessarily seen as inauthentic and fake. Emotional, aesthetic and performative labour skills matter and the use of humour is often important too.

environment which they represent as computing and networking technology that is embedded in everyday objects such as furniture, clothes, vehicles and buildings. From the user perspective they suggest that such developments will permit individual needs to be met faster with more responsive and tailored solutions to information. A linked idea is that of ubiquitous technology (Greenfield, 2006). In a Tokyo application of this approach buildings and surfaces in prominent shopping districts are embedded with computer chips which enable tourists with hand-held readers (entitled ubiquitous communicators) to access information in several languages about directions, store guides, and interpretive material. The designers of the project which was a part of the unsuccessful Tokyo Olympic bid for 2016 describe their work as forcing computers to live out in the world with people. They view this approach as shifting the pattern of use beyond both the mainframe approach of one computer and many people, and the personal computer style of one computer and one person, to the newer world of one person and many computers (Ubiquitous Computing, 2009). As Buhalis and O'Connor point out there are detailed research opportunities in establishing what is both intelligent to the tourist user and what kinds of technologies will work best for these new developments (Buhalis & O'Connor, 2006: 201).

Directions

The trajectory of research concerned with technology and tourist behaviour can be considered in terms of some of the key organising concepts presented in Chapter 1. In particular, we can assess the kind of research which has been done and point to what needs to be done by examining the etic-emic distinction, the use of theoretical approaches and conceptual schemes, the paradigms of research being employed and the wider issue of the sampling of the phenomenon. These directions may be seen as united by proposing a greater emphasis on the tourists' experience of using the various communication and service instruments.

In terms of the etic–emic distinction an observer of the research world which links technology and tourists can suggest that the voices of the tourists themselves could be louder. As will be suggested presently the style of work which imposes categories and requests ratings from technology users is often linked to the post positivist paradigm. Undoubtedly there is much useful, some powerful and certainly some sophisticated statistical work in this area of tourism study. Opportunities exist however to access more of the tourists' views of their experiences.

For example adopting the procedure of having a range of tourists (not students as in the Zhang et al. study) think aloud while searching through the TripAdvisor kind of material could offer other insights (cf. Ramey & Boren, 2001; Zhang et al., 2008). The think aloud approach asks the individual to talk about what they are reading thus mixing their comments, attitudes and emotional reactions to the text and revealing their unfolding decision-making process. A valuable addition to this activity for the researcher, which avoids overly shaping or controlling the process, is to use a number of non-directive prompt questions such as please tell me more about that or do you think something else about that. The reporting of this kind of study, which is in line with much constructivist writing, would benefit from having multiple researchers working on the project as a team and combining their insights across a range of respondents and materials.

Additional circumstances where the views of tourists could be developed were mentioned in relation to the use of in-vehicle guiding systems. Opportunities for field work-based studies of user responses to mobile guiding devices can be noted. A stress was also placed in the discussion concerning tourism entertainment in this chapter on the potential benefits of researchers gathering both what tourists think of the technology employed and at the same time how they evaluate the content delivered to them or meant to engage them. In general terms, a stronger experiential perspective represents an opportunity to embellish the existing studies; it suggests ways to expand the study approaches and prompts fresh questions. Importantly an emic orientation to tourists' experiences provides a check that any elegant systems devised by using researcher-derived variables and built on structural equation-based models are dealing with the factors that matter when users assess the technology.

A considerable diversity of small scale theories and conceptual schemes are used in the array of tourist behaviour and technology studies. These include but are not limited to social identity theory, pro-social behaviour, attitude theory, innovation theory, and technology acceptance. There is some select use of motivation theories and communication theory in the selection of variables to study. In the terms used by Smith and Lee (2010: 33) to describe theories in tourism research, the approaches underlining the tourist behaviour and technology studies are really theories of the third type; that is descriptive accounts which are then used to build empirical generalizations. A particular note can be made of the strong links among researchers in this sub-field of inquiry. There is a tight network of researchers attending common conferences and publishing in quite selected outlets. There is, though, not much work from this field penetrating the more general tourism research journals such as *Annals of Tourism Research* or *Tourism Recreation Research*. One consequence of this pattern of publishing is that opportunities may exist to link more frequently the findings from the tourist behaviour-technology studies to pre-existing and broader questions in the larger field.

Some examples of the potential integration among the findings and directions of the tourist behaviour technology areas of study and broader concerns were noted in this chapter by outlining the erosion of the concept of liminality and suggesting its replacement with digital elasticity. Additionally the amelioration of culture shock into a simpler form of cultural confusion and potentially culture exchange was also noted. It also appears that there are spirals of comfort and acceptance in using technologies in tourism applications and a systematic appraisal of use levels employing earlier notions of specialisation, self-efficacy and skill could prove to be valuable. It was noted that technology may induce a behaviour which can be identified as gaze switching which has implications for memory and recall of tourists' experiences. Additional comments were made in this chapter about expanding the heuristics of tourist decision making and the application of tourist motivation to technology use. Much work too can be done with a fuller treatment of digital identity, both in reading it and creating it. We also do not yet know how tourists' memory of their travels and its recall are shaped by the digital mobile recommender systems compared to the personal touches delivered by a skilled tour guide. The identification of what is lost and gained by the two approaches represents a clear area of future research inquiry. The fuller development of these ideas represents just a small fraction of the benefits and possibilities in a consideration of how the work on technology can modify and be integrated with existing studies.

A key pathway to develop a richer trajectory of technology studies lies in extending the paradigms within which such work is conceived. Researchers have shown clear preferences for post positivist work both in the dominant journals where the work is available and in the supporting conferences. It can be suggested that interpretive and constructivist styles of work can be usefully reconsidered. Key topics of interest which can be addressed when considering this tourist linked technology include the time it takes to employ the devices, the number of cognitive steps or effort involved in accessing material, the trust in the information and the integrated issue of the values expressed in the content and style of delivery.

From a critical theory perspective there are also multiple questions to be asked, some of which can be confronting to the researchers engaged exclusively in the dominant lines of work. Such questions include who is benefiting from this sort of study, who is being made richer by the research effort and possibly who is being displaced from a job in tour guiding or travel agency work by the recommender systems.

An important theme in examining research in Chapter 1 was the topic of the sampling of the phenomenon. This was described as directed by the goal of being able to categorise, rate or provide a pattern of the key dimensions creating variability within the phenomenon of interest. An awareness of this issue was introduced in the consideration of context for mobile technology devices in the work of Tan *et al.* (2009). Nevertheless further descriptions of the patterns and links among studies are needed in the tourist behaviour technology field so that individual studies do not become isolated pockets of inquiry which cannot be related to other work. This recommendation would seem to be particularly important as more field studies of mobile recommender devices and interpretive tools are trialled in different locations. Similarly an understanding of reactions to tourism entertainment would benefit from identifying the similarities among types of performances and products.

In Chapter 1 it was also suggested that understanding tourists' experiences was analogous to understanding the music produced by a full orchestra. In particular, an emphasis was placed on the contributions of varied components each of which contributes at different times to achieve the full effect. In the studies of tourists and the technologies which are coming to shape their world, there remains considerable scope to pursue further the roles of the sensory qualities of the technology, the affective reactions to its use, the cognitive mechanisms employed to think about and understand the tools, the actions undertaken and generated by the new devices and their effect on the relevant relationships which define the participants' world.

3   The Tourist in Trouble

Introduction

A few tourists seek to live dangerously. Most do not. The structure of material to be considered in this chapter follows the premise that an understanding of tourist motivation is necessary to describe how tourists evade or become involved in the dangers of travelling in the contemporary world. A view of tourist motivation will therefore be presented at the outset of this chapter. An understanding of the patterns among tourists' needs is a preliminary requirement in working out why some have trouble-free travels and others court or encounter risks. The excursion into the field of tourist motivation study in this chapter serves not only to provide insights for our consideration of the tourist in trouble but also enriches our store of concepts to consider other topics such as sustainable behaviours and personal growth in later chapters. Motivation is the perquisite study topic for assessing many tourists' experiences and thus is a core concern not only for this chapter but of the entire volume.

Following the discussion of motivation the issue of personal responsibility will be considered. This area blends ideas from attribution theory and recent developments in positive psychology concerned with character strengths and personality. The review of individual responsibility will assist in the understanding of the roles of the tourism and government sectors in providing reasonably safe settings for tourists to fulfil their holiday motivations. Research on a number of topics will then be considered. Some of the material will reflect the efforts of previous researchers while other material constructs new information and calls for further investigation along novel lines of inquiry. The scale of the problem varies from the more mundane but still troubling issues of crime and tourist scams to the traumas and crises of health problems, natural disasters and terrorist attacks.

Motivation Theory

What tourists do frequently amazes other tourists, the citizens in the community they visit and the civic authorities responsible for managing the settings. Questions about the motivation of other travellers are common in such contexts. Why would tourists run through the streets of a Spanish town being chased by semi-wild bulls? Why do some tourists get so close to the edge of the volcanoes that they risk being asphyxiated? (Heggie, 2009) And further, why do numerous tourists skydive from planes, plunge down waterfalls and expose themselves to a bewildering array of risks and uncertainties? For the casual observer speculating about people's motives is a good way to pass the time, while for the site manager it involves regular challenges in matching the tourism experiences available at their location to people's needs. Additionally for tourism academic researchers it is a topic rich in history, methodological challenges and opportunities for refining our understanding (Figure 3.1).

The question 'Why do people travel?' is, in both an academic and applied sense, an inadequate question. It is akin to asking the equally bland question 'What are the impacts of tourism?' A better approach for those seeking a rich understanding of motivation is why certain groups of people choose certain holiday experiences. And importantly we need to do this without invoking circularity in our discussion. Circularity is evident when assertions are made that people choose risky or adventurous activities because they are motivated by sensation or risk seeking. It can also be noted here that we are not assuming that a specific destination, whether it be Pamplona or Paris, meets only one travel motivation. Instead we are trying to determine a relatively

Figure 3.1 Motivation patterns
Bungee jumping, swinging across canyons and skydiving represent classes of activities which tourist motivation seeks to explain. Circular notions that tourists decide to bungee jump because they are sensation seekers do not offer any substantial insights. Motivation theories in tourism tend to explain classes of activities and seek patterns of motives at a more general level rather than motivation for a single activity. There are also attempts such as the TCP (Travel Career Pattern) work which seek to trace individuals' careers in leisure travel.

convenient number of common driving patterns or themes describing the forces prompting people's travel.

Tourist motivation is a special subset of the wider interest area of human motivation and can be defined as the total network of biological and cultural forces which give value and direction to travel choice, behaviour and experience (Pearce *et al.*, 1998). The key implication for all those considering tourist destinations and their management is that it is tourist motivation which energises and generates people's behaviour (Hsu & Huang, 2008; Mansfeld, 1992).

In order to tackle this topic several preliminary perspectives are needed. A professional view of motivation requires the analyst to be mindful that other travellers may not be driven by the same social, cultural and biological needs as the observer. An enduring challenge for students, professionals and academics researching motivation is to allow the possibility that other people may see the world in other ways, their needs may be different and their approach to the destination they visit may be unconventional. This issue repeats our earlier concern with the importance of taking an emic perspective, which amounts to seeing the world from the insider and participant's point of view (Cohen, 1979; Pike, 1966).

There are some defining characteristics of tourism which shape the kind of explanations we are seeking when assessing tourist motivation. Contemporary tourism in its many forms permits individuals some freedom to choose how to spend their time (and money). Tourism provides scope for the expression of well-being and an embodied, performative opportunity to enhance one's perceived life satisfaction (Harris, 2005). As a consequence, tourist motivation analysis needs to be cast within a framework of considering the importance of preferred future states for individuals. Further, the influence of close relationships in particular can be a powerful moderator of individual motivation in tourism experiences. These characteristics of tourism have solid implications for the study of tourist motivation. The episodic, dynamic, relationship dependent, future-oriented and varied experiences inherent in tourism imply that there is likely to be a complex pattern of learning about being a tourist and what satisfies the individual. The importance of these key characteristics will be reconfirmed in subsequent discussion.

There exist multiple reviews of travel motivation theory in tourism studies (Bowen & Clarke, 2009; Hsu & Huang, 2008; Pearce, in press a). This work considers the history of the field and notes the use of related terms such as benefits, which are the post-travel consequences relevant to classes of motives (Ryan, 1995); expectations, which are anticipatory beliefs about the attributes of destinations and the likelihood of experiences being achieved (Kozak, 2001); and values, which are summary statements integrating people's attitudes on a topic (Pearce *et al.*, 1998). Additionally some of the typologies of tourists which have been central in writing about tourism have implicit motivational components. A hybrid blend of motives, interests and travel types underlies Cohen's well-known division of tourists into recreational, diversionary, experimental, experiential and existential categories (Cohen, 1979). Much of the attention using this scheme has been on whether or not special subgroups of travellers such as backpackers were best described by the existential category or by the other labels (Maoz, 2005; Noy, 2004). The category scheme devised by Cohen has been and remains influential and it is really like an intuitive or a priori factor analysis of sets of motives which are then linked to traveller characteristics.

These other expressions all offer indirect approaches to studying the driving forces as to why people undertake their behaviour. For the precise topic of tourist motivation, the approach favoured and emphasised in this volume is that of the TCP (Travel Career Pattern). It is an approach which meets many of the requirements specified in the above comments by essentially providing a rich description of motives and then asserting that they function as a driving pattern of forces modified by travel experience and the life stages (Hsu & Huang, 2008). The 14 core factors which describe travel motivation were built on items of interest from a rich array of previous studies and identified across the two large international samples (Pearce, 2005; Pearce & Lee, 2005). The defining forces were, in order of importance, novelty, escape/relax, relationship strengthening, autonomy, seeking nature, self development through involvement with hosts or the site, stimulation, self-development of a personal kind, relationship security (enjoying being with similar others), self-actualisation (getting a new life perspective), isolation, nostalgia, romance and recognition (prestige of travelling). These motive categories reflected many of the forces described in previous studies and together provide one of the more complete motivation inventories undertaken in the tourism field. The key feature of the TCP approach was then to use the levels of travel experience and the stages of the travellers' life cycle reported by the respondents to formulate a three-part model which described the relationships among the 14 motives and the key career factors.

The varied importance of the motives suggested that a pattern could be imposed on the data such that for all travellers there was a core layer of motives which were very important. These motives were to escape and relax, to experience novelty and to build relationships. These motives were relatively unaffected by how much travelling the participants had experienced or where they were located in the life cycle. These findings were in close accord with the early studies in the field especially the work of Crompton (1979). There were further motives which were structured into a middle and outer layer of importance. For the most experienced travellers, the middle layer of motives was more important than the outer layer. By way of contrast those with limited travel experience tended to see all motives as quite important. It was noted further that for the middle and outer levels of the pattern the phases or stages of the travellers' life cycle were also linked to the travellers' motive patterns but here there were some Asian and Western cultural differences. For Western travellers later stages of the life cycle also tended to be linked to more travel experience and the alignment of motive importance as already described. By way of contrast in one study younger Koreans had often travelled more than older Koreans so the links between travel experience and later stages of the life cycle were not strong. This discrepancy is readily explained since the availability of travel as a discretionary leisure pursuit is a more recent phenomenon in Korean society (Kim *et al.*, 1996). Indeed most of the variability in the Korean data was better explained simply by the amount of travelling rather than by the age and life cycle stage of the respondents. Overall the motive structures were broadly consistent both for Asian and the Western travellers. Further confirmation of the relative importance of the motives in the TCP has been provided in a study of tourists in South East Asia (Pearce & Panchal, 2010) (Figure 3.2).

How might we summarise the value of the TCP work for our consideration of the tourist in trouble? The value of any tourist motivation approach, as Gnoth (1997: 294–297) observed, lies in being able to deliver a degree of specificity rather than merely outlining general categories. Most importantly, it is the shifting patterns of motives which can be insightful as we study why tourists jump from bridges, venture into back regions and risk attacks from bulls, bears and bothersome locals. For example, the pathway to understanding the tourists venturing to Pamplona lies not in simply seeking to document a simple travel motive which underlies this holiday activity choice but instead suggests that we contrast the whole pattern of motives among those who are about to participate, for those who have done it and will continue to do it again, to those who have done it and now no longer want to participate and those who will never participate. It is necessary in this process to use the multiple items which define the 14 factors, to be inclusive of the full range of motives and to assess the perceived importance of the motives along scales which permit individuals to express change in their perspective. While this work has not been done for the particular setting and activity of interest, we can speculate that there will be differences and shifts in importance among the groups outlined in terms of the relative importance given to outer layer motives such as status and achievement. The TCP approach would also predict that these different groups will vary along life cycle and travel experience dimensions. Recent work on the motives which underlie tourists' participation in spa tourism suggest that the shifting patterns of motives do coincide with varied levels of travel experience (Pearce & Panchal, 2010). There is the possibility that the common career patterns we find empirically amongst groups with different levels of participation and varied interests in set activities may reproduce patterns of motivation similar to those described by Cohen and others in qualitative terms.

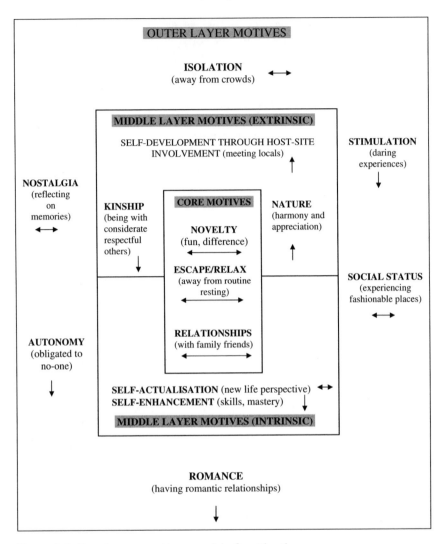

Figure 3.2 Travel career pattern model of motivation
The core structure of the TCP approach
(The highest loading item(s) for the factors are in brackets and the direction of
the arrows indicates changing emphases (greater, unchanging, less) with increasing traveller experience)

Attribution Theory

An additional approach to enhance our understanding of tourist behaviour and particularly the problematic behaviours in which tourists may be
engaged can be developed from extending the powerful work in social

psychology on attribution theory. This approach is a key consideration in explaining behaviours when there is a surprising element such as an ambiguity or a puzzle in what people do and how events turn out. Attribution theory is closely linked to the study of achievement motivation and has been used for over 50 years to describe how individuals respond to success and failure in meeting status and achievement needs (Weiner, 2010). The theory comes into particular play and prominence for subsets of tourist behaviour, notably those where achievement is involved, particularly when troubles develop and the unexpected prevails.

A succinct review of the concept which has occupied so many researchers in social psychology is needed to appreciate its underused power in certain kinds of tourism contexts and research. The metaphor which best makes sense of attribution theory is life as a courtroom (Siegel & Shaughnessy, 1996). The core idea here is that when puzzling outcomes occur we judge ourselves and others judge us. Several kinds of errors or biases have been identified in these judging processes, although it might be more appropriate to call them heuristics or rules of simplification (Hewstone, 1983). The actor observer bias suggests that the perceived causes of an outcome will be affected by who is making the assessment. This specific variation in explanations and judgements is referred to as the fundamental attribution error. In particular, external observers tend to favour explanations of the behaviour of others in terms of internal factors rather than situational factors. Thus the tourist whose wallet is stolen while he is in a crowded subway may be seen as negligent for not being more careful of his property. Individuals tend to explain their own behaviour in terms of a self-serving heuristic with favourable outcomes attributed to themselves and unfavourable effects due to the situational factors.

Courtrooms have formal rules for what is admissible as evidence. Similarly, everyday explanations of human conduct appear to work within rules as well. Fundamental components of these heuristics were first identified in the work of Kelley and Weiner. Kelley (1967) for example proposed that individuals use three rules of thumb when assessing the puzzling behaviours of others; the extent to which other people behave the same way in that setting (consensus), the degree to which individuals behave the same way in the same setting (consistency) and the individual's repetition of the behaviour across different settings (distinctiveness). In the case of our wallet losing tourist he or she will be 'blamed' more often if there is low consensus (few others are pick pocketed in that subway), high consistency (this is the third time he has had his wallet stolen in a subway) and low distinctiveness (he is repeatedly having items stolen).

Weiner's work, again over a long period of study, focused more specifically on achievement and affiliation situations. He provided a model and much supporting evidence that the stability and controllability of the factors involved in the explanation produce different psychological consequences in terms of emotional outcomes (Weiner, 2008). Examples of the outcomes of the judging process for puzzling achievement and affiliation outcomes which Weiner *et al.* (1978, 1979) identified include; internal causes of success (ability) generate pride, internal controllable causes of failure (lack of effort) produce guilt and regret, internal uncontrollable causes of failure (low ability) give rise to shame and humiliation, stable causes of failure (unfair others) result in hopelessness, and unstable causes of failure (bad luck) are associated with immediate resignation but in the longer term hope). In turn these emotional outcomes reshape subsequent motivation for the behaviour involved.

The work of Kelley and Weiner and the many researchers who have followed their core ideas helps to address two fundamental components of puzzling behaviour – how do we infer or work out causality and what are the consequences in terms of behavioural outcomes. Broader and different kinds of question arise with the inclusion of a social representations framework. Expressed succinctly, social representations are 'ways of world making' (Moscovici, 1988). They are shared, publicly communicated, everyday belief systems of meaning (Moscardo & Pearce, 2007; Quenza, 2005). They exist for large-scale public issues and topics such as unemployment, sex, health and public behaviour. Social representations exist outside the individual as well as in the minds of individuals (Howarth, 2005). When this approach is applied to the topic of dealing with puzzling (tourist) behaviour it helps address the issue of the origins of our ideas about what are appropriate explanations. Moscovici and Hewstone (1983) suggest that the everyday explanations we have are a blend of popular science and various forms of folk wisdom including aspects of theology and, at least in Western culture, ideas about sin and guilt.

Social representation approaches also inform the important topic of dealing with scapegoats and punishing those whom we deem responsible for negative outcomes either legally or in terms of social disapproval. Bains (1983), amongst others, relates these explanations to the need societies have to control their in-group behaviour (cf. Habermas, 1987). Tourism and particularly international tourist behaviour provide many opportunities to witness the operation of competing explanations of responsibility with a consequent set of practical implications and actions taken by the outside observers, in this case business and civic authorities, to prevent or limit key troublesome behaviours.

It is quite apparent in reviewing studies of tourist behaviour that few researchers have employed attributional frameworks to buttress their studies. A few examples do exist. Pearce (1989) used an attributional framework to examine tourists' complaints, while Jackson *et al.* (1996) used the approach to assess how tourists accounted for their best and worst experiences. More recently, Yoo and Gretzel (2008) provided evidence that the ideas were valuable in understanding why individuals provided internet travel stories.

Nevertheless in studies of consumer behaviour generally as Weiner (2000) himself pointed out, there remains considerable scope for using an attributional framework.

The exploration of tourists in trouble in this chapter will employ both motivational and attributional approaches to provide explanations of responsibility and suggest pathways for multi-stakeholder action in response to a variety of scenarios. The kinds of troubling situations of most interest in this exposition will be tourists subjected to scams which will be defined in detail presently. A consideration of the distinction between scams and criminal behaviour against tourists will be noted. Some consideration will also be given to the more generic risks inherent in travelling associated with health issues, natural phenomenon, civic unrest and social upheaval. It will be a central concern of these discussions to consider the issue of who is responsible for the troubles tourists may experience.

Tourist Scams

A tourist scam for the purposes of this volume can be defined as essentially fraudulent practice intended to gain financial advantage from a tourist where that targeted individual is initially a willing participant. Not all scams are illegal. Nevertheless, many involve barely legal behaviours and include instances of deception, false promises and ruses designed to extort cash or goods from the target. Tourist scams exist in many countries and while the forms differ outwardly it will be suggested that the principles of exploiting tourists are similar. Stajano and Wilson (2009) note the use of a fairly widespread 'trade' language to characterise the players in these social situations. The target is referred to as the mark, the perpetrator is labelled the operator or sometimes the hustler, and if there are accomplices, they are known as the shills. Tourist scams are allied to crimes against tourists but in tourist scams there is an element of culpability since the tourist targets are usually trying to gain their own personal advantage from the interaction. As an illustration, a tourist whose property is simply stolen is a criminal victim, whereas a tourist who buys gemstones from a jewellery trader in the hope of profiteering by on-selling them but who later finds that half are worthless because the vendor has substituted cheaper products in the package, is the victim of a tourist scam.

A sample of common tourist scams is provided in Table 3.1. The examples are a subset of anti-social and exploitative acts against tourist taken from unpublished work in 2009 by the author and colleagues Focken, Kanlayanasukho, Smith and Semone in Thailand (Pearce et al., 2009).

Contemporary studies on the nature of scams in general provide some psychological insight into the way tourists are deceived and implicated in these troubling circumstances. In a publication prepared for the British Office of Fair Trading, researchers at the University of Exeter (2009) focused

TABLE 3.1 TOURIST SCAMS IN THAILAND

Service deception

Taxis: In this scam airport taxi operators approach new arrivals and offer the cheapest fare into the city. By adding surcharges and tolls, tourists actually can pay considerably more than metered and regulated taxis. Arguably the culpability of the tourist is low and the degree of seriousness of the scam is modest.

Airport porters: Smiling and physically strong airport porters assist passengers with luggage by physically taking hold of heavy bags and lugging them to nearby taxis. They then ask for money for the service and undoubtedly get some further rewards from their unregulated taxi colleagues. Tourist culpability here is low and the seriousness of the attempt to scam the marks is low.

The fake reception call: Late in the evening the reception calls the hotel guest suggesting the need to recheck credit card numbers which were a little hard to read on the first scanning to get a recently announced discount. The guest is simply asked to read out the credit card number again then the eventual bill can be changed in their favour. The call is a fake and the provision of credit card details sets up the hustler with the bases for fake credit card production. Tourist culpability is moderate and the consequences potentially expensive and serious.

Cash confusions: Payment in an unfamiliar currency can lead to a suggestion that the tourist pay in cash US dollars or Euros and receive change in the same currency, thus saving on exchange rate conversions. The notes in US dollars or Euros which the hustler holds are counterfeit so all change from larger notes become a profit. The tourist is a little culpable and the consequences can vary from trivial to expensive depending on the cash margins involved.

Shopping deception

The age old Thai gem scam: Tourists purchase what they believe to be good quality gems but in fact are sold inferior products. This may be because the gems are of low quality in the first place or there is a product substitution. There are multiple versions of this scam with varied other products from carpets to antiques, some of which come with supposedly valid authentication certificates. Culpability of the tourist here is moderate to high since the aim is often to make easy money in a reselling the items and the seriousness of the scam can be considerable with large amounts of money involved.

Purchasing pirated goods: Tourists purchase goods (e.g. watches, handbags) they know to be copies of famous brands. At times the goods are so cheaply made that they fall apart or stop working within a short period of time. Both the mark and the hustler are equally involved in maintaining this activity.

(Continued)

TABLE 3.1 CONTINUED

Non-arrival of purchases: Items which are bulky or which take time to make are bought on a 50% down payment and 50% on receipt basis. The goods never arrive at the home destination thus leaving the tourist with little recourse except to write off the money initially spent. Hustlers may operate this scam only infrequently allowing them to continue to trade in a legitimate way.

Interpersonal deception

The friend and the police: Tourists are befriended by a local or locals and share an enjoyable evening or entertainment-based outings. The tourist mark is then given pirated goods or drugs as a part of the friendship. Later police arrive at the hotel/accommodation location and search for the goods demanding payment to keep the matter quiet. The police may be corrupt officers or shills masquerading as police. The tourist mark is seriously in trouble with this scam since large payments may be requested and if drugs are involved the potential consequences are extreme. The tourist being scammed is at fault to the extent that they believed in the friendship and accepted the gifts as appropriate.

The massage service extras: Male tourists in particular using massage services are the mark in this scheme which sees the legitimate body massage turn into the offer of sexual services. Customers refusing to pay the extra money and use the sexual services have their massage terminated and are asked to leave. Complaints about the exploitation are deflected by threatening the arrival of the police or private security and associated suggestions that the tourist will be accused of harassing the female staff member. There is minimal fault here on behalf of the tourists, except perhaps in trusting the legitimacy of the operation, and some seriousness for them if the complaint is pursued.

The international romance: Romantic attachments between the mark and the operator are built on time together and intimacies established during the tourist's holiday. There is the promise of a continuity of the relationship and further contact but requests for supporting money for the operator and her/his family are involved. The operator may be simultaneously having multiple international partners who are being exploited to varying degrees with promises of future contact and long-term relationships. The cost to the mark here are financial and emotional and their culpability is testimony to the skill of the operator in building the trust in the relationship.

attention on the motivational and cognitive drivers which lead to consumer involvement in scams. Their work was concerned principally with email approaches to consumers. They suggested that appeals to trust and authority were important in influencing participation in the activity. Motivational factors which they described as visceral triggers – greed, fear and the desire to be liked – formed an important pattern in leading the marks to be involved. The study which included experimental and questionnaire work conceived of scam involvement as errors in consumer judgement. They noted that the perpetrators were skilled in using the authority criteria and relying on the visceral triggers. While these notions are promising in considering public scams in general, the University of Exeter studies did not engage with the very social nature of tourist scams such as those depicted in Table 3.1. It is likely that additional errors, attributions and motives may also be involved in close social interaction.

Some indication of the forces at work when scams have a more social nature is provided in a study by Stajano and Wilson (2009). Their work was based on a thorough analysis of the British TV documentary series *The Real Hustle*. The study was written by a computer scientist (Stajano) in collaboration with a professional hustler (Wilson) and was carried out to provide insights into human error underpinning computer security systems. They derived seven principles from their study of a considerable number of scams, some of which were tourist scams closely resembling the scam of the friend and the police, the cash confusion scam and the international romance scam already described. Many of the other scams they describe involve extracting pin card numbers, using sleight of hand to play marks at games of chance and extracting money from shop assistants through fake authorisation from their bosses. The principles are summarised in Table 3.2.

Responsibility and its Implications

A consideration of both the tricks of the hustlers and the motivational patterns of those they exploit, provide rich resources for our common-sense or everyday ways of judging others. We have already suggested that the fundamental attribution error comes into play when judging others and is likely to make us place more responsibility on the internal characteristics of others. Thus while we acknowledge the role of the hustler and his or her shills in exploiting the tourist, we are also predisposed to relate to the stories of exploitation by assigning quite a bit of blame to the tourists. The consensus and consistency principle is used in many of our social judgements in these circumstances, summarised in part by the cliché: 'Scam me once, shame on you. Scam me twice, shame on me.'

Our metaphor of the courtroom and the rules of evidence we use to decide who is most responsible for the tourists' troubles can be seen in operation in the multiple postings about global tourist rip-offs, scams and bad experiences. There are usually numerous commentators and threads of discussion following these stories of ill fortune. Commonly the stories move from assessing who is to blame to a consideration of how to behave and how to solve the problem in the future.

TABLE 3.2 SEVEN PRINCIPLES LEADING TO SCAM VICTIMISATION

The distraction principle
While you are distracted by what retains your interest, hustlers can do
   anything to you and you won't notice
The social compliance principle
Society trains people not to question authority. Hustlers exploit this
   'suspension of suspiciousness' to make you do what they want.
The herd principle
Even suspicious marks will let their guard down when everyone next to them
   appears to share the same risks. Safety in numbers? Not if they are all
   (shills) conspiring against you.
The dishonesty principle
Anything illegal you do will be used against you by the fraudster, making it
   harder for you to seek help once you realise you've been had.
The deception principle
Things and people are not what they seem. Hustlers know how to manipulate
   you to make you believe that they are.
The need and greed principle
Your needs and desires make you vulnerable. Once hustlers know what you
   really want, they can easily manipulate you.
The time principle
When you are under time pressure to make an important choice, you use a
   different decision strategy. Hustlers steer you towards a strategy involving
   less reasoning.

In posting his reactions to a web listing of Bangkok scams, an internet
commentator, labelling himself as Jeff, writes:

> Why on earth in a foreign country would you entertain talking to anyone
> that you do not know? ANYBODY who approaches you is out to get
> something. They either want you as a customer or a soft touch. Ignore
> them all no matter how innocent or innocuous they seem. It is contrary
> to western nature to ignore a smile and offered handshake from a tuk-tuk
> driver but in your own best interests smile and say 'Mai ouw' meaning
> DONT WANT. Smile and keep walking. Don't stop or hesitate.

(http://www.bangkokscams.com/scams-in-bangkok/khao=san-road-
indina-sikh-mind-readers.html#jc-allComments Sun 31 Oct 2010.)

We can usefully redeploy the theory of social representations to consider
how these public attributions of responsibility become the basis for citizen
action or government control of tourist-linked activities. A strong social representation that gullible tourists are at fault and that they get themselves
into trouble is a responsibility attribution which permits public authorities

to ignore some scam operators. If on the other hand, a widespread tourist attribution is that many hustlers exist, as in the views of Jeff the internet commentator, then the recommended best practice is that it is desirable to avoid all contact with local people. This representation may be particularly damaging to the international appeal of a destination if it becomes enshrined in destination images.

The attribution of responsibility can also produce some surprising responses given the initial culpability of the marks. In the case of the 'age old Thai gem scam' there have been organised delegations to the Thai police and authorities wanting the operators involved to be closed down. The protest action can be seen as deriving from the marks' shared view that the gem operators are at fault for failing to deliver cheap goods from which they as participating tourists may profit. This is a self serving attribution made in the marks' favour buttressed by their in-group representation. No responsibility is being taken here for the tourists' implicit 'visceral' motivations such as greed and a planned willingness to profit in the future.

Several strands of further thorough academic work can be identified in the context of tourist scams, how attributions are made about them and the potential consequences which follow from those attributions. A first kind of study could involve coding and categorising scams according to the frequency with which they use the principles outlined by Stajano and Wilson. Additionally, as outlined succinctly in the previous paragraphs, the internet description and commentary on tourist scams is a source of research information. Using naturalistic data of this type could be productive in classifying the kinds of attributional statements made in commentary on others' experiences. The value of using naturalistic data in accounting for explanations has been recognised for some time and methods to assess the available information have been proposed (Harvey et al., 1988). Further, taking versions of tourist scenarios and asking select groups with varying levels of involvement and authority to consider who should be held accountable for troubling outcomes is another potential line of work. Such studies may provide subtle insight into some of the public debates about who should be responsible for and what actions should be taken to promote safer tourism settings. Tourist scams are at one end of a spectrum of threats to tourists' good times and their further study could usefully explore the exact influence mechanism which underpins them. Such operational information combined with an understanding of the motives, character strengths, and personalities of those who get involved may also be insightful for both future travellers and site managers.

Crimes against Tourists

In the same preliminary study on scams undertaken in Thailand, the research group collected broader anti-tourist crime statistics for the last three years (Pearce *et al.*, 2009). Before reviewing this material and related studies, an important caveat on the nature of the phenomenon we are considering is required. All data about crime rates are subject to error. Much criminal activity goes unreported and key organisations providing the data may have strong interests in representing information in ways that favour their efforts to reduce crime (Ambinder, 1992). At an even broader level, while any criminal activity against tourists is too much activity, the number of tourists who fall prey to criminal activity needs also to be put in the context of the millions of safe and relatively uneventful tourist trips undertaken annually.

In the data collected from the Thai tourist police in our research team's work it was established that while crimes reported to the Thai tourism police had declined by almost 50% in the period 2005 to 2008, there were still more than 4000 notified cases of property and document loss. Together these categories constituted more than 90% of the crimes reported. The major improvements occurring in the designated period were in the category of property losses. Data from diverse locations confirms some of the patterns noted in our statistics from Thailand (George, 2010; Pizam & Mansfeld, 1996, 2006). The categories used in these studies of crime perception and crime statistics are usually framed within the kind of definition of crime offered by Ryan (1993); that is, crime consists of 'actions contrary to written or case law applying either in the tourist generating or the tourist receiving country' (Ryan, 1993: 174). Further, crime is subdivided into what are referred to as the Big six categories – murder and aggravated assault, rape, public violence, burglary, robbery and car theft. It is consistent with data from Hawaii and the Caribbean as well as West and South Africa and our Thai data that tourists are four to six times more likely to be robbed or burgled than encounter the other extremely negative experiences (Chesney-Lind & Lind, 1986; de Albuquerque & McElroy, 1999; Ferreira, 1999; George, 2003).

The empirical studies which examine official statistics represent just one style of work in this field. There are also analyses of the perception of crime in various locations with some of these studies being inspired by dramatic media reporting of major crime incidents with tourists as victims (Boakye, 2010; George, 2003, 2010; Howard, 2009; Pizam & Mansfeld, 2006). It is notable that tourists of different nationalities rate their perceived levels of safety and comfort and their overall concern with crime in destinations differently. As Ferreira (1999: 319) reports, German tourists are approximately 15% less worried about crime in South Africa than their Australian fellow tourists and 26% less concerned than tourists from Asia.

Howard (2009) studying the dangers to tourists in Thailand provides evidence which strongly suggests that there is a tight correspondence between the crime statistics and the tourists' perceptions of and experiences of crime. He reports that the dominant criminal activity experienced in Thailand was being robbed, sometimes through being drugged or mugged.

Howard's study also confirms the prevalence of scams and what he describes as hazards in terms of the reported prevalence of overcharging, problems with taxis, police corruption and approaches from touts and bar girls or would be companions. It is notable that his sample was 85% male and consisted principally of United States, Australian and United Kingdom tourists, so perhaps the more resilient or less concerned German tourists noted in the Ferreira studies might have been less concerned with the activities under discussion.

Michalko (2003) provides further evidence from Hungary which suggests that some nationalities are probably less cautious in their tourist behaviour. He analysed the nationalities of crime victims in Hungary and found that German and Austrian tourists were disproportionately the victims of crimes especially burglary compared to the tourists from neighbouring eastern European countries. Michalko's explanation was two fold: tourists from the Western Europe are more affluent making them better targets but they may also be more careless since they are less used to the high levels of crime still persisting in developing Eastern European nations.

It is possible to move beyond descriptive information and empirical data to formulate a more complete understanding of the forces at work in the tourism crime interface. A first step towards formulating a more conceptual understanding of the tourists in trouble linked to criminal activities can be found in a five-part classification scheme offered by Ryan (1993). One category identified by Ryan views tourists as incidental victims; here the crimes against them are not due to their tourist role but they are simply in a situation where anybody could have been a victim. A second category Ryan identified was later labelled as the crimogenic factor (Ryan & Kinder, 1996). In essence the term suggests tourist locations can become specific venues for crime. The kinds of location being specified as crimogenic include entertainment strips where businesses serving large crowds of passing tourists. Such settings include a mix of bars, nightclubs, markets, cheap shopping and gaming opportunities. Crime and tourism links may be thought of in these settings as involving multiple criminal activities including money laundering and, in some countries, prostitution and drug dealing. A third kind of link between tourists and crime is simply numerical; more tourists provide more people for criminals to prey upon. This category differs from the incidental tourist category since in this case the physically identifiable characteristics of those who are out of their normal surroundings makes them softer targets. Ryan's scheme does not neglect the direct involvement by tourists themselves in generating crime particularly in creating a demand for stolen or pirated goods and possibly illegal services. Finally the presence of tourists in prominent hotels, at attractions or at transport nodes can provide identifiable targets for public violence including individual acts of insanity and planned acts of terrorism.

A number of authors have repeated the themes underlying these categorisations. Crotts (1996, 2011), as well as other commentators, has used the notions of hot spot theory and the routine activities approach to describe the same kinds of tourism – crime links as has Ryan. There is an incremental value in these two formulations with the concept of hot spots being used to identify specific locations within the crimogenic places where the criminal activity is most prevalent. Additionally, the routine activities approach suggests that criminals will exist irrespective of the presence of tourists and that provided three enabling conditions are met (easy victims, motivated criminals and low levels enforcement) crime will take place. Tourists may or may not get caught up in these routine criminal efforts. The routine activities approach reinforces the perspective that the extent to which tourists' appearance and behaviour single them out as soft targets will be matched by the extent to which they are victims of attempted crimes.

Boakye (2010) has provided evidence for the relevance of the routine activities approach by noting that the distinctiveness of tourists in certain settings of tourism institutionalisation makes them more susceptible in some instances and less in others to criminal efforts. He notes that in Ghana, West Africa, for example, travelling on buses offers criminals occasional opportunities to access relatively unprotected luggage and may promote theft whereas when tourists stay in quality accommodation they can benefit from security which criminals do not bother to try to breach.

There is additional work of interest which develops further ideas about the tourism crime relationship and it contains the seeds of proactive responses to the situations in which tourists might be enmeshed. Tarlow (2000, 2006) considers the tourism crime relationships from the broader perspective of ideas in sociological theory and criminology. He concludes from his foray into the associated literature that tourists are susceptible to criminal attack because they tend to trust those they should not and that in some senses they are alienated from the place they visit. He argues that Durkheim's concept of anomie applies to tourists (Jones, 1974). The term anomie is used to suggest that tourists are not as mindful of their setting since they are potentially preoccupied with struggling to deal with the society in which they find themselves. Tarlow also views tourists' stress, specifically the stress of taking care of valuables which they may not usually have to carry such as passports, extra bags and cameras, as playing a role in making them less aware of immediate dangers. Although these ideas are all plausible they effectively restate the simple issue that tourists are less mindful of the dangers in the situations confronting them due to unfamiliarity (Figure 3.3).

A more important dimension of the sociological and criminology literature derives from an appreciation of the economic disparity between tourists and hosts and how this gap may be seen as partially legitimising certain kinds of robbery and burglary. In this view there is a 'Robin Hood' element – the notion of wealth being redistributed from the rich to the poor – in these

Figure 3.3 Mindfulness of danger
Tourists occupied with finding their way in crowded settings also often carry
more items of personal baggage than they might in their own home location.
They can become targets for pickpockets seeking to steal handbags and wallets.
Commonly scam artists work in pairs with one creating a distraction capturing
tourist attention. In such situations tourists can be temporality less mindful of
their possessions enabling criminals to be successful in their regular work. The
tourists here may be incidental rather than focused targets of the activity.

kinds of anti-tourist crimes. The implication of this view is that such a perception may be partially shared by local law enforcement personnel who
may therefore soften their approach to pursuing offenders. The value of the
sociological material is to reinforce the view, now widely espoused in tourism development studies, that tourism is not a phenomenon which can be
studied in isolation (Arntzen *et al.*, 2008; Harrison, 2010; Jafari, 2005;
Moscardo, 2008). As Tarlow suggests:

> The economic undulations of the host community will have an impact
> on the local tourism community. (Tarlow, 2000: 146)

Of particular interest in this context is that the well being of the local community and its subsections will have significant implications for the nature
and extent of tourism-related crime. De Albuquerque and McElroy (1999) and
Cohen (1996) both add the further perspective that subcultural predispositions
to violence and deception shape the form of anti-tourist crime.

TABLE 3.3   ACTIONS TO COMBAT TOURIST CRIME

Cooperative planning

The development of a tourism and safety team comprising law enforcement, local government and tourism interests

Pro-active police participation on hotel and tourism boards

National coordination of criminal activity to monitor movement of tourism linked crimes

Other partnerships among law enforcement, tourism authorities and the private sector (e.g. marketing activities and safety campaigns)

Development of community safety plans

Media Communication

Develop links with the media to resolve problems of lack of cooperation/ sensationalism

Provision of crisis management consultations regarding negative publicity

Training

Employee security training

Police tourism training-sensitivity to and communication with tourists

Development of tourism safety courses for the industry

Surveillance

Increase of manpower – especially if community economic times are difficult

High police visibility – 'out of car' patrols recommended

Police talking with tourists to build confidence

Property inspections to prevent crime hotspots

Personnel checks – workers in the industry to be thoroughly vetted for criminal connections

Academic analyses of the tourist crime relationship can often conclude with rather vague suggestions for managing crime. As yet there appear to be no author collaborations between tourism researchers and criminals or between police and tourism researchers such as that provided in the study of scams. One major exception to this criticism of a lack of specificity in anti-tourist crime recommendations is provided in the work of Pizam *et al.* (1997) who offer a pragmatic 15-item list of suggestions. The list they provide can be conveniently reorganised and slightly modified under four headings (see Table 3.3).

Directions

For the purposes of this chapter some issues remain for further analysis and research. The recommendations offered by Pizam and colleagues may not really attack the most far-reaching issues in a community which drive crime. In particular, the government policies which shape the permitted forms of tourism development and the distribution of wealth and well-being in a country are salient macro-level issues which need to be considered. From a critical theory perspective one view of the measures proposed in Table 3.3 is that they are 'band-aid' measures dealing with the symptoms rather than addressing the driving cause of the pain in the community. In this view investing in tourism police or security guards may be less necessary if there are more jobs and better employment options than burglary, robbery and prostitution.

The kinds of research which have been conducted in this area favour descriptive statistical reporting of crime figures or perceptions of crime. New routes to refresh the research on the topic can be identified. McElroy *et al.* (2008) suggest some directions. They propose a much closer examination of the situations in which tourist find themselves harassed or targeted by local unsavoury characters. Their suggestions include an analysis of the social interaction sequences and the non-verbal behaviours involved, possibly followed up by focus group reinvestigating how tourists felt about and understood the interaction. This is one line of promising line of work and could be matched by a closer examination of the physical settings and defensible space in which criminal acts occur. This kind of micro-treatment of crime scenes could follow the foundation work of Newman (1972, 1995) and offer pathways for managers and civic authorities to use architectural solutions as well as boosting electronic and personal surveillance of the most troublesome locations. Other research possibilities also exist, particularly in the area of evaluating the messages which tourists receive about safety and crime avoiding skills. The rich and extensive catalogue of persuasion tricks which hustlers use could be depicted in lively training and educational packages with a special focus on building tourists' skills to recognise warning signs (cf. Cialdini, 2001). The research undertaken in the area of scams and much of Cialdini's work on social influence could be used to isolate key social situations where specific tourist advice can be clearly communicated. How to guard one's valuables, avoid the spiking of drinks and how to deflect gaze are all teachable behavioural routines which offer the prospects of reducing criminal attacks. Researchers could be closely involved in designing such programs of influence and then use their skills to see how well tourist can recall and then practice the behaviours demonstrated. Efforts to participate in this more action oriented research might serve the well-being of tourists and support civic and business crime prevention efforts more effectively than conducting recurring studies of crime statistics.

Health Challenges

Tourists can be hurt, seriously injured or indeed die while travelling. Tourists' mental and psychological health is also of interest in this volume but a consideration of the more cognitive and affective impacts of travel will be treated in subsequent chapters. The field of travel medicine has evolved to deal specifically with the impacts of travel and the tourism setting on the human body, its immune systems and functioning (Jones *et al.*, 2009; Zuckerman, 2009). It is functional in this chapter to travel lightly in terms of citing only a representative subset of studies from this considerable volume of travel medicine work. In effect, we are concerned with only some of the highlights of this work and even then much more from the perspective of studying tourist behaviour than diagnosing and treating medical problems.

There are arguably two dimensions – one describing level of risk and one defining the tourists' degree of responsibility – which serve to characterise many of the tourists' health-related incidents. In the high-risk and high-responsibility category there are numerous adventurous recreational behaviours which may result in accidents and tourism health problems. For activities such as white water rafting, remote area hiking, ocean swimming and canyoneering, tourists do place themselves in a high-risk environment and elect to do so, sometimes with very bad outcomes (Heggie & Amundson, 2009: 246). In the low-risk and low-responsibility category tourists may contract uncommon but serious diseases or infections or be injured during kidnapping or terrorist attacks. In these instances tourists may have little control over the situation and their responsibility is low. Examples include the unfortunate cases of catching primary amoebic meningoencephalitis through swimming in warm freshwater. In an attribution of responsibility sense this must be considered to be a very unlucky outcome since the number of globally reported cases amongst tourists is restricted to a mere handful of reports (Heggie, 2010).

Traffic accidents, a relatively high frequency and common cause of medical problems for tourists, may be seen as high risk but the responsibility can vary from quite direct such as unsafe driving behaviours to very low such as when others generate the accident (Wilks *et al.*, 2000). The fourth and final category is when the risk is low and the responsibility is high. Promiscuous sexual behaviour when the participants use condoms may be seen as relatively low risk (health risks do remain), but since such behaviours are explicitly sought by both parties the responsibility is high (Bauer, 2007). Intimate behaviours when unprotected sex is involved and the participants are likely to have had multiple partners changes the situation into the high-risk, high-responsibility category (McNulty *et al.*, 2010; Rogstad, 2004).

Another large subset of work relevant to tourist behaviour lies in the strengths and frailties of the human body and its sensory systems. This work too has important implications for human health and evades easy categorisation in the four-cell model outlined above. The limitations of the physiology of human beings as a species is in one sense not a direct personal responsibility but it is sometimes possible to manage one's behaviour to avoid being stressed by hypothermia, hyperthermia, dehydration, altitude sickness, various forms of motion sickness, diarrhoea and decompression sickness (Ashcroft, 2000; Greenfield, 2000).

There are also debilitating issues which repeatedly put tourists into trouble and can produce life-threatening health challenges. Tse (2006) labels these forces as the crises of tourism and four broad categories may be distinguished. There are extreme and well-recorded challenges to tourists and tourist destinations arising from (1) natural catastrophes; (2) terrorism and civil unrest; (3) regional and multi-nation epidemics; and (4) technical problems such as airline crashes and disasters (Beirman, 2003; Timothy, 2006). The scale of these problems can vary from global impacts to events with a more confined set of implications. There is substantial documentation of these tourism concerns in key books and reviews (cf. Hall *et al.*, 2003; Pizam & Mansfeld, 2006).

It is consistent with the style of this volume to highlight some directions in which the work on tourists and their health challenges may be developed. An overriding conclusion from many of the travel medicine studies and some of the research on safety generally is to propose better information dissemination to tourists about the risks and the challenges which might confront them. These kinds of cautionary advice mechanisms vary from the well-known government travel advisories to specific brochures and websites with travel tips. Compelling questions which have been asked and which need to be asked repeatedly in this field are do these efforts and communications make a difference? Bauer (2005) expresses her concern that they do not. It is clear from the voluminous work on travel medicine, including studies of infectious diseases and tourist activity induced trauma that tourists continue to participate in much unsafe behaviour.

In a colourful and dramatic illustration of the unsafe behaviours of tourists Ghiglieri and Myers (2001) review all of the known fatal mishaps in the Grand Canyon. They observe that standing on the rim of the canyon is often a prelude to a fall and almost inevitable serious injury or death. Falls within the canyon are common but so too are drownings on the river at the base of the canyon especially when flash floods and sudden rains change the parameters of tourist activities. Lightning and venomous creatures take their toll as well. They conclude their considered review of all the incidents as follows:

> The take home lesson here is that people who die traumatically in the Grand Canyon die mainly-almost universally due to their own or their guide's poor judgment. It is impossible for the rest of us to protect them fully from these personal failings ... Forewarned it is then up to the personal responsibility of each of us to avoid killing ourselves and thereby also tacitly accusing the wilderness of being our murderer. (Ghiglieri & Myers, 2001: 366–367) (Figure 3.4)

Figure 3.4 The Grand Canyon and responsibility
The cumulative toll of people who are injured and killed at open tourist sites such as the Grand Canyon is considerable. The quest for the better photograph is inherently dangerous as crumbling and unstable rock edges, wind gusts and wet surfaces are unpredictable sources of danger. Access to a natural setting does not mean that the setting, however spectacular and well used, is reliably safe. Tourists need to adopt an internal rather than an external attribution of responsibility when explaining what can go wrong in such settings.

It is possible to return to the introductory sections of this chapter on motivational patterns and explanations of conduct to search for further answers to these continuing problems. The motivational patterns of the more adventurous tourists suggest that the drivers of travel switch only gradually and with considerable travel experience. Importantly there are life cycle influences at work too and fulfilling stimulation, status and achievement needs generated by participating in risk relevant behaviour is likely to persist as enduring profile of motives for some subgroups. Even when negative outcomes occur it is unlikely that many tourists with this motivational profile will blame themselves as the self serving attributional bias operates to protect individual's view of the choices they make. Further, in some cases the health challenges are commonly held by all judging parties to be outside of tourists' control since the attribution for what has happened in these instances lies with the larger forces at work in both the natural world and the conduct of commercial businesses.

Food poisoning, for example, occurs occasionally in cruise ships and in aircraft (McMullan *et al.*, 2007). Identifying what has gone wrong with the management quality controls is important in these kinds of instances. Perhaps the most cautious of tourists could improve their probability of not being affected by such outbreaks if they avoided cold meats, mayonnaise and salads sourced from Africa and Asia (cf. MacLaurin, 2003). These items may contain *Salmonella* and *Staphylococcus* causal agents and appear to account for over 70% of the problems. Nevertheless, the list of other foods which have caused problems is long and short of avoiding all food provided by transport companies there remains some probability of negative outcomes. This kind of hyper vigilant or total avoidance behaviour sometimes emerges as a recommendation in the travel medicine literature. Heggie (2010), for example, commenting on primary amoebic meningoencephalitis contracted through swimming in warm fresh water suggests that simply not undertaking such water-based activity is advisable. For tropical tourism and the spa industry, as well as all those who love the activity, this represents an unrealistic option.

Given the logic outlined above, effectively that patterns of needs will continue to push some travellers into riskier behaviours and from attribution theory that they will reduce their own responsibility for negative outcomes, a serious question becomes how to still influence those most at risk without simply suggesting that the safest travel behaviours are virtual experiences conducted at home (cf. Tussyadiah & Fesenmaier, 2009). One answer to this conundrum might lie in a closer liaison between medical and safety researchers and tourist behaviour analysts. Medical science is a highly specialist, respectable and avowedly technical enterprise but could benefit from more incisive treatment of the social interactions which shape behavioural choices.

Directions

Wong *et al.* (2007) illustrate some of these possibilities in their work considering the issue of unsafe sexual behaviour by international tourists. They note how the immediate dynamics of the encounter override broader attitudes towards condom use. Their work contains clues as to how people decide to participate in unsafe behaviour under conditions of 'hot' or affect laden decision making. It appears the men in their study were taking cues from the women with whom they were interacting and their use of safe sex behaviours was nearly always adopted if the woman suggested that condom use was required. These considerations are very close to the time pressure factors influencing sound judgement noted by Shapiro and Wilson in the study of scams. The concepts here are fully in accord with the thorough psychology analyses of the heuristics of rapid decisions (Cialdini, 2001). In essence, decisions in these settings are somewhat 'automatic'. They are influenced by the participants' behavioural repertoire which is their knowledge of what to do and having the skill to do it efficiently. In this view, unsafe or safe behaviour is not the outcome of a personal internal debate about the probabilities of the behaviours consequences. Following these considerations there appears to be a genuine research and applied opportunity to communicate skills, routines and rules of thumb which can be implemented under the most pressing and emotion-rich conditions. This approach provides a continuity of approach in this chapter because the same kind of implication was drawn from the consideration of the review of tourist scams. For researchers in both the medical science and the tourist behaviour field the possibility of collaborative effort to assess the effectiveness of these hot decision heuristics and how best they might be communicated are significant directions.

Other links between medical science research and tourists in trouble can also be formulated. Much of the work conducted in these two fields is a snapshot – the studies provide accounts of what happens or has happened at a point in time. More longitudinal work can be proposed. Shaw and Leggat (2009) for example track illness and injury among affluent and older travellers on a seniors' tour through Indochina. A small component of their study suggests that there are patterns of illness and injury which vary across the duration of the tour. A link can be made here to the psychological profile and the nature of tracking the emotions and psychological well-being across the duration of the tourist experience (Coghlan & Pearce, 2010). It should be possible to undertake more longitudinal work on group tour and cruise operations for example to document the way fluctuations in risky behaviour occur thus linking physical outcomes more closely to psychological states and social interaction.

The perspective on tourist experience offered in earlier chapters also repays attention when considering the tourist in trouble. In the earlier formulation it was noted that it is appropriate to consider tourists' sensory systems and emotions, their attitudes and their understanding of the setting as well as how they interact with others and move in space and time. The orchestra of experience analogy suggests that for the scams, for the crimes against tourists and the health issues they encounter these elements vary in their power to influence the prevailing pattern of experience. The motivational and attributional frameworks discussed in this chapter provide insight into how tourists understand and select the settings which they choose and in which they find themselves in trouble.

It can be suggested that the role of others and the forces exerted by key relationships (immediate contacts and companions in this context) may be understudied as one component of the experience array in the area of tourists' troubled times. The social pressures and powers of others to incite unsafe behaviour or fail to act judiciously to support tourists or travel partners may be important in setting up improved practices to encourage safe behaviour. There is interesting evidence that a sense of the mere presence of others in the form of an image of a pair of eyes can limit small scale anti-social behaviours such as theft (Bates *et al.*, 2006). It would seem that both those who commit crimes against tourists and tourists themselves who participate in unsafe or illegal behaviour might be influenced by the greater presence and persuasive efforts of others rather than relying on their own character strengths to keep them out of difficulty. The implication here for educational and promotional programs to deal with troubling situations may be usefully thought of as targeting not just individuals but the reference groups and relationships which surround the individuals causing the problems. The application of these ideas about the multifaceted nature of the tourists' experiences is a solid illustration of Lewin's maxim that a theory or conceptual scheme is often a very practical resource for thinking in fresh ways about an issue.

4   The Tourists' Footprints

Introduction

Our concern in this volume is with contemporary tourist behaviour and experience. Nevertheless, it is valuable to recognise that much of what tourists do today reiterates patterns of the past. In this spirit, we will explore how tourists follow the footsteps of some of those who have gone before them. The expression 'the tourists' footprints' will be considered in three ways in this chapter. A first meaning will consist of exploring the symbolic value of the expression with a focus on how tourists follow the routes of others. This analysis will consider spiritual journeys as well as the popular walking tracks and routes which become personal quests for many tourists. A second area of interest will lie in empirical approaches to tracking tourists as they move through spaces. Such studies emphasise observable behaviour more clearly than most other lines of work described in this book. This work will consider queues, pedestrian movement and the use of space in such settings as theme parks and attractions. A model of tourist crowding and its relation to congestion will be included in these considerations. A third approach to considering the tourists' footprints will lie in the dissection of the term ecological footprint. The body of literature which accompanies this term is centrally focused on assessing, in a holistic and comprehensive manner, the resources consumed by contemporary tourists.

In this chapter it will then be suggested that by understanding some of the symbolic meanings of travel, by considering the specific behavioural patterns which are evident in tourist locations and by providing an overview of the wider set of resources which tourists use, it is possible to formulate some suggestions for sustainable tourist behaviour. These tactics, suggestions and practices will form the final part of the chapter. It is appreciated that much work has been conducted in all of these areas of interest but, in the spirit of this volume, an attempt will be made to integrate some existing work and then identify research opportunities which might advance the way tourists can tread lightly.

Symbolic Paths

There are both religious and secular traditions influencing the paths some tourists choose to follow. As van Egmond (2011: 125–128) has observed,

Western tourists (and researchers) should not assume that their understanding of common tourist behaviours is valid for tourists from Arab, Asian and African worlds. For example, the world's major religions provide master narratives which shape where many followers choose to walk. For the most devout there are prescribed routes which have become a mandatory part of their life experience. The five pillars of the Islamic faith include undertaking the hajj- an Arabic word which means to travel with purpose (Ahmed, 1992). The hajj specifically refers to the journey to the Ka'aba, the structure near the centre of Mecca. This plain cube-shaped building is usually covered in black cloth inscribed with sayings from the Koran. Of equal importance is the black stone which is the remnant of the shrine of the Prophet Abraham and the spiritual heart of the Muslim world. The call to visit the Ka'aba originated with Abraham being instructed by God to tell people to undertake a pilgrimage to the shrine he had built, but it was Muhammad's two pilgrimages to the Ka'aba 1500 years ago which truly 'enshrined' the practice. In the contemporary world the hajj is a spiritual trek which is unmatched in terms of the number of people following in the footsteps of others. Over 150 countries provide more than 2.5 million visitors to this specific part of Saudi Arabia for the 10 days of the hajj (Sulaiman *et al.*, 2009) (Figure 4.1).

While there is a small body of work in the English academic literature on the management issues surrounding the continued growth of the hajj, little work has yet been published outside of the Arabic world on the meanings and experiences of those who travel to Mecca. Questions of interest in such future studies could include the ways in which the experience confirms the tourists' values. Is it the case that the actual experience richly augments the fundamental beliefs thus establishing a spiral confirming both the Islamic faith and personal fulfilment, or is it indeed the case that modern Muslims bring a worldly and critical eye to the experience, finding it less rewarding than anticipated? If the answers are not yet available in the published English literature about the hajj, there are some indications of what might lie at the centre of hajj tourist experiences from analogous studies of Christian and Jewish tourists.

A second site of pilgrimage on the grand scale is Jerusalem. Again there are prescribed paths for the faithful to follow. Mark Twain wrote about his 19th century experience of visiting Jerusalem and walking around the Holy City:

> We are surfeited with sights. Nothing has any fascination for us now but the Church of the Holy Sepulchre. We have been there every day and have not grown tired of it, but we are weary of everything else. The sights are too many. They swarm about you at every step; no single foot of ground in all Jerusalem or within its neighbourhood seems to be without a stirring history of its own. It is a very relief to steal a walk of a hundred yards without a guide along to talk unceasingly about every

Figure 4.1 The Prophet's Mosque, Medina

This image supplied originally to *The Journal of Tourism Studies* by the Saudi Arabia Embassy, Australia, highlights the spectacular architecture which inspires pilgrims as a part of the hajj. Access to such sites is restricted to those devoted to the faith and the image has been taken at a point of low use. In the height of the hajj these kinds of sites present a carpet of white as the devout pray in unison at regular daily intervals throughout the duration of the hajj.

stone you step upon and drag you back ages and ages to the day when it achieved celebrity. (Twain, 1864: 393) (Figure 4.2)

The struggle that tourists may have to find a balance between provided and personal meanings when following the footsteps of others is a considerable one. Epstein and Kheimets (2001) studied Russian Jewish tourists travelling to Israel and came to several conclusions from their participant observation studies and interviews of tourists on 15 such tours. They discovered that many tourists were motivated to follow the paths laid out for them in a major novel, a tale of fantasy and political satire by the author Mikhail Bulgakov. The importance of his major work *The Master and Margarita* for tourist study lies in the fact that it was set in part, in Jerusalem and was available to the Russian Jews at a time when the Bible was banned by the communist regime of that country. Bugakov's novel was therefore a de-facto

Figure 4.2 Church of the Holy Sepulchre
Mark Twain found the Church of the Holy Sepulchre the only lasting structure in Jerusalem to maintain his interest. By way of contrast 21st century tourist pilgrims follow devoutly the many other footprints of the saints and saviours. It is noteworthy that for some tourists actually visiting sites they have imagined for so long can be disappointing either due to scale issues or to modern surrounds. The resolution to the disappointment seems to lie in investing meaning in personally discovered insights or other features of the setting.

guide to the sites of the Holy City and numerous respondents in the study felt drawn to the key sites described in the novel with great eloquence and imagination.

It is pivotal though to record that some famous sites are physically unimpressive. For the Russian tourists used to splendidly decorated churches, luxurious summer gardens and grand-scale historical structures the reality of visiting the sites in Jerusalem was often a very unremarkable experience. Mark Twain, whose observations we have already considered, provided a direct view as to how tourists deal with places which are less impressive than they imagined. He suggested his tourists simply mimicked the words, feelings and phrases of those who had gone before them and whose reactions they had read (Twain, 1864: 356–357). Epstein and Kheimets found that tourists turned to other experiences in Jerusalem to augment their longed for spiritual and identity affirming experiences. For many of the Jewish tourist from Russia, Yad VaShem, the museum which presents the horrific events of the Holocaust, became the central highlight of the visit and acted as a powerful compensation to the lesser experiences of seeing the historical religious locations.

Selwyn (1996) has noted that an overload of guide-delivered information as well as other forms of presentation can compress or distort the time lines of history. These interpretive efforts can make it difficult for tourists to appreciate what they are viewing. In some visited settings where tourists are following the paths of others they may have to work hard at personalising their experiences and surmount the limitations of the site and the way it is presented (Ballantyne, 1998; Horne, 1992). The opportunity to closely monitor visitors' on-site experiences at significant locations and to observe how they manufacture and create their own personalised story about the visit represents an emerging opportunity for future tourism studies.

Edensor (2000) explores the ideas underlying the meaning of walking in a more secular British context. His analysis considers the purpose and practice of walking in the countryside which he contrasts with the rapid, mechanised and functional walking witnessed in urban environments (cf. Simmel, 1971). Edensor suggests that it is by walking in the countryside that we rediscover our sensory capacities. This argument can be located within the context of evolutionary psychology thinking. As a species with excellent binocular vision and an upright stance we have evolved to move through environments on foot and by ambling, strolling and sauntering through landscapes, our exploratory and orienting systems are reactivated (Grandin & Johnson, 2009: 6–7).

Additionally, our walking practices in the countryside arguably represent the opportunity to adopt a romantic gaze, a perspective which Urry (1990, 2000) has emphasised as central to understanding much of the individual tourist experience. In this view walkers have the time to contemplate the natural environment and to reflect on their role in the physical world and the lives they are leading. These views of walking identify contemporary tourists, and possibly especially certain classes of English speaking tourists, as following in William Wordsworth's footsteps. It was Wordsworth who was not only an active walker but a significant poet in the Romantic Movement and who articulated the search for the sublime in nature. These kinds of deep motives for walking and the escape from the mundane world are not disconnected from our earlier consideration of spiritual journeys since a common theme in the lives of prophets and Christ is the contemplative time such figures spent in the wilderness.

A second kind of contemporary walking style and purpose can also be identified. While a casual stroll in the countryside offers its participants a chance to contemplate the setting and the world they live in, there is also strenuous, achievement-oriented walking where the physical challenge of completing the journey is important. These kinds of challenges exist in numerous countries and some of the famous examples include the Appalachian way (USA), the Kokoda trail (Papua New Guinea), the Milford track (New Zealand) and El Camino de Santiago (Spain). There are many more. Some of these challenging walks appeal because of the environmental beauty of the setting. Others define the very concept of a physical challenge and yet others retain spiritual and symbolic value deriving from historical events or mythical qualities arising from the literature of the society.

Fielding *et al.* (1992) conducted a study of tourist behaviour which provides some insights into the interaction among tourist motivation, perceptions of time and enjoyment for these arduous kinds of tourist treks. The specific study site was Uluru (formerly Ayers rock) in central Australia and the study was of the now controversial climb to the top of the rock rather than a walk (du Cros & Johnstone, 2002; Hueneke & Baker, 2009). The Uluru climb is physically challenging but provides striking views of a unique physical and spiritual landscape. It also has a specific start and finish. Researchers in this study were positioned at the start of the climb and also at its highest point. They asked those who reached the summit as well as those who did not, a set of questions about their motivation, their enjoyment of the activity and their estimates of the time taken to undertake the task. For many visitors it is a 2–3 h expedition and quite challenging because temperatures are usually high. The perceived time was later compared with the actual time recorded for each tourist's trek. The pattern of motivation responses was assessed and climbers divided into those expressing more intrinsic motivation responses and those more concerned with status and achievement. In a broad sense this study anticipated the distinction between emphasising some of the intrinsic motives which characterise the middle layer of the travel career pattern approach and motives which are in the outer layer of that system (Pearce & Lee, 2005) (Figure 4.3).

The climbers with the different motives reported their experiences differently. Intrinsically motivated climbers were more satisfied with the experience and their satisfaction was not influenced by whether or not they made it to the top of the climb. They also tended to perceive the time they had taken as less than the actual time they had spent during their Uluru experience. By way of contrast, extrinsic or achievement motivated tourists were satisfied if they reached the summit but markedly less so if they failed to complete the full trek. They tended to overestimate the time taken to achieve the full experience.

These results provide some interesting connections to Edensor's work and the ideas of the walk as a life metaphor in either fast or slow time. For some walking enthusiasts, and particularly those for whom fulfilling achievement goals are very important, the walk or climb may be approached as a test of character. Wainwright (1969) suggests that giving up on a walk, such as the Pennine Way, is like giving up on the harder parts of life. This perspective of achievement can be found in reports by tourists in their online comments:

Figure 4.3 Climbing Uluru/Ayers Rock
It is a physical challenge to complete the whole climb from the base of Uluru, central Australia, to the top. There are multiple plaques at the starting point commemorating those who have died in the attempt, usually from heart attacks brought on by physical stress. Uluru is 348 metres in height and the climb is a 1600 metres return trip with some steep and hazardous sections. The climb is still possible but the local indigenous community prefer tourists to walk around the base of the rock. This 9.4 kilometre circular walk is increasing popular and still challenging.

Reporting on walking the Kokoda Track, a route made famous by Australian soldiers in World War II, James a 45-year divorced man reports:

> I knew if I could do this (get to the end of the track) I could do anything. That is what kept me going. One foot after another … This walk could

help me start afresh. be a talisman for what I have to confront back in Australia. Yes, the other walkers on the track were my companions but it was really about me and what I can take out of this experience forever.

The results reported by Fielding *et al.* also provide some other insights including the relevance of the concept of time in understanding the tourist experience. Walking, climbing, trekking all involve the possibility that the tourist becomes absorbed in the experience and time becomes distorted. Edensor suggests:

> An extended period of walking perhaps for 12 hours is a long time to be alone ... without being distracted by entertainments and demands. The different temporal structure means that time can be difficult to comprehend. Periods of walking seem much longer or shorter than they are and other influences produce a temporal pattern when to rest, to eat – which is shaped more by physical contingencies, the rhythm set by the legs and the nature of the terrain than the clock. (Edensor, 2000: 102)

Being absorbed by an experience or feeling that it lasts much longer than one wants is a major part of the psychology of our perception of time (Zimbardo & Boyd, 2008). For Csikszentmihalyi (1990), a defining feature of his concept of the flow of experience is the rapid passing of time while for Fraisse (1963) it is filled time which passes quickly. Fielding *et al.* suggest that researchers should routinely include time estimates in satisfaction studies since, if it is possible to compare estimates with actual time, such measures can provide interesting insights into the nature of the experience as seen by the participant. We will return to the importance of time in a later section of this chapter in terms of understanding tourist queues.

A final consideration in our discussion of tourists and walking emphasises the embodied nature of the behaviour. We have already referred briefly to Urry's concept of the tourist gaze. In his first major work on this topic, Urry (1990) distinguished between the tourists who can be said to engage in a romantic gaze, a more private and searching inspection of their settings for the deep values such vistas contain and the collective gaze which, by way of contrast, is a shared, even crowded, public celebration of a setting informed by a dominant sense of seeking good times. For studies of tourists and walking this perspective draws attention to whether tourists are in groups or alone and, if in groups, to what extent are they sharing the experience? Alternatively, as in the case of the individual reporting on the Kokoda track, are they really undertaking a private journey? Irrespective of whether the tourist is truly social or wrapped up in their own experience, it also clear that the gaze and outlook received from walking is embodied and in this important sense differs from viewing the world through a coach, car or train window. For the walking tourist the sensory experience is not limited to gaze alone. Walking requires effort and energy, and sometimes involves pain and physical discomfort. It is tactile and involves the senses of smell and hearing more acutely than the insulated traveller viewing the world from a vehicle. It also follows certain social norms of how we perform the behaviour in different contexts. The following section of this chapter provides some details from studies which have looked closely at how tourists walk through the settings they visit. The concern here is less with the experiential components of the walking and more with the way human bodies interact in public.

Patterns of Tourist Movement

One different line of work on how tourists walk through spaces was initiated in the world of museum studies (Melton, 1972; Robinson, 1928). As suggested in Chapter 1, at times researchers concentrate on only component parts of the full experience of tourists. This does not lessen the value of their work but it does give it a tight focus. In particular, the work arising from the museum traditions, unlike the more symbolic and affective issues discussed in the previous section, is very much about the observable behaviour of the tourists. In summarising the findings of movement patterns in these kinds of exhibition spaces, Bitgood (2006) suggests that an interactionist perspective is required to integrate visitor factors and design or layout considerations. He argues that the evidence supports a view that we are drawn to objects which are especially interesting to us but that key architectural features such as doorways, windows and open spaces will also influence the steps we take.

Importantly, Bitgood extracts a general principle from numerous specific studies in art galleries, museums and attractions (Bitgood, 2003, 2006). He argues that the concept of a general value principle is helpful to explain the conscious and subconscious choices made by the viewing public. The core elements of the approach are captured by emphasising that the choice of viewing exhibits (or parts thereof) is influenced by the actual or perceived benefits of viewing divided by the costs such as physical effort or inconvenience. He argues that many objects are viewed because they are in the visitors' circulation pathway and thus require no additional cost – that is, little extra mental or physical effort is required. A few exhibits which are especially attractive to individuals and which are not on the main provided pathway may merit the effort of visitors changing direction and walking further. It is noteworthy here that there is a cognitive explanation (an algebra of supposed mental effort versus attractiveness) invoked in the explanation of the tourists' behaviour.

There are also links in the Bitgood general value principle to a more evolutionary explanation of visitor behaviour and movement as proposed by

Rounds (2004). In the latter explanation, tourist behaviour is also strongly influenced by the amount of effort involved but three specific heuristics are identified which control curiosity seeking. Search heuristics prompt visitors to explore and seek out items of interest. Attention heuristics control focused attention on an exhibit and, all importantly, quit rules provide guidelines for moving on to a new area. While these rules of thumb have a descriptive appeal and in Round's work are linked to survival needs in human evolution, they lack detail and do not provide predictive information about when the three rules come into play.

It is possible to suggest a more thorough explanation of this kind of tourist and visitor behaviour. The approach first identified by Langer (1989) and applied in tourism studies by Moscardo (1999) offers a richer cognitive psychology view of visitor attention and processing. The mindfulness model is not incompatible with the decision rules identified by Rounds; it is simply that the full mindfulness model provides more detail of what drives the three rules. In essence, the mindfulness model distinguishes two states of mental functioning, one in which tourists are fully engaged which is termed mindfulness. When mindful, visitors are mentally absorbing information whereas when they are mindless they are following existing scripts and while they appear to be processing material they are in fact not really taking in new information (Langer, 2009; Moscardo, 1999; Pearce, 2005).

For the purposes of our discussion on visitor movement the mindfulness model suggests that certain key factors promote mindfulness and it is these elements of both the display space and the individual which will activate the search and attention heuristics proposed by Round. Key characteristics which make tourists mindful include surprise, novelty, questions, clear themes, violence and sex as topics, opportunities for visitor control and interaction, new forms of sensory input, and change or discontinuity in a pattern. The opposite of these factors leads to mindlessness. Exhibit spaces which are familiar, provide nothing new, are dominated by text or repetitive talks, have no opportunity for visitors to ask questions or offer no visitor control, have a theme which is confusing or not lively, provide one-dimensional sensory input (e.g. just looking) and have display formats which are predictable will induce mindlessness.

These factors may operate alone or together to induce mindlessness. In Round's terminology mindfulness inducing characteristics are the attention heuristics while the quit heuristic is activated by the mindless inducing factors.

Bitgood (2006) summarises a number of findings of further interest from the museum and attractions literature. The review builds on extensive studies by Loomis (1987), Falk (1993) and Serrell (1997) as well as his own papers and research collaborations (e.g. Bitgood & Cota, 1995; Bitgood & Dukes, 2006; Bitgood & Lankford, 1995). His review suggest that there is a dominant behaviour of turning right at choice points but qualifies this generalisation by adding that this finding is applicable only when it is the choice that involves the least amount of movement or effort. He neglects to mention that all of the studies he reviews are from North America. It can be suggested that there is the potential for left turning dominant patterns at choice points in cultures where traffic and pedestrian circulation is on the left. Nevertheless, in these cases a left turning preference pattern may still be explained by the same underlying principle of effort and familiarity.

A second generalisation lies in the tendency for people to walk in relatively straight lines. It has been found that walkers only tend to divert occasionally from this pattern when 'pulled' away by highly attractive exhibits. Additionally people moving through open courtyards tend to approximate straight line movements but many do sometimes cut the final corners of diagonals as they move in their chosen direction.

Bitner also notes that visitors are reluctant to backtrack and recommends that exhibit spaces avoid requiring visitors to move into long passageways or rooms where they have to retrace their steps. Another finding which is consistent with the general value principle is that visitors often inspect exhibits along only one side of a two-sided display room or corridor. Undoubtedly this is regulated in part by traffic flow and whether other visitors are moving in the opposite direction but a persistent preference for not criss-crossing a display space has been identified (Weiss & Boutourline, 1963) (Figure 4.4).

Studies of tourists' and people's movements in outdoor environments complement the research undertaken in museums and exhibition spaces. Ball (2004) reports that people moving in public spaces behave in ways which are consistent but possibly unknown to them as participants. For example, tourists moving along a promenade are likely to proceed in what Ball terms loose counterflowing streams, organising themselves with collision avoiding manoeuvres to preserve their personal space while achieving their directional goals. Mechanistic models of particle flow adopted from core physics principles provide some insights into how these flowing streams behave (Helbing et al., 2001). It appears, for example, that when restrictions such as doorways, exit points and narrow alleyways impede visitors' movement, alternating bursts of small tourist groups pass through the common point of restriction. The work of Batty et al. (2003) has demonstrated that when a crisis occurs such as a fire, terror attack or riot, then the pulsing behaviour of visitors leaving a space becomes dysfunctional, the interpersonal distances breakdown and attempts to move faster become slower and potentially hazardous.

Public Movement Patterns

Other shapes and forms can be detected when examining the broad movement patterns of tourist behaviour. The length and organisation of tourist queues is important in shaping tourists' experiences at many junction points. The psychological and information needs of those waiting in line

Figure 4.4 Pulsing of traffic flow
In many public and tourist settings the movement of people is described well
by the notion that there are pulses of people moving through entertainment
and attraction places. Pulses occur at the conclusion of events and when people
move between key sites. Settings need to be designed to prevent congestion
by considering the likely maximum numbers of tourists. Clear directional and
instructional signs (as well as a measure of patience) are needed to prevent
panic when stressful or dangerous situations arise.

combine with the physical demands of standing or queuing in taxing conditions can affect the tourists' subsequent evaluation of their whole day
(Pearce, 1989). The tight clusters of visitors attending to the instructions of
tourist guide provide another formation of interest. On this occasion the
ability of all in the audience to hear the guide's conversation dictates such
issues as the physical closeness of the group. Yet again the ways in which
tourists claim territory and organise space on even the most crowded of
beaches is a further instance of settings which offer opportunities for tourism researchers to uncover patterns of public behaviour (Figure 4.5).

Perceived Crowding

The cumulative effect of these movement patterns is often of most interest when actual congestion (too many people in an area to permit free flow)
or perceived crowding (a personal sense of there being too many people)
confront tourists. Crowding management is a long-standing issue in tourism

Figure 4.5 Queue management
The best forms of tourist queue management look after tourists' mental and physical needs. Attention to both components of tourists' needs can reduce the boredom and discomfort of the queuing process. Physically, the queue space may be incorporated into the attraction as a precinct or sheltered area thus limiting public exposure to the elements. Providing information about the waiting time and using entertainers, showing films or having interpretive signs can all assist visitors in mentally "filling" the time required.

and recreation studies. Undoubtedly the dominant tradition in this field derives from the work of North American researchers who have pursued this topic largely in outdoor recreation contexts. The work has its origins in the 1970s (Stankey & Lime, 1973) and much attention has been focused on key concepts such as carrying capacity, limits of acceptable change and crowding norms (Donnelly *et al.*, 2000; Manning *et al.*, 1999; Rouphael & Hanafy, 2007; Vaske *et al.*, 1986). While many of these concepts have helped researchers understand key aspects of crowding attitudes and, further, provided suggestions for limiting numbers, the dominant North American context of the work negates its immediate relevance to many other settings where tourist crowding is important. In other countries and in urban settings the forces may differ and the applicability of the foundation concepts might need readjustment (Gillis *et al.*, 1989; Rustemli, 1992; Yagi & Pearce, 2007). For example, the development of both international and domestic tourism in countries such as China, India, Brazil and Indonesia, where the presence of large numbers of people is a way of life, may alter the way individuals respond to the presence of others. One way to develop this study topic is to use the available evidence to build a model of the key factors shaping tourist crowding. The usefulness of such a model can then be trialled in multiple locations.

Fundamental Points in Crowding Management

The actual numbers of people in an area is a starting point for any model of crowding management. A considerable body of work has documented how rising numbers of visitors bring problems in site management, notably in areas such as ecological impacts, including but not limited to soil erosion, trampling of vegetation, water pollution and facility damage (Manning et al., 1995; Ormiston et al., 1997; Shelby et al., 1988; Thomas et al., 2005). From the earliest studies in recreation it was appreciated that in addition to the environmental impacts of rising numbers of people, there were also social implications of the growth of numbers of people to an area (Shelby & Heberlein, 1984). The social implications include the conflict among users with different goals such as those who seek solitude and those who prefer a more social atmosphere in their leisure and tourism pursuits (Manning, 1997). The historical and cultural forces which underlie these views were documented extensively in Urry's work on the tourist gaze which has already been mentioned in this chapter. Urry (1990) identified the positive value of the collective gaze where the emphasis was on the value of having other people present at the site since they added atmosphere, consolidated the reputation of the location and could be co-participants in the experience.

An enduring characteristic of the North American work on crowding management is the implicit location of most of this work within a managerial romantic gaze. More specifically, in natural environment recreation contexts and in Western culture, there are strong traditional values asserting that non-urban settings and especially national and state parks should be the preserve of those who want to contemplate nature and benefit psychologically from the refreshing, aesthetic functions of the natural world (Sax, 1980). This view, which pervades the approaches to natural environment management and the social perception of crowding in many Western countries, tends to view rising numbers of people as a negative force, something to be countered and limited by management action. Management actions can then effectively filter, hide and segregate large numbers of people from one another. By way of contrast those who manage tourist attractions tend to see rising numbers of visitors as good for business, at least to the extent that such numbers can be managed profitably without too many rising costs. The implications of these two somewhat contrasting views of the desirability of more visitors is that researchers on crowding management always have to look beyond the actual number of visitors in their studies. While recognising that the foundation work in North America was developed in a different context to that of many contemporary tourism sites, it remains important to review the conceptual work deriving from the Western studies.

Conceptual Foundations of Crowding Studies

The existing contributions to crowding management can be conceived at two levels. At the larger scale there are a number of visitor and crowding management systems or approaches which provide a framework for this area of analysis. The key concepts here are carrying capacity, limits to acceptable change and, in a slightly more specific context, the tourism optimisation management model. Rouphael and Hanafy (2007) and McCarthur (2000) provide reviews of these concepts. This kind of work has been adopted at a policy level in tourism with the United Nations World Tourism Organization offering the following definition of carrying capacity:

> the maximum number of people that may visit a tourist destination at the same time, without causing destruction of the physical, economic and socio-cultural environment and unacceptable decrease in the quality of the visitors' experience. (UNWTO, 2004: 3)

While the carrying capacity approach has had a general appeal as a guiding statement, there is a lack of specificity when the terms it contains are closely scrutinised. This has led to the more detailed 'limits to acceptable change' approaches where there are empirical measures of concepts such as visitor experience or satisfaction and better defined parameters of environmental impacts. The limits to acceptable change approaches, in common with other systems such as the tourism optimisation model, recognise that there are inevitable impacts of tourism and visitor numbers. These approaches also appreciate that there are values involved in deciding whether negative outcomes are justified by the optimising of tourism income, employment, alternate social and environmental achievements and visitor well being.

The second tier of work identifies specific concepts to deal with how visitors react to the presence of others and is dominated by perceived normative theory (Donnelly et al., 2000). The normative theory has been used in over 50 studies to understand the relationship between encounter norms and perceived crowding (Donnelly et al., 2000; Manning, 1999; Shelby et al., 1996; Vaske et al., 1986, 1993). The relationship between actual use levels and perceived crowding is mediated by the number of reported encounters and visitors are said to have standards or norms for the acceptability of the number of these encounters. In this approach when people report more encounters than their norms, they felt very crowded. Those who reported less encounters than their norms felt not at all crowded. Vaske and Donnelly (2002) also report that these relationships can be described as having a mid-point of acceptability – this is where the number of groups encountered equals the number expected.

The value of much of the previous crowding management research lies not just in these foundation concepts but also in the close attention to the labelling of the response scales which are used when assessing visitor attitudes. Acceptability is not the only evaluative dimension in the normative literature. The evaluative dimensions which have been related to use levels include preference, desirability, tolerance, ideal and favourableness (Hammit & Rutlin, 1995; Manning et al., 1999; Watson, 1995; Young et al., 1991). One clear finding from the use of these multiple assessment scales is that these evaluations tend to be related to one another in predictable hierarchies. Manning et al. (1999) report that preference and ideal are terms which consistently produce lower crowding norms (fewer people) than absolute tolerance. Acceptability appears to lie between preference and tolerance. Management-based tolerance norms are sometimes higher than visitor-based tolerance norms.

The literature also reveals that perceived crowding norms are not static but changeable because of a suite of factors (Higham & Kearsley, 1994). Such factors include demographic variables like gender – women are more tolerant (Friedman et al., 1972; Jain, 1992; Ross et al., 1973), education – better-educated visitors are less tolerant (Fleishman et al., 2004) and socio-economic status – the higher status individuals are less tolerant (Hayduk, 1983). Further factors of influence on perceived crowding norms include time pressure (Schellinck, 1982), spatial arrangements (Oldham, 1988), the social environment (Rustemli, 1992), motives for the experience (Bellenger & Korgaonkar, 1980) and perceived control (Hui & Bateson, 1991). Some initial research outside of the North American and Western contexts suggested that individuals of Asian and African origin have a better ability to deal with noise than Europeans and White North Americans (Gillis et al., 1989; Pearce, 1995; Rustemli, 1992). The further questions about the relationships between tolerance and preference for Asian visitors remain unanswered with studies of Japanese visitors suggesting a preference for larger numbers at popular tourist sites, especially when these numbers were made up of Westerners (Yagi & Pearce, 2007).

Heberlein (1992) has pointed out that it is not only the characteristics of the individuals and social groups which affect the perceived attitudes to others but that the information available in the setting and the setting design also have roles to play. In particular in studying festivals, Heberlein noted that the application of good waiting in line practices and keeping patrons well informed could reduce the negative perceptions.

Additionally several forms of crowding can be distinguished. Crowding can be continuous such as when a site experiences large and continuous levels of visitation. When crowding is constant, the site may require continual attention to facilities to support the tourist experience especially in areas such as access, parking, arrival areas, entry and ticketing, public spaces and viewing areas, interpretation and visitor facilities. It may also require upgrading of management, staff, information management and financial resources. Alternatively, congestion and crowding may only occur at certain well-determined times, such as weekends, public or school holidays, and festivals. This form of tourist pressure can be labelled fluctuating crowding. Such pressures occur when a site has tours arriving at specific times during the day. These bursts of visitor numbers may require additional staffing, transportation, security, and food and beverage resources for these short periods (Figure 4.6).

Congestion and perceived crowding may diminish visitor satisfaction. In combination they can prevent tourists from having the time and the opportunity to appreciate and enjoy their surroundings, including the local culture and the values of the places that are visited. Additionally simply accessing key goods and services may become problematic. Other consequences of

Figure 4.6 Congestion

Narrow passageways at popular tourist sites have a physical limit on the number of people who can pass through them. Congestion occurs when literally no more people can fit into the space. Many tourists are also likely to see this setting as crowded. Crowding, however, may be perceived by some people when only a few others are present. The photograph is the entrance to the square below Juliet's balcony, Verona, Italy – a popular site for romantics and lovers. It also is the site of graffiti, now managed in part by designated walls for messages.

congestion include potential damage to the flora and fauna; scenic values; physical fabric or special values of the place; adverse impact on conservation or presentation programs; stress on the local community through competition for local services; increased litter and pollution, and an overall reduction in the efficiency of tourism services.

Congestion, the physical restriction of movement, is most likely to occur at entry and exit points, at the most popular parts of an attraction, or within certain areas such as stairs, doorways, narrow passages, at toilet facilities, near food and beverage stalls, or where visitors need to make a choice about something, for example a retail product. These pressures are exactly those identified in the work of Batty *et al.* (2003). Congestion is therefore a product of the number of visitors present, the space available and the behaviour of crowds, as well as the cultural background of the tourist. By using these ideas from the literature as well as data from original studies conducted at tourist attractions in China and Australia, Jin and Pearce (2009) constructed a model of tourism crowding. Figure 4.7 presents the approach.

The model suggests multiple pathways to consider when understanding and managing tourist crowding and its further use in integrating and stimulating research in this area is recommended. More specifically the way to employ this kind of concept map of crowding is for researchers to track specific links among the categories of variables by conceptualising the later variables in the system as dependent measures. For example an interest in tourists' tolerance for the crowding experienced can be seen to consist of their pre-existing attitudes and key demographic and travel characteristics. The factors identified in Figure 4.7 can assist researchers to image and select the variables to measure for the outcomes of specific academic and, at times, managerial interest.

Broader Movement Patterns

There is a further level of analysis about tourist movements which also exists in the tourism literature. On this occasion the concern is with how tourists move around larger destination areas rather than specific sites. Some of this work is done with patterns of tourists driving from a base destination while other work is concerned with mobility by public transport (Lue *et al.*, 1993; Parolin, 2001; Xia *et al.*, 2010). Lau and McKercher (2007) provide a study which is typical of the latter level of interest. They take as their base geographic unit the destination of Hong Kong. The researchers used a diary technique to ask tourists to recall the places they had visited and then using a geographic information system converted their data into a format which enabled them to search for common movement patterns. The patterns obtained for the Hong Kong site are quite complex with the main regularities lying in a tendency to stay close to the accommodation base initially, disperse more widely on days three and four and limit travel on the final two

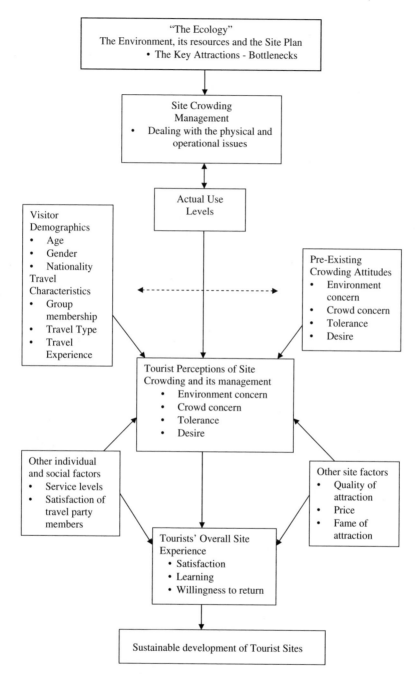

Figure 4.7 Model of tourism crowding

days of their stay. The variability in the movements of visitors is undoubtedly heavily influenced by the same kinds of interaction perspectives observed
by Bitgood (2006); specifically the combination of individual interests and
the structure of the environment. In the latter category, the location and
access to the main attractions of the city may be very important in shaping
the routes taken. Cooper (1981) suggested that in other locations there may
be a hierarchy of visiting key attraction with the most important attractions
in a location visited first and the minor sites being inspected if time
permits.

There needs to be a keen awareness, however, that these kinds of studies
may be aggregating multiple sub-patterns of tourist movement. We are not
just dealing with a pre-selected group of tourists to a museum but all kinds
of visitors motivated by multiple travel career patterns to all manner of attractions. It would be reasonable to suggest that future research in this area might
examine closely the comparative patterns of tourist movement within a destination. The kinds of comparisons of interest will undoubtedly depend on
either applied or conceptual research goals but could include differences
amongst demographic groups with varied motivational profiles. Additionally,
large samples of visitors are needed in these kinds of studies to overcome
issues of seasonality, weather fluctuations and tourists modifying their travel
due to the congestion and perceived crowding issues outlined in the earlier
section. In line with the developments in contemporary tourist behaviour and
technology noted in Chapter 2, there are developing opportunities to track
tourist behaviour with an array of mobile digital devices but the caveat about
using large numbers or limiting the generalisability of the study to very specific groups remains powerful. One value of developing detailed records of
tourist movement patterns lies in the potential use of this information in
assessing the environmental impact or ecological footprint of visitors.

Ecological Footprints

The essence of the concept of ecological footprints is that researchers can
construct a measure of the impacts of human activity on the natural systems
of the planet (Hunter, 2002). Importantly the totality of the impact is
expressed as one simple number. The notion of a footprint has much intuitive appeal, since it both symbolises and records the pressure of human activity. Many applications of ecological footprint analysis take a big picture view
of human activities and are concerned with nations and cities (Venetoulis
et al., 2004). Over time the term has increasingly been used as a benchmarking concept among different economic activities so that different sectors can
be seen as having different footprints (Gössling, 2002; Gössling et al., 2002;
Hunter & Shaw, 2007; Sonak, 2004). Individual behaviour and one's lifestyle
can also be described in terms of a personal ecological footprint. Patterson
et al. (2006) provide a succinct summary of the measure:

The ecological footprint is an accounting model of resource consumption and waste production, and relies on comprehensive and reliable data sources available at the relevant scale. (Patterson *et al.*, 2006: 749)

The process of constructing ecological footprints for different economic sectors and at other scales of analysis requires a translation of all activities into a common denominator which is referred to as a gha unit. This measurement in ecological footprint methodology refers to the demands upon natural resources in terms of an equivalent biosphere area (Hunter & Shaw, 2007). The gha values can be itemised for particular aspects of an economic activity (such as food consumption or water use or travel) but often the interest is in the total effects of the activity so the component scores are aggregated to produce an overall footprint. In the work reported by Venetoulis *et al.* the ecological footprint for citizens of different countries was documented with the summary scores ranging from 0.50 gha per person for Bangladesh to 9.57 gha for the United States. A commonly used benchmark for assessing the meaning of this scale of values is that a figure of 2.0 is described as a good estimate of the global average area of productive land available for each human being annually. Following this metric, citizens of Bangladesh are operating on 25% of their share of the earth's resources and the United States citizens at over 470% of what might be seen as their natural resource entitlement.

Perhaps not surprisingly, given the contemporary importance of the concept of sustainability and efforts to measure and assess human impacts on the planet, the concept and specifically the technical measurement issues surrounding the use of the ecological footprint approach have attracted considerable commentary (cf. Hunter & Shaw, 2007; Rees, 2000; Wackernagel, 1999; Wackernagel & Yount, 2000). The technical discussion is relatively complex and for assessing tourism's ecological footprint includes specific attention to nagging concerns on how to establish equivalence among the areas of impact, how to include the impacts of all travel and how to offset the behaviour of the tourist which would have occurred in their home destination. It is particularly important to consider closely the type of tourist activity involved in a region (Patterson *et al.* 2006).

For the purposes of this volume and our specific interest in tourist behaviour, a consideration of the ecological footprint approach contains two powerful implications. One form of impact lies in the now ready availability of derivatives of the formal academic assessments which enable individuals to calculate quite easily their overall footprint from their lives. A small sample of these resources are indicated in Table 4.1.

The public communication power of these tools is considerable. In addition to the global whole of life calculators which tend to try and quickly summarise all aspects of lifestyle, there are specific versions which just focus on carbon footprints and sector versions which assess individual footprints for life at work, domestic activity and travel. The latter category

TABLE 4.1 EXAMPLES OF ECOLOGICAL FOOTPRINT WEBSITES

Eco-*Footprint* - *Earth Day* Network

Welcome to the Earth Day Network Footprint Calculator! Take an important
step and sign up to be an Earth Day Network activist! ...
*www.**earthday**.net/**footprint**/*

***Ecological Footprint* Quiz by Center for Sustainable Economy**

After answering 27 easy questions you'll be able to compare your Ecological
Footprint to others' and learn how to reduce your impact on the Earth. ...
www.myfootprint.org/

WWF *Footprint* Calculator

Worried about your impact on the environment? The way we use the planet's
resources makes up our ecological footprint. Measuring yours takes less
than 5 minutes ...
footprint.wwf.org.uk/

Personal *Footprint*

How much land area does it take to support your lifestyle? Take this quiz
to find out your Ecological Footprint, discover your biggest areas ...
www.footprintnetwork.org/en/index. . ./personal_footprint/

Ecological *Footprint* Calculator

Best Foot Forward uses the ecological footprint methodology to help
businesses ... To estimate your footprint, please select those options that
most closely match your life ...
www.ecologicalfootprint.com/

---

includes a range of tools which enable tourists to compute the tons of carbon
their travel incurs and some sites feature options to offset this environmental impact by providing money to organisations which then invest that
capital in environmentally responsible ways. Additionally some sites provide specific hints about personal and individual behaviours which can
reduce the levels of consumption which generate large tourist-related
footprints.

The ecological footprint approach also offers implications for tourist
behaviour study. The consideration of tourism impacts has been dominated
by studies of how experts assess impacts or how communities appraise the
outcomes of tourism. Relatively few studies have considered how tourists see
their own impacts (Hillery *et al.*, 2001; Priskin, 2003). The few studies which
have been conducted from this perspective reveal that often tourists are
unaware of or underrate their influence (Priskin, 2003: 199). Such findings
are consistent with the self-serving attribution bias but there are undoubtedly tourists with motivational patterns who are keenly aware of the consequences of their actions while others may be less attuned to their effects.
Studies of such self-awareness are arguably important. Awareness of one's

influence is a prerequisite for change (Cialdini, 2001). It can be suggested that many more studies of tourists' awareness of their impacts could be conducted and comparisons then made between their interpretations of their behaviour and the views of other stakeholders. The ecological footprint calculators could be used in such studies with tourists who differ in their motivational patterns and who travel to diverse destinations asked to estimate tourists' footprint in various ways and then actual calculations being made to assess the accuracies in the self-ratings. More effective persuasive messages might be able to be designed if a thorough knowledge of how tourists view their impacts in specific locations could be established.

At different levels of human activity and with different purposes there remains an inevitable outcome that tourist behaviour leaves traces on or extracts resources from the setting visited. More than the material in most other chapters, the discussion in these sections including that on ecological footprints has placed an emphasis on the physical actions of the tourist. The mindfulness model has also addressed the cognitive mechanisms building their understanding of the visited settings. A further emphasis on the behavioural routines and the cognitive and affective responses of tourists may underpin more enduring and sustainable actions. Nearly two decades ago, Bramwell and Lane remarked:

> It is easy to discuss sustainability. Implementation is the problem ... The time has now come to 'walk the talk'. (Bramwell & Lane, 1993: 4)

While academic analyses generally avoid condensing complex topics into simple formulaic approaches to behaviour, there is plenty of scope to suggest more responsible tourist behaviours. The largest issue in all of the ecological footprint studies is clearly that of the effects of the tourists' air travel (Hunter & Shaw, 2007). There are developing attitudes and changing views of what is responsible behaviour in this domain with some efforts to reduce the footprint of aviation by airline companies and for tourists to offset their inevitable carbon burdens by the exchange processes already mentioned. Goleman (2009) believes that one step towards a better sustainability outcome for air travel and for many other consumer purchase lies in what he has termed the notion of radical transparency. He argues that the true costs of many purchases have been hidden from tourists and others for a long time and that only by explicitly pursuing these costs and forcing public disclosure of what is being sacrificed can more intelligent consumer choices be made. It is for this reason that Goleman advocates and foresees products, including tourist purchases, being branded with green barcodes which provide information about the products' contribution to a personal ecological footprint. The most regulatory approach to this system of measurement may begin to consider and potentially implement capacity limits for individuals on how much of a footprint they can generate in their adult life and hence how far they can travel.

While these more restrictive practices' may still be seen as futuristic possibilities it is also possible to identify action items which take up some of the on-site sustainability challenges implicit in Bramwell and Lane's call for walking the sustainability talk. Some of the websites noted in the previous section suggest specific behaviours and broadly follow the 'reduce, re-use, recycle' approach. As noted in Pearce (2005: 144) these ideas can be expanded into a wider net of 10 actions beginning with the letter 'R'. The continued relevance of these ideas in contemporary tourist behaviour makes it worthwhile to repeat the actions and further to suggest that they can be used not only as advice guidelines but as guides to further research. The specific suggestions are:

- Recognise: This action stresses the need for tourists to be self-aware and to recognise and identify that their behaviour creates a problem for example feeding wildlife may encourage animals to become dependent, potentially unhealthy and occasionally aggressive.
- Refuse: Faced with purchasing products from endangered animals or being offered illegal products, simple refusal is a sustainability enhancing action by reducing demand, for example for all animal products on banned or prohibited lists.
- Reduce: Lowering consumption of local resources by reducing needless use of lights, power, water, for example turning off room air conditioners, if possible, when exiting a hotel for the day.
- Replace: Finding substitute experiences with fewer or no impacts on environments and settings, for example using photography rather than extractive souveniring to record one's experience.
- Re-use: One-time use of products can be costly and environmentally unfriendly, for example reusing conference badges, towels, soap, bed linen, china cups rather than disposing of and requiring a new round of products can be recommended.
- Recycle: Finding a different use for a line of products, for example recycling paper, cans, bottles and clothing as handbags or art decorations.
- Re-engineer: The restructuring of behaviour and where it can take place through active personal intervention. The concept can be applied to a hard architectural solution to a problem such as recommending that a guard rail be put in front of objects or trees which could be easily touched or damaged.
- Retrain: Develop physical and personal skills to cope better in new situations, for example learning how to snorkel well so there is no need to stand on sensitive corals.
- Reward: Taking advantage of incentives or use one's personal resources as an enticement to promote sustainable activities, for example becoming a donor or sponsor of organizations supporting the environment.
- Re-educate: Long-term changes to personal behaviour resulting from tourist experiences may help the overall sustainability effort, for example

on returning home visitors may change their consumption of certain products including stopping their long-term use of plastic previously experienced as a hazard to marine wildlife.

The adoption of any and possibly many of these behaviours will go some way towards reducing the tourist's ecological footprint at a destination. There is of course more to the outcomes of tourist behaviour than environmental and ecological consequences and subsequent chapters will pursue these personal, social and cultural effects of contemporary tourist behaviour (Figure 4.8).

Figure 4.8 Re-engineering for sustainable behaviour
The Rs for sustainable behaviour – effectively the tactics for promoting a minimal footprint at tourist sites – include re-engineering settings to reduce pollution and manage site aesthetics. The photograph taken at Head Smashed in Buffalo Jump, a world heritage site in Alberta, Canada, reflects the requirement that tourists must walk to the core attraction from a relatively concealed and slightly distant car park. The sign is a reinforcing message thanking tourists for their behaviour. It also effectively prepares visitors for further responsible actions.

Directions

The topics reviewed in this chapter have emphasised the observable behaviours associated with the tourist experience. Through the mindfulness model the key cognitive components explaining and underpinning some tourists' experiences were considered. Nevertheless, the kind of work reviewed pays only some attention to the affective and sensory components involved in these activities. Additionally the ways in which relationships mediate the walking experiences, the crowding, the waiting in line, and the desirable actions which tourists can undertake all represent options for further consideration. The experience agenda in this book suggests that many of the studies described in this chapter could be embellished by considering the multifaceted experiential nature of the activities and behaviours already considered. As discussed in Chapter 1 there can be divided loyalties in tourism studies between providing research which seeks primarily to understand contemporary tourism and equally high-quality work which has practical applications as its goals (cf. Aramberri, 2010). The kinds of topics discussed in this chapter do have significant managerial implications. It can be argued that as managerial imperatives become more sophisticated and in line with the tenets of the experience economy the goals of sound business become to provide superior experiences (cf. Schmitt, 2003). A research focus on observable behaviours alone in these kinds of tourist settings may not yield sufficiently rich information for the desired goals of practical intervention. The opportunities for the richer appreciation of the topics reviewed and how these other components of experience might enhance our full understanding of the actions tourists undertake as reviewed here may offer a fruitful future for tourism studies.

5 Dimensions of Personal Change

Introduction

All tourists travel with a sense of hope. They are hopeful in the teleological sense that they can imagine themselves at a brighter point in their imminent future. Some may simply want to meet their hedonistic holiday goals while others may possibly seek to learn more about the world or create new identities. Further still, a select few may be seeking to support or even change the relationships in which they are involved. In exploring the essence of hope and personal change we will revisit some of the ideas underlying motivation. Both the roots of human emotion as outlined by Panksepp (1998, 2005) and the further articulation of the travel career pattern model of motivation (cf. sections of Chapter 3) will be considered in this analysis. An additional contribution to this discussion lies in incorporating the positive psychology ideas of character strengths (Dahlsgaard *et al.*, 2005; Park *et al.*, 2005). Some commentary on the potentially confusing concept of identity will also be noted in the context of these deliberations.

Attention will then be directed to studies reporting empirically the impact of tourism on the tourist. Both the topic of learning and the issue of the importance of relationships to the tourist experience will be central to this chapter. In particular, we will be concerned with what tourists learn or more specifically what they believe they learn from their travels. Recent studies, including some by the author and colleagues, will be used to explore tourist learning. Such studies will act as specific illustrations of how tourists come to view themselves differently after travelling. For our consideration of tourists and the influence of travel on their relationships, more indirect routes to considering the processes involved and their outcomes will be explored. In this section, reliance will be placed on the representation of relationships in traveller blogs and in the cumulative interpretation of tourists' relationships in select popular fiction.

In these considerations of tourists travelling with a sense of hope, either directly or unknowingly on a track of personal change, we will try and not overestimate the scope and scale of tourist learning or view the management of their relationships as an obsessive interest. Tribe (2004) has argued that tourist researchers filter the world around them to explore topics which they find inter-esting and which meet the career-linked requirements of journal publishing and peer approval. It is important at the outset of this chapter not to fall into the trap of over-emphasising the cerebral nature of the time tourists spend on holi-day. Others have reminded us of this issue. Huxley (1925) commented 'we travel not that we may broaden our minds but so that we may pleasantly forget they exist'. Huxley's remark still applies to the contemporary tourist but pos-sibly we should also allow for some clear outcomes in learning and relationship enhancement for those who travel today with a sense of hope.

The Roots of Personal Change

Any consideration of human behaviour and the systems surrounding social activities immediately tends to select a specific level of analysis. That level may be biological, psychological, social psychological, sociological or anthropological. It is also argued that some functional areas of interest such as tourism management move across these disciplinary emphases (Hofstede, 1995). In considering the personal change dimensions pertaining to tourists' experience there are at least three levels of analysis which can be considered. At the first level there is emerging work in neuroscience on the primary emotional response systems which can assist in understanding what under-pins tourist motivation. The second level, and one already considered in this volume, is the work by tourism researchers on tourist motivation. The fuller specification of the operation of one of these approaches, the travel career pattern work, will be reconsidered. Additionally some brief comments will be provided on other tourist motivation schemes. A third level of work which is pitched more at the sociological level as outlined by Hofstede is concerned with identity. Some of the values and problems with this concept for tourist experience will be highlighted.

In an extended and highly productive career Jaak Panksepp, together with a suite of colleagues, has identified and provided evidence for the exis-tence of seven neurologically identifiable emotional systems (cf. Panksepp, 2005; Panksepp & Biven, 2010). These subcortical emotional circuits coordi-nate instinctual actions that include affective, cognitive, behavioural, expres-sive and physiological changes in the individual. Panksepp refers to and labels these states in capital letters; a communication tactic he employs to avoid suggesting that his interest in these topics covers all higher-order interpreta-tions which human reflection and higher-order consciousness can bring to the systems he has unearthed. The states he discusses are SEEKING, FEAR, RAGE, LUST, CARE, PANIC and PLAY. Together with his colleagues, Panksepp approaches the study of these core emotional states with the view that consciousness is a tiered multilevel process (see also Greenfield, 2000: 21–23). The interests here are in primary process consciousness which reflects raw sensory feelings and motivational imperatives.

For our understanding of tourist behaviour there are particular points of interest in the development of the SEEKING, LUST, CARE, PANIC and PLAY systems. The SEEKING system refers to one of the best documented, hard-wired, emotional neural clusters in the subcortical levels of human and animal brains. Berridge and Robinson (2003) have described this system as a 'wanting system' as it is characterised by a coherent urge to explore the environment and seek resources both in response to bodily needs and external incentives. For readers more familiar with considering the studies of tourism researchers, these descriptions might not seem all that remarkable. Similar phrases and labels occur in other studies of motivation. The distinguishing feature of the neuroscience work is that three precise levels of evidence are used to document the appropriateness of their description. First, there is solid evidence that there are common trans-species emotional and behavioural response styles in the form of actively searching the immediate locale – foraging is an appropriate term – when the system is activated (Panksepp, 1992). Secondly, the results are the same for different species when very specific parts of the brain are stimulated using electrodes (Olds, 1977). Thirdly, when specific drugs are administered, notably in this case dopamine, the system reliably becomes more active and greater seeking efforts are observed (Volkow et al., 2002).

In reviewing a large amount of evidence for this basic emotional system, Panksepp notes human beings in this SEEKING mode report feelings of being engaged with the environment with a strong sense of excitement and being alive. In particular these feelings describe the affective world of research volunteers when they receive specific stimulation to key parts of their subcortical emotional circuits. The parts of the brain involved in this emotional circuitry are the limbic system, especially the hypothalamus and the amygdala. It is also notable that the nerve cell clusters in this system are more responsive to the anticipation of rewards rather than the receipt of reward. Supporting evidence for this view comes in the form of high rates of firing to novel stimuli and attenuated firing to repeated stimuli or predictable triggers. These specific results speak to the kinds of autonomous, self-sustaining hedonic nature of some behaviours noted in early social motivation writing by Allport and others (Boring, 1950). It is the chase rather than the capture which is the most emotionally rewarding.

The LUST, CARE, PANIC and PLAY systems while not as well understood as SEEKING, FEAR and RAGE are also described as coherent emotional subcortical circuits (Panksepp & Biven, 2010). For any tourism researcher, PANIC might not seem to be an appealing motivational foundation for our hopeful tourists but the term is used to describe the need for contact with others and emphasises attachment to members of the group. It is in effect the supporting emotional system for relationships and builds on earlier work by Bowlby (1972) on maternal attachment and the socialisation needs of children. In explicitly human applications the emotional system of

PANIC could be relabelled RELATE. The systems represented as LUST, PLAY and CARE are more self-explanatory and it is notable that continuing work in all of these areas is slowly reproducing the full complement of common behavioural patterns, the uniformity of outcomes as a consequence of electrical stimulation and the common effects of drug influences.

How might the work of the neuroscientists be applied to tourist motivation study? Or expressed differently, how might we use multilevel analysis as Hofstede (1995) suggests, and combine insights into the phenomenon in which we are interested? As a starting point for the application of the neuroscience work to other levels of analysis it is important to defend such ideas against zoomorphism. This expression suggests that we are overly ascribing animal attributes to people – it is an inverse of anthropomorphism which is seeing human traits in animals. The charge can be rejected because the work explicitly includes human studies and research evidence about the way all animal brains work. Further, the researchers acknowledge that shades of perceived meaning of affect are fostered by higher-order cortical processes. We are not dealing here with naïve reductionism and a simplistic conversion of the neuroscience work on the older parts of the brain into tourist behaviour without recognising fully that there are major higher-order brain inputs. Instead, a compelling reason to integrate the neuroscience work into motivational studies is that by having an alignment between brain-based processes and reported experiences we can avoid the messy consequences of dualism. In brief, we are not trapped into proposing motivational systems with no linkage to how the physical world of brain functioning works. Importantly, when we do propose abstract drivers of action such as status they can be seen as combined outcomes of higher-order processes building on two or more interacting core emotional circuits-in the case of status possibly SEEKING and PANIC/RELATE.

The systems of tourist motivation which have been applied in the tourism field for some time include the Plog-based system of allocentric and psychocentric needs, the Iso-Ahola model of preferred levels of arousal and the Pearce and Lee travel career pattern approach (Hsu & Huang, 2008; Iso-Ahola, 2011; Pearce, 1992; Plog, 2011). Only the travel career pattern approach fits well with the neuroscience groundwork on motivational states and affect. The Plog approach is based only on the FEAR system while the general arousal model of Iso-Ahola considers the one emotional circuit of SEEKING as an adequate core system. The travel career pattern approach places SEEKING and PANIC/RELATE at the heart of the model and then peripheral motives in the system are underpinned by LUST, PLAY and FEAR. Middle level motives are much more to do with CARE than other emotional substrates. The remaining system of RAGE is not included as it is not applicable to the world of tourist motivation.

A compelling aspect of the application of these emotional systems to the travel career pattern approach lies in the specific ordering of core, middle layer and peripheral underpinnings of the previously reported travel motives. These layers represent the pre-eminence of SEEKING and PANIC/RELATE as dominant emotional drivers for human beings. Less common but occasionally powerful emotional routines are consigned to peripheral roles. In proposing these links between the neuroscience work and the travel career pattern, the emotional states are linked to the factors in the earlier representations. There is a clear admission that the linkages now being specified are serendipitous – the original travel career pattern work was conducted without explicit knowledge of the neuroscience material. These core systems are represented in Figure 5.1.

The further development of these ideas may provide some fresh pathways for tourist motivation work which some see as lacking in recent innovation and development (cf. Hsu & Huang, 2008). An important and pragmatic consideration for researchers will be to confirm and work with enough travel motivation items to capture the full details of the travel career pattern approach.

It has already been suggested that some neuroscientists follow an integrationist approach to motivational studies and recognise the rich interplay between core emotional circuits and more abstract cortical inputs. What

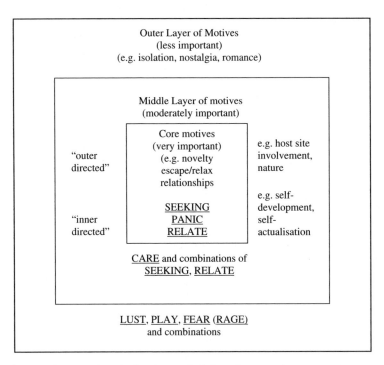

Figure 5.1 The emotional circuits underlying the travel career pattern model of tourist motivation

kind of cortical inputs are we describing? The notion that human beings are driven by visions of themselves as better people or at least people with different character strengths has been another strand of psychology work for several decades. Maslow, whose work was one input into the travel career pattern studies, offered such a view; in essence that people could be described as developing a pattern of motivation in which the apex of their personal growth was self-actualisation. Others have had less influential but similar views of human ambition and growth either in the sense of higher levels of moral functioning (Kohlberg, 1986) or a well-managed social life earning respect and avoiding contempt (Harre, 1979).

The development of the new and integrative field of positive psychology has usefully assembled the character strengths which many now see as functioning across cultures and motivating human striving (Park *et al.*, 2005; Peterson & Seligman, 2004). The positive psychology literature through its characterisation of human strengths and virtues offers a comprehensive checklist, another frame of reference when the 'top down' motivation of experience is considered. For example in the work of Peterson and Seligman (2004) overarching character strengths include seeking wisdom and knowledge, employing courage, showing a concern for humanity, respecting justice, showing temperance and pursuing some levels of transcendence. In the schematic framework of emotional circuits outlined in Figure 5.1, we must graft the moderating and future-oriented views tourists have of themselves to the core system. When viewed in this way, the original travel career pattern model proposed and outlined in Chapter 3 is effectively a model of the integration for tourist motivation of these multiple levels of influence on the hopeful tourist. Like all explanatory systems it remains in need of continued empirical support and further conceptual deliberation but it is at least encouraging to report that recent assessments of the importance of the motive items amongst South East Asian tourists confirmed the relative importance levels of the three motivational layers (Pearce & Panchal, 2010).

Approaches to Identity

The additional construct of identity is also popular in tourism research. Sexual identities, ethnic identities, identity amongst those who are disabled and changing personal identities are all studied in the tourist research literature (Harris, 2005; Maoz, 2005; Noy, 2004; Venedig, 1997; Waitt & Markwell, 2006). There is a close connection between our interest in identity and character strengths. The values and ideals represented in such concepts as wisdom, courage, concern for others and showing restraint may be seen as components of personal identity and represent aspirational goals for some tourists. More generally in connecting ideas in this area of identity, personality and character strengths, it is necessary to emphasise the explicit purpose of our interest. All of our concerns with the way tourists currently view themselves and further, how they envision themselves in the future, can be depicted as the rich operation of higher-order cortical processes which moderate and provide sophistication to the core-affective motivational systems described in the work of Panksepp and others. There are though multiple distinctions among the terms in the field of identity research which provide subtlety, power and insight into the influence of these higher-order considerations shaping tourist behaviour.

One widely recognised distinction is that between personal identity and social identity (S. Cohen, 2010; Harris, 2005). Personal identities are the way individuals view themselves. In particular they represent a kind of reflective personal overview of the physical and psychological characteristics of our make-up. Social identities refer more explicitly to the way others see us and our membership in groups or collectives. Such membership is both determined by birth and heritage and forged in social life. Harris (2005), amongst others, argues that the master identities, such as those originating in class distinctions, religious practices or ethnic origin, which once defined many people's sense of their place in the world, have partially dissolved in contemporary society. The weakening of these once clear categories has facilitated the ability of individuals to create and work at new hybrid and often consumer-influenced identities (cf. Desforges, 2000). This process of identity creation is perhaps best illustrated through queer theory which emphasises that gender is a performance to be understood as a rich social process rather than interpreted through narrow approaches to categorisation (de Lauretis, 1991; Seidman, 1996). For tourism study the views that we create and make both our personal identities, and to some extent, our social identities are important. The options to recreate one's identity are somewhat constrained for most people by personal financial considerations which limit the choices and the consumer expression of who we might want to become. Leisure and tourism have been recognised as providing the spaces and the fresh opportunities for identity work. For tourist behaviour and experience researchers it is predominantly personal or individual identities which are of most interest although studies in tourism community interaction pursue the broader social level of interest (Moscardo & Pearce, 2003).

In the well-developed area of identity research in psychology and sociology there are two specific theories which have been developed. Both share the view that individuals are constantly constructing their identities and that identities have multiple components or aspects. Both see an interplay between society and the individual in shaping identity. The terminology which has been used to label these theories can cause some confusion. Social identity theory is a social psychological approach to understanding the dynamic formation of identities (Hogg et al., 1995). Both social identity theory and its main derivative social categorisation theory (J.C. Turner, 1991) show a strong concern with cognitive processes such as categorisation perceptions and the power of context relevant prototypes (stereotyped-like images of in-group and out-group members) to guide behaviours. The origins of the approach lie in the minimal group identification studies undertaken by Tajfel who showed that groups can be formed based on the most trivial ways to assign membership. Importantly, once groups are formed individuals show strong in-group favouritism in subsequent behaviours (Tajfel, 1982; Tajfel & J.C. Turner, 1979). These inherently psychological mechanisms shape behaviours towards out-groups and can produce conformity to social norms beyond the research laboratory and highly relevant to the worlds of tourists.

From travel blogs collected in Pearce et al. (2009) we can see the processes at work;

> Jane (a pseudonym), a self-confessed divorced New Zealand traveller, reports;
> 'I was in Milan and just having coffee at the airport. I noticed a dark haired tall stranger looking at me in a very friendly way. Normally I avoid such contact but it was late and I was tired so I smiled agreeably. He moved towards me. The cut of his clothes, the way he held his coffee immediately I thought he was French. The way he said Bonjour confirmed he was all that the charming stereotype can offer. I was prepared to take a few chances.'

The responses and judgements indicated in this example reveal the power of categorisation and assignment of group identity to guide select behaviour (Figure 5.2).

The second approach of interest, that of identity theory, as distinct from social identity theory, is a micro-sociological approach which seeks to explain the ascribed roles people are given and how individuals work within these role constraints and boundaries. Its roots lie in symbolic interaction and the follow up work of Stryker, R.H Turner and colleagues (Stryker, 1987; R.H. Turner, 1978). It is core to identity theory that the self is seen as multifaceted and reflects society. Terms such as role commitment and identity salience account for the impact of role identities on behaviour. Role identities are organised hierarchically in an individual's self-concept and have power according to their respective level in the hierarchy. Thus the father who is a fireman and rushes into the burning building to save his son is enacting the dominant father role rather than his employment role of fireman, even if in the latter professional role he knows that the behaviour is very unsafe and he would not undertake the actions in normal circumstances.

Importantly when comparing the two approaches of social identity theory and identity theory the latter tends to downplay context issues and underemphasises the extent to which individuals are drawn to respond favourably to others in their category (Hogg et al., 1995). That is, identity theory operates at a more general level and provides a direct reciprocal link between individual and society through the construct of role identity. The roles of father and son,

Figure 5.2 Group identity and personal meaning
Long treks to spiritual shrines can see individuals involved in enormous physical hardships and cost them a lifetime of savings. One component of the spectrum of tourist experience is emphasised in the photo at a Buddhist monastery near Xining, China; the devotion to an ascetic ideal. By way of contrast indulgence may also confer meaning and status amongst one's peers for some tourists, even though hedonistic enjoyment is a very different pathway to fulfilment and one quite a few researchers studying well-being would question

for example, are important in identity theory but less so in social identity theory which is more concerned with in-groups and out-groups. Fathers are not a meaningful out-group in the same way as French men or older Japanese tourists. The core implication of this discussion, which is quite extensive in modern social psychology, is that what kind of identity we study and what theoretical approach we choose to pursue in that study will influence the extent to which we emphasise an array of constructs such as roles, social context, psychological processes, role hierarchies, identification and favourableness towards others. There is a cryptic piece of advice sometimes proffered to those who contemplate the future: be careful what you wish for. For tourism researchers it might be reworded as: be careful what you borrow. One direction will take tourism researchers concerned with identity to issues of how categorisations are formulated and associated consequences in terms of favourable behaviours, the other to how roles are defined in terms of all the components of social worlds and how these roles are acted upon.

Some further notes of caution about employing identity-related motivations for studying tourist behaviour are necessary additions to this discussion. Tourists may be aware of identity issues or their identities may be covert and only appear in a surprising way. Other people may create an awareness of identity issues where none existed. For example, living in and having grown up in Australia I do not think about being Australian on a regular basis. When I am fortunate enough to travel in China it is a prominent part of who I am, how others see me and how I come to represent and see myself. Researchers too may ask questions about identity in a way which raises questions and contemplation about personal identity challenges which were not a concern to the tourist. In particular if researchers assume that identities must be wholly and satisfactorily integrated and driven by harmonious conceptions that individuals hold of the totality of their being, they may be making the same kinds of mistakes which once troubled such theories of social functioning as balance theory and cognitive dissonance (Furnham, 2008).

More specifically it seems that researcher built models of balance, integration and holistic functioning are just that, constructed models of one way of functioning whereas in everyday life many individuals, including of course tourists, are able to function quite well with apparent contradictions in their cognitive and self-appraisal systems. To cite an example, a western tourist may view herself as a generous and socially concerned individual yet aggressively bargain with a local street vendor in a developing country with the sole aim of saving a trivial amount of money (van Egmond, 2007). Further, and beyond the issue of simply saving a small amount of money, the tourist may be ignoring the exploitative practices and labour conditions which have produced the cheap items which they are purchasing (Goleman, 2009). It seems unlikely though that this bargaining act would alter the identity component of being socially concerned to one of being exploitative, and only when called upon to explain inconsistencies does a rationalisation process occur. In brief, tourists carry out their activities and while some of these activities may have repercussions for their own conceptions of identity, researchers have to be cautious not to see forests where only trees exist. This commentary can also be seen as providing a stimulus for researchers to expand their observational and unobtrusive approaches to tourism study and not overly rely on direct and potentially reactive direct questioning.

Tourists and Learning

The interest we have in tourist motivation and how tourists might change as a consequence of fulfilling their more complex motives is partly dependent on the process of learning. This study area has not been a dominant theme in tourist behaviour and experience studies, possibly because the tourism industry concerns about repeat business have prompted researchers to focus on understanding satisfaction. By way of contrast tourists' learning and personal growth relate only marginally to performance and profitability and arguably such issues have been understudied by the more pragmatic and business-oriented researchers.

For the kinds of learning in which we are interested two linked concepts from the mainstream study of psychology need to be considered. The first concept is the learning of complex material. A consideration of memory and remembering is the second associated interest area. The concept of learning has been conceived for a long time as an enduring change in behaviour particularly as shown by altered responses to the world surrounding the individual (Boring, 1950). This older definition of the term places most emphasis on physically observable acts as opposed to cognitive understandings of the world. Some elaboration of this earlier view is required to include knowledge-based changes. A broader and contemporary perspective defines learning as an adaptive process in which the tendency to perform a particular behaviour or interpret information is changed by experience (cf. Martin *et al.*, 2007: 267). It is important to note that the changes induced by learning are not transitory or limited and, for learning to be established, the individual must retain the ability to respond to the world in novel ways for at least some time.

A consideration of the time element in learning requires a discussion of memory. Long-term and short-term memory are key distinctions made in this area of study. Short-term memory represents the ability to hold sense impressions and immediate material for, at most, a matter of only some minutes. Learning, as we are interested in it as tourism researchers, is mostly linked to long-term rather than short-term memory gains, although the ability to recall such facts as a set of directions may be largely about short-term memory functions.

Another classification of interest in the memory research is between shallow and deep processing. This concept, which has become an important one in the field of education, distinguishes between attending to the surface elements of the material under review as opposed to considering its underlying principles and insights (Biggs, 2003). Immersion in the activity, reflecting on the material and taking personal control of the information are all factors which encourage deep processing. These active cognitive processes can be seen as opposed to the more passive approach of simply accepting the received or supplied messages. The fundamental process which underlies deep processing has also been identified as mindfulness (Langer, 1989, 2009). Personality factors which seem to be linked to learning success and mindfulness include openness to experience and agreeableness (Farsides & Woodfield, 2003).

Research in the field of memory has also suggested that there may be two kinds of learning involved which operate differently and which are stored differently in human brain systems. These distinctions are of particular interest to the theme of this chapter as a distinction is made between information pertaining to issues outside of the individual's own functioning and personally relevant material. The first kind of memory has been referred to as semantic memory and describes knowledge about facts and specific details. In the travel context this would be equivalent to remembering that Singapore has a population of 4.4 million people or that the flight time from London to Dubai is 6 h.

A second kind of long-term memory has also been postulated. On this occasion the term employed is episodic memory. This label is somewhat misleading as it is not simply episodes which are being stored but more specifically events which are related to or have strong meaning for the individual (Tulving, 1983, 1984). For this reason episodic memory is also known as autobiographical memory. An illustration of autobiographical memory is provided in existing tourism studies where travellers who recall their journeys between cities frequently report the social events and activities in which they participated along the route (Pearce, 1981, 1999). Despite the appeal of this simple division between memory for factual information and personally relevant material, debate persists as to whether they are truly separate systems (Martin *et al.*, 2007: 318). It is perhaps not so important in the tourism research context to explore the definitive neural basis for these two systems, but rather to be mindful of the need to at least collect the two different kinds of learned information.

The topic of intentionality is another distinction in the learning and memory research which matters to the tourism context. In the psychology literature this construct is framed as explicit and implicit memory. It is sometimes also referred to as incidental versus purposeful learning. The core of the distinctions being addressed here are whether the individual has set out to learn the material or has, in a more general way, 'picked up' the information through ongoing activities (Cleermans, 1993). Implicit or incidental learning can be thought of in the tourism context in the terms outlined by de Botton. He observes that even those travellers on business trips and without the time to take in, for example, Rome's history or art still learn much detail about the visited location:

how much they would notice nevertheless; the fascinating roadside advertisements for fruit juice on the way from the airport, the unusually delicate shoes worn by Italian men, the odd inflections in their hosts' broken English (de Botton, 2009: 37).

A question of some interest here is whether or not these simple observations provide a cumulative power in the formation of beliefs and change tourists' perspectives on the locations and people they visit. Additionally the reflective value of learning about others for one's own life is a pivotal topic for tourism researchers seeking to establish studies of personal growth and change. A further point to be considered in this context is that an explicit motivation to learn about a visited society may not be required or implicated in the learning process. Arguably, if travellers do seek to study a location or an aspect of the visited culture then their involvement in that exercise should produce deep process learning and be entrenched in long-term memory. Nevertheless, the research on incidental learning also offers the view that tourists may acquire new insights without intentionally setting out to do so.

Cutler and Carmichael (2010: 17–18) report some growing interest amongst tourism researchers in learning issues. In their own review they recognise cognitive development such as knowledge and communication skills; affective development such as dealing with the emotions surrounding stress; psychomotor development in learning specific new skills; and personal development gains which include building character strengths such as open-mindedness and adaptability.

One set of outcomes missing from Cutler and Carmichael's list is learning about the locational issues – the explicit construction of a richer cognitive map of the setting visited (Falco-Mammone, 2005; Lynch, 1960; Pearce, 1977, 1981; Pearce & Thomas, 2010; Walmsley & Jenkins, 1992; Young, 1999). In studies of tourists viewing cities, traversing small towns and travelling through the countryside, it has been established that they do build layered representations of the locational, physical and emotional components of the places encountered (Oliver, 2001; Pearce, 1999). The technique to access locational information has often involved asking tourists to draw sketch maps of the visited environments. The kind of learning indicated in the maps is about remembering how streets are organised and where key resources are located as well as establishing the size and scale of the settings. The maps drawn by tourists while they are in these settings or shortly after they have returned to their home base provide tangible evidence of locational learning. Sets of maps drawn by travellers enable researchers to ask further questions about the commonality of tourists' experiences (Pearce & Thomas, 2010). A map drawn by one younger tourist after a two-day visit to the remote northern Australian location of Cooktown illustrates the kind of material found in many previous studies. The tourists' experiences of place as revealed by these kinds of maps highlights the cognitive and sometimes the affective components of tourist experiences as well as the selectivity of personal interests, memory and the role of motivation (Figure 5.3).

Besides, other work of interest in this chapter reports the broad skill-related benefits of tourist travel. Skills may be thought of as an eclectic mix of abilities and competencies which help individuals cope in their daily lives. For example, Gmelch (1997) observed that students of university age returned home from their trips abroad with an increased sense of self-confidence, adaptability and an improved ability to cope, survive and deal with surprises. In an analysis employing a non-travel control group, Hansel (1998) found that students who travelled appeared more independent, more aware of their home culture as well as less materialistic and less conventional than their

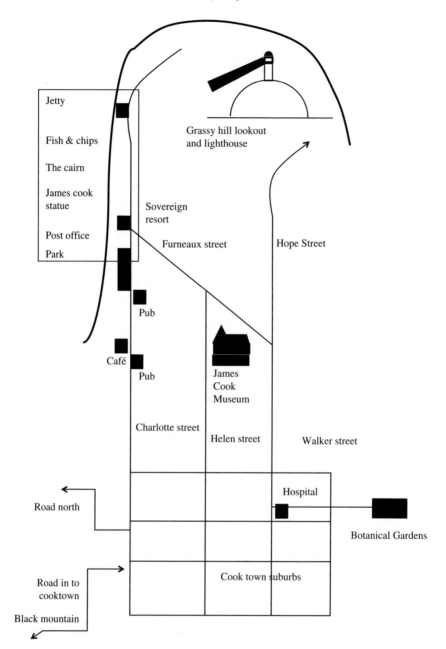

Figure 5.3 Jack's map of Cooktown

non-travelling counterparts. Earlier, a tourism-based study of young travellers in Europe demonstrated that those returning home (again by comparison with a control group) had different and more tolerant views of their own nationality as a consequence of their adventure group travels (Pearce, 1982).

A limited number of researchers have focused just on business and leadership skills. Many of these contributions provide arguments and anecdotes about skill development rather than detailed empirical evidence. Kuh (1995) noted that travel was a powerful contributor to particular business skills for some students. In particular, he argued that the skills required in out-of-class experiences were those required in an increasing number of jobs including leadership. The value of travel-related experiences as a precursor to corporate and political leadership has been emphasized by Hunt (2000) and Oddou et al. (2000).

Some of the existing literature on the learning of generic skills through travel does more than simply document the skills which seem to increase for certain groups of travelers. It also describes the contextual conditions necessary for skill building to take place. Factors of importance in fostering experiential learning include internal motivation, self-initiated activity, involvement in the experience, the experience of novelty and opportunities to reflect on the experience with others (Boud et al., 1985; Foley, 2000; Gmelch, 1997; Mohsin & Christie, 2000). These conditions for learning are very applicable to many younger student travelers and the types of experiential travel they pursue (Murphy, 2001; Pearce, 1990).

In seeking to extend work in this field there are a number of challenges raised by these kinds of studies. The challenges lie in researches identifying a comprehensive range of skills and using a framework which links their findings to information arising from other studies. There is also the further considerable difficulty that most studies in this area focus on perceptions of skill development rather than measuring actual skilled performance. This is a consistent limitation of the whole area of work and analysts should be constantly mindful that it is actually respondent perceptions that are involved in these skill assessments.

Pearce and Foster (2007) have attempted a thorough audit of generic skills. They use the term generic skills to refer to the abilities, capacities and knowledge one requires to function as a sophisticated professional in an information-rich society. They extracted generic skill items from a comprehensive literature review of the skills topic area and supplemented this information with self-reports of skill development from traveller websites to develop a 42-item framework of generic skills. In a second part of their study young budget travellers were shown a list of the skills and asked to identify skills they thought they had developed due to international travel. The top three skills that the respondents perceived they had developed included effective communication (84.7%), being open-minded (84.1%) and gaining in self-confidence (79.3%).

The majority of Pearce and Foster's 372 respondents felt that travel had substantially increased at least 10 of their generic skills. A powerful contribution of this study was the identification of clear relationships between tourists with different patterns of motives and the amount of skill and character strength learning they reported. Four groups of backpackers were identified using a factor-cluster approach built on travel motivation items derived from the travel career pattern approach. There were consistent differences amongst these clusters in the amount and kind of skill learning perceived to have taken place. In particular, high thrill-seeking younger males were seen to develop fewer generic skills while less socially oriented older females reported the highest generic skills acquisitions revolving around independence, self-evaluation and resource management.

Learning skills and building character strengths was identified in Cutler and Carmichael's list as some of the learning outcomes we can explore. Factual knowledge and improved understanding of the visited setting are other topics. Here the work of researchers concerned with interpretation and tourists' responses to such settings as zoos, national parks and heritage areas offers further insight into tourist learning. In an earlier summary of this field of work it was observed that the amount of factual learning recorded in a range of studies depended heavily on the techniques employed to ask the questions and the detail required in the answers (Pearce, 2005: 174–180) (Figure 5.4).

Learning from places, particularly appreciating the value of environments for contemplation and spiritual restoration, has been a topic of enduring interest in the studies of western tourists. Urry's term, the romantic gaze, captures some of this interest and traces a path in western culture which emphasises the perceived values to travellers of contemplating (in relative isolation) the majesty of physical settings (Sax, 1980; Urry, 1990). Such ideas pervade North American studies on wilderness and the tourism-linked appreciation of natural environments (Gunn, 2004 and see Chapter 4, this volume: 96).

Much of the work has been conducted in an area known as informal learning or free choice learning. The work in this field consists of a combination of highly specific learning outcomes in such specialised settings as zoos and museums. This area of research also provides some frameworks or models which attempt to integrate the influences on learning which occur in these informal settings (Falk & Storksdieck, 2005; Roggenbuck et al., 1991). These frameworks include many important factors which can be used to build an overview of tourists' learning and personal development issues. The models provided by these research groups focus more on domestic travellers rather than addressing learning by international tourists.

Setting aside the issue of cross cultural variability, the ideas offered by Roggenbuck, Loomis and Dagostino highlight key influences shaping leisure learning. In their work they identify the individual's personality, the social expectations and the physical setting itself as well as the amount of

Figure 5.4 Existing knowledge and learning
The basis for sound communication and interpretive efforts lies in recognising how much tourists already know about a topic area. This principle applies to guided tours where the beginnings of such tours should quickly gauge partici- pants' knowledge levels. The notion is also applicable in brochures, visitor centres and for signs. For a full treatment of signs see Moscardo, G., Ballantyne, R. and Hughes, K. (2008) *Designing Interpretive Signs*. Golden, Colorado: Fulcrum for an accessible and appropriately visual summary of good practices.

interpretation in the location as influencing the likely amount of learning. Roggenbuck and colleagues then suggest that seven outcomes are the possible result of leisure engagements. They are behaviour change and skill learning, direct visual memory, information (factual) learning, concept learning, sche- mata learning, metacognition learning and attitude and value learning. This approach provides a broad framework for considering the types of learning which may also be possible in tourism settings.

The development of these ideas has led to the Contextual Model of Learning. This approach serves as a device for organizing the complexities of learning within such free-choice settings (Falk & Dierking, 2000; Falk & Storksdieck, 2005). The Contextual Model of Learning provides the large- scale framework with which to organize information on learning. There are multiple factors deployed in the framework, so many in fact that Falk and Storksdieck are prompted to write 'the total number of factors that directly and indirectly influence learning in museums probably number in the hundreds' (Falk & Storksdieck, 2005: 747).

The issue of context is the key feature of this framework (Falk & Storksdieck, 2005). More specifically they highlight 12 groups of factors as influential for museum learning experiences. Five of these factors are subsumed under the heading of personal factors and include tourists' motivation, prior knowledge, prior experiences, prior interests and the amount of choice and control they exert in the setting. Two sociocultural context factors of importance are the within-group interaction of the travel party and mediation by others outside the core group. The physical context factors identified as important to tourist learning identified by Falk and Storksdieck are the advance organisers provided to the tourists, orientation to the physical space, the architecture of the setting, the way the exhibits and programs are designed and subsequent reinforcing events outside the museum or attraction.

In addition to this area of work, Falk and Storksdieck (2005) have shown that individuals with the least prior knowledge have shown the greatest learning gains in these museum and interpretive contexts. While this is not surprising, their work also adds to this literature by comprehensively identifying factors they consider as critical to the uptake and retention of information.

It is possible to summarise our contemporary understanding of tourist learning as an amalgam of the elements already considered. It can be argued that there is evidence of learning about locations, of learning about oneself and developing some skills in the specific acts of travelling and there is research demonstrating that in some settings where information is being directed at tourists then within certain contextual limits some of the material presented is retained. We can expand upon an observation of de Botton (2002) in this context since he reported that travel did indeed offer learning opportunities but the curriculum is a chaotic one. The learning environments with which most of us are familiar are structured according to disciplines and well organised fields of study. Further there is a gradation of difficulty in learning in these areas with formal subjects and courses building upon the foundation ideas and in time tackling the sophisticated topics. The tourist who is already dealing with the sometimes distracting issues of cultural confusion (Hottola, 2004) is not usually following such a structured learning path. Even if a guide is providing a level of instruction for most tourists the information with which they are dealing is a rich array of history, anthropology, sociology, biology, architecture, art, urban issues and natural processes.

Like the studies of the impacts of tourism or questions about what motivates tourists, general queries about what tourists learn are very difficult to determine. We can establish lines of work which provide specific answers for targeted tourist groups. As a way of assisting future studies, a flow diagram of tourist learning is provided in Figure 5.5. The material builds upon earlier studies of leisure learning by Roggenbuck *et al.* (1991) and the research already reviewed by Falk and Pearce and Foster. The value of the diagram lies in concentrating researchers' attention on what kinds of context, tourists and learning outcomes they are seeking to investigate. The opportunities for original study in this area of tourist experience are considerable and attention to the particular groups being considered as well as the processes used to investigate the different types of learning offer promising future options for investigation. The usefulness of this kind of conceptual map will be explored

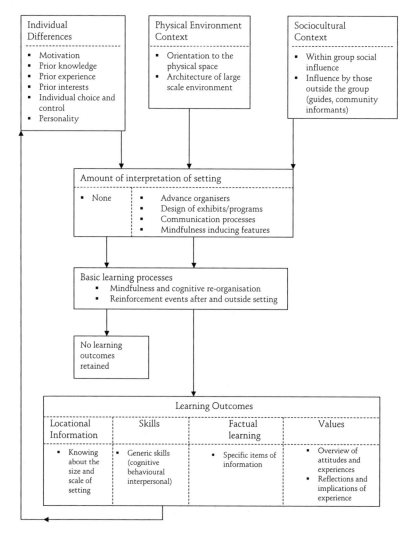

Figure 5.5   An integrative model of tourist learning

further in the final section of the chapter under the integrative section labelled Directions.

Tourists and Relationships

The building of new relationships and the enhancement of existing social bonds are key personal growth opportunities associated with tourism. It is apparent from the travel career pattern model of motivation that many tourists travel to enhance their existing relationships as well as to build new links. The process is multifaceted and involves a consideration of encounters with local people as well as fluctuations in existing relationships. It is relatively easy to document overall attitudes towards strangers at fixed points in time with structured questionnaire response formats. This kind of work underlies much of the study of tourists' attitudes towards the people they visit (Bowen & Clarke, 2009; Murphy & Murphy, 2004). Some of the assumptions underlying this kind of work will be considered in a subsequent section where new research approaches are highlighted.

It is not so easy to study the perceived quality and ongoing changes within existing relationships. For example, research attempts to study intimate relationships are very likely to be perceived as invading the privacy of respondents. Nevertheless, the importance of close relationships is a theme running through many travel commentaries and personal reflections (De Botton, 2002). (For readers interested in this literary commentary, the classical works of Mark Twain, Ernest Hemingway, John Steinbeck, Joseph Conrad, and D.H. Lawrence repay attention. Additionally, the popular travel writers such as Michael Palin, Paul Theroux, Jan Morris, Eric Newby and Bill Bryson make for entertaining and at times insightful reading about what motivates travellers and their relationships.)

The significance of relationships to tourists is affirmed in several ways. Diener and Biswas Diener (2008: 53–55) suggest relationships support people through difficult times and that the mere presence of others can be soothing. Nawijn (2010) reports that holiday stressors are reported quite frequently. Nevertheless, such concerns do not appear to affect the generally elevated moods which tourists report while on vacation. It may be that the presence and actions of others is all important in managing these stressors, possibly through the process identified as Katabasis – the small acts of kindness offered to strangers. Other people also provide social comparisons thus expanding the creative ways we can approach our travels. Not insignificantly other people make us laugh which is good for our immune systems and sense of well being (Cohen & Janicki-Deverts, 2009; Solomon, 1996).

Other more specific evidence confirms the importance of relationships to the travel experience and well-being. Pearce and Lee (2005) view close relationship building as a core motive in their travel career pattern model of motivation thus repeating a common theme highlighting the social needs of travellers (cf. Crompton, 1979; Driver *et al.*, 1991; Klenosky, 2002; Mannell & Iso-Ahola, 1987). In addition to suggesting the importance of enhancing close relationships, such as amongst family, friends and emerging partners, the travel career pattern model suggests that the building of closer relationships with the people in the visited community becomes a more important middle order motive as travellers become more experienced (Pearce, 2005). The argument that relationships matter to travellers is clear and the logic to be applied for personal development considerations is that the fulfilment of these important motives may be central to the travel experience.

For some groups in particular, travel provides the time, the new venues and the opportunity to affirm their identities and potentially promote a sense of well-being. The importance of time to all relationships is a pivotal consideration. Zimbardo and Boyd (2008) have argued that the way we view time is a complex pattern of integrating the way we treat the past, live in the present and anticipate the future. Zimbardo and colleagues devised a set of time-related questions – the Zimbardo Time Perspective Inventory (the ZTPI) – which enables researchers to assess the emphases people place on different time periods (Zimbardo & Boyd, 1999). Five time perspective scores are calculated; past negative, past positive, present hedonistic, present fatalistic and future. The separate components describe scores for being negative about the past (e.g. showing regret, remembering painful events, wishing mistakes could be corrected); positive about what has happened before (e.g. enjoying wonderful memories, relishing stories about the good old times, enjoyment of rituals and traditions, being nostalgic about childhood); maximising present enjoyment (e.g. being impulsive, living for now, taking immediate risks, preferring spontaneity); being fatalistic about day-to-day life (e.g. beliefs in the importance of luck and the influence of other forces, reporting a sense of powerlessness to influence the course of events); and being more oriented to the future than the present (e.g. an emphasis on goal setting, delaying immediate gratification, working before playing). In developments of the work a transcendental future time perspective has been added and this orientation records people's belief in an afterlife, divine laws and beliefs in an enduring human soul.

The pivotal considerations for tourism and the tourists' experience are that the holiday periods offer a time transforming opportunity. Freed from the daily pressures to consider the future time perspective, one closely associated with work, planning and conserving one's resources for anticipated future difficulties, tourists have the immediacy of their present circumstances as the foreground for their attention. The management of present time then becomes an opportunity to foster intimacy and possibly confront the adequacy of existing relationships. Pearce and Maoz (2008) report that inexperienced backpackers, like other tourists, sometimes struggle with the shifts in the amount of time they have to contemplate their travels and their relationships. They cite the work of Hicks which depicts the interaction between an inexperienced traveller and those now accustomed to their time horizon:

'Slow down, Ben. Time's on your side ... you've got lots of it for once' said Maca.

'Walk the middle path, seek Nirvana'

'Yes, but how exactly? Ben asked slightly puzzled.' (Hicks, 2004: 61)

Merely having the time to work at relationships may not be enough since the skills to undertake this task, as identified in this example, are equally necessary.

The perception of time and its challenges is one influential factor with the potential to reshape relationships. Another key consideration is the different social rules and novel contexts for certain types of behaviour. For example, Waitt and Markwell (2006) show that travel opportunities to gay-friendly destinations offer a kind of context and space where individuals can develop new relationships with locals or other gay travellers. Their study of gay destinations suggests that there are discourses for approving and encouraging some types of gay relationships, and by implication the well-being of those travellers. The favoured groups are the high spending, western gay males while the unwanted gays include the disabled, those with special needs and those without much disposable income. Identities for women and the satisfaction they experience on holidays as influenced by their relationships have also become key tourism research topics (Swain & Momsen, 2002). This research area too, affirms the interdependence of relationships, travel and personal development.

A further and final consideration amplifying the importance of considering relationships and their role in tourism's influences on personal development lies in the highly affective and emotional impacts associated with dealing with others. Difficulties in ongoing relationships are regularly considered to be among the most stressful of life's events while the commencement of new close relationships can generate the most euphoric of feelings (Argyle & Henderson, 1985; Armstrong, 2003). While it is challenging to study these issues among travellers, some initial evidence suggests that when holiday makers' relationships are in difficulty and arguments prevail, the enjoyment of the destinations is seriously compromised (Pearce & Maoz, 2008). Several commentators have followed the observations reported in the classical poetry of Ovid, that travellers change their sky not their soul when they cross countries (de Botton, 2002; Bowen & Clarke, 2009). It can be added that either implicitly or directly, tourists' relationships travel with them as well.

Pearce and Maoz (2008) approached the study of close relationships by studying the way interactions among tourists and others were presented in six backpacker novels. They noted that novels about backpackers do emphasise powerful themes revolving around relationships. In assessing the six novels, three from the popular works of English writers and three from successful novels about backpackers written in Hebrew, they noted the themes of fantasy and longing, relationship formation and disintegration, acknowledgement of unusual romantic attractions, sexual misadventures and family bonds. The novel insights generated by these explorations assist the wider view of tourist behaviour-specifically how tourists variously disconnect and reconnect themselves to their families and pre-existing relationships. De Botton (2009) writing a small monograph about Heathrow Airport comments on the anticipation of holidays:

> Our capacity to derive pleasure from aesthetic or material goods seems critically dependent on our first satisfying a more important range of emotional and psychological needs, among them those for understanding, compassion and respect. We cannot enjoy palm trees, and azure pools if a relationship to which we are committed has abruptly revealed itself to be suffused with incomprehension and resentment. (De Botton, 2009: 41)

The full complement of tourist relationships which affect tourist behaviour are summarized in Figure 5.6. The possibilities are inherently either positive or negative in all domains of interest.

Directions

The focus in this chapter has been on the personal outcomes for individuals which develop as a consequence of their tourist experience. Several components of the tourist experience emerge as interacting powerfully when examining the personal development outcomes arising from the multifaceted components of the tourist experience. The nature of motivation and its links to core emotional systems supplemented by a cognitive readiness to appreciate a setting and benefit from it are key components of the learning studies. The immersion in the setting and often the multisensory experience accompanying this immersion are seen to be important in activating mindful processing. This kind of active deep cognitive attention to identity issues, to diverse facets of learning and to relationships shapes how much of the tourists' experiences is encoded in their long-term memory store and may help reshape the tourists' sense of who they are, what they know, and both with whom and how they react to others. Nevertheless like many of the other relatively fresh topics reviewed in this volume there are still many unanswered questions in the emerging effort to enhance studies and improve our understanding of the dimensions of tourists' personal change.

A feature of this chapter has been the development of two organising frameworks to assist researchers contemplate the array of factors which matter when undertaking studies of learning and relationships. In Chapter 1 of this volume it was suggested that using a set of flexible conceptual schemes to address and attack clearly contextualised tourist behaviour issues is preferable to pursuing a monolithic goal of building overarching theory. The frameworks

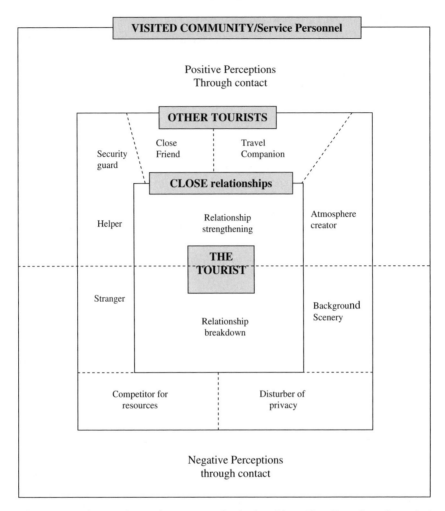

Figure 5.6 The tourist and an array of relationships. The diversity of tourist's relationships

constructed in this chapter represent an array of factors in which these nimble and targeted mini theories can operate. That is, there is not a theory of tourist learning or relationships but insights generated by linking component parts of the systems outlined.

It can be proposed that three key conceptual schemes and approaches may help develop the study of personal development. The topic of mindfulness has been explored already in the consideration of tourists' learning. Two other powerful schemes for understanding the learning and relationship experiences are storytelling and the role of social representations. The ideas are applicable to both areas of interest.

Our efforts at describing relationships, for example, are dependent on to whom we are speaking, the context of the conversation and its implications. It has already been briefly suggested in Chapter 1 that the concept of narrative or storytelling can be seen as central to the tourist experience (cf. Moscardo, 2010a; Woodside *et al.*, 2007). Stories are effective summaries of the travellers' experiences, packaged and delivered to others in discrete units to suit particular time frames and circumstances. Core attitudes and perspectives on relationships and evidence of learning lie entangled within these narratives. Such accounts are distilled attitudes in the sense that through recounting incidents, tourists can highlight what they have learned and how they feel about others (Pritchard & Havitz, 2006). Importantly travel stories are often told more than once and in the telling and retelling they act as a solid data unit in the individual's memory. In this retelling process the actual people and places encounters are re-imaged and re-imagined and take on the special character of confidently held core facts.

When seen in this way attitudes about relationships are more than sets of evaluative responses to structured question formats but packages of information which are selectively traded among key individuals in the tourists' world. The content of these packages is shaped by further concepts in tourism analysis. There is now a legacy of ideas about the tourism experience derived from more than 30 years worth of work on authenticity. Cohen (2007), Olsen (2007) and Pearce (2007) note in particular two kinds of subjective authenticity both of which are highly relevant to the reporting of relationships. Setting aside the older notion that authenticity can be objectively measured from physical elements of the scene, Cohen has proposed that most commentators in this area now recognise the importance of subjective authenticity which amounts to people's imposition of their judgements on the viewed people and places. Within this subjective authenticity notion, existential authenticity is recognised as describing special numinous moments when the traveller is shocked surprised and often transformed by what they see, learn and hear.

Additionally, the concept of mundane authenticity has been proposed where the ordinary, everyday events and contacts associated with others also have a strong impact on the travellers' memory (Pearce, 2007). This realm of interest was described by de Botton when he noted how travellers, without necessarily intending to do so, will tend to notice small features of their visited location. Mundane authenticity focuses on simple observations such as how people eat their food or how they greet one another. Such observations are the learned facts of our earlier discussion on tourist learning. Travellers construct from these everyday observations and scenes clear, incident-based stories and views of people's lives. Existential authenticity by way of contrast focuses on what Wordsworth once called spots of time, where the traveller is overwhelmed and dramatically influenced by the scene and or contact with significant people. It is through the operation of existential authenticity and mundane authenticity that the traveller forms a summary of relationships and things observed and has a basis on which to construct the relevant illustrative stories.

The stories reported by tourists and frequently built on their moments of existential and mundane authenticity can have a wider influence in shaping tourists' social representations about other people and places. The term social representation warrants some explanation. At core, social representations are everyday theories or branches of knowledge (Moscovici, 1984). They are held by individuals and shared by social groups. Social representations are often summarised and communicated by powerful images and succinct phrases. Moscovici proposed that social representations should be applied to knowledge and belief systems that exist in ordinary communication rather than to specialist knowledge domains such as science or religion.

Jaspars and Fraser (1984) note that social representations are social in at least three senses; they originate socially, they describe or represent a coherent, easily labelled aspect of the social world and they are shared with others. A fundamental aspect of social representations for the present interest is that these dynamic systems of knowledge contain values, beliefs, stereotypes and attitudes and are explanations of how any interest area is mentally organised. Applying this concept of social representations it can be suggested that travel stories and accounts circulating in the community become a part of the information array underlying social representations towards other groups and can ultimately influence personal responses to those the tourist meets. A previous excerpt from one of the younger tourists travelling in Milan and commenting on a French stranger illustrates the categorisation process through a defining incident which was reported as a travel story worth telling.

Sometimes the advantages and benefits of studying one topic reap rewards in an adjacent area of interest. More specifically, in developing an interest in the less well-researched areas of tourist learning and in particular tourist relationships, some insights into the dominant interest area of tourist satisfaction may well have been generated as we come to appreciate the pre-eminence of travel stories rather than Likert scale responses to experience.

6 Tourists Connecting to Others

Introduction

The final stage of this expedition into the research world of tourist behaviour is preoccupied with three broad concerns. We will be concerned at first with tourists and their views of poverty. Tourists' reactions to poverty can be related to the Millennium declaration of 2000 and the poverty reduction goals which were established at that event to enhance the life of millions of the world's less fortunate citizens (United Nations, 2000). The concern is not with explicit voyeuristic travel where tourists are motivated by a desire to gaze at the dispossessed or view struggling communities, but rather our interest is in noting how in their multiple activities tourists can be sensitised to a globally challenging issue. The second topic connecting tourists to others is that of volunteering. We will explore the motives and experiences of those who volunteer their time and expertise but who do so while paying for their participation. In this part of the chapter the issues of equity and altruism will be examined in order to uncover the value and complexities of volunteer tourism. Examples drawn from tourists' accounts of their experience will be incorporated into both the considerations of encountering poverty and being a volunteer. The third topic to be treated in some detail which connects tourists to those who entertain them and lets them mix with those they visit is the analysis of humour.

Tourists and Others: Reacting to Poverty

It is necessary at this juncture to define more precisely the use of the expression poverty in this chapter. Most formal definitions of poverty specify local people earning or having access to very limited amounts of income per day or per year (Sen, 2000). Rather than restricting our definition of poverty to set monetary amounts, the approach in this chapter lies in using the subjective appraisal and uses of the term poor and poverty by the travellers (cf. Scheyvens, 2001). This approach to the term poverty and the related expression poor people is not identical to the term poverty tourism, which can be reserved for the somewhat sinister and voyeuristic gaze at those who are destitute (Earth Times, 2009; Scheyvens, 2007). Our interest is in situations where tourists encountering very poor people may be an unexpected by-product of visiting places.

Arntzen *et al.* (2008) argue that researchers attempting to understand tourism to developing countries need to specify carefully which countries are being studied. They noted that tourists encountering poverty even within regional destinations such as Southern Africa or Central America can experience considerable localised differences both in people's circumstances and the challenges individual communities face. Bandyopadhyay (2009) and van Egmond (2007) both add that tourists' views of the circumstances of others may be driven by their vestigial colonial views of other nations. These considerations are not trivial since the reactions to poverty may in part reflect the self-justification which accompanies a neo-colonial view of others as less able than members of affluent societies. It is also highly likely that traveller definitions of poverty include more people and communities than the application of the term by developmental bodies and agencies.

In a recent study conducted by the author the relative frequency of the reporting of encounters with poverty in Southern Africa was assessed by considering the travel blogs written by western visitors (Pearce, in press b). The 297 blogs together constitute an impressive array of material amounting to over 1000 A4 pages of text and photographs. The blogs were selected by examining a comprehensive website www.travelblog.org. In this site over 7000 blogs have been recorded which are specifically concerned with Southern African destinations. The four destination countries studied in this analysis provided the following number of stories for each location: South Africa 3920, Mozambique 890, Namibia 678 and Botswana 417. It was decided to examine 5% of the stories from each of these locations in the first phase of the study and to follow this preliminary examination with more intensive analysis of material most germane to the examination of tourists' reactions to poverty. The basis for the selection of 5% of the stories was to ensure a comprehensive data set, akin to the sample sizes used when representative and random samples are drawn from published marketing studies of travellers' attitudes and perspectives (Smith, 1989; Veal, 2005). The study required an efficient yet comprehensive way to code the material. A coding scheme was devised as follows. Fifty blogs were read and considered, resulting in a sense of saturation of the themes being reported (Krueger & Casey, 2000). That is, after reviewing these 50 blogs a repetition of themes and content in the stories was apparent.

Based on this initial scan of the material a seven-part coding scheme was constructed to reflect the dominant emphases in the blogs. It consisted of the following themes: wildlife; scenery, scenic sights, attractions and activities; transport experiences; accommodation experiences; food; friends and fellow traveller contacts; contacts with local people. Those blogs reporting contact with local people were then set aside and a further coding scheme was put in place.

While the first coding scheme was simply an ad hoc construction serving the purpose of sorting the available data, the second scheme was structured according to the existing literature on social contact and group behaviour. Following Bales (1950), as well as that of Argyle *et al.* (1981) and associated work on social interaction, a multi-category coding scheme to describe how tourists interact with those they meet was formulated. Aspects of this scheme were proposed in an earlier monograph (Pearce, 2005: 115) and were reconsidered in Chapter 5 in Figure 5.2. The reactions to poverty study adapted the categories into the following components: simply seeing others as background scenery with no direct interaction, and being directly concerned with different emotional reactions to the situation being viewed. For further details see Pearce (in press b). Two researchers were involved in coding all the blogs and the percent of matching codes for commonly coded material was 92%. Five themes were identified from a detailed interpretive consideration of the poverty linked instances. Following the observations made by Antzel *et al.* (2008) on being specific about the country effects it can be noted that proportionately more instances of poverty reports were provided by tourists to firstly South Africa and then Mozambique. The following themes summarise the key findings of the study.

The Disengaged

For quite a large number of travellers the Southern African experience was all about wildlife, adventurous activities, beautiful sights, food, transport, accommodation arrangements and the social lives of themselves and their companions. The explicit mention of local people was higher for Botswana and Mozambique but as stated previously the relative frequency of poverty comments was highest for South Africa. The category scoring scheme may slightly overrate the percentage of travellers who are truly indifferent to or disengaged from the people they see, since the general term culture was coded as a part of the label scenery/sights if there was no explicit mention of individual contact or experience. Cultural shows or performances by way of contrast were coded as a part of the mention of local people. Undoubtedly nearly all travellers do have interactions with local people, even if it is only tourism service personnel, but in the sometimes succinct blogs they write, many do not comment on the personnel involved.

Compartmentalisation

In the focused assessment of the data and in the subdivision of those people who do mention contact with the local people whom they perceive to be poor, the authors of the internet accounts often note the situation and move quickly to other topics. There were emotional reactions here of distaste, disgust and occasionally indifference. The emotional tone is captured by the remarks from a British traveller, Simon;

> We arrived in Namibia after a long wait. It was tedious and there were lots of quite poor kids and families around but we moved quickly past them to get to our adventure trek.

The Lucky Self

One set of responses prompted by viewing poverty and local people involved a reflection on the tourist's home society and affluence. This category frequently used words such as privileged, spoilt, lucky and eye opening to describe the encounters. Common emotional reactions here were relief and guilt. A notable illustration comes from a younger woman Rebekka travelling in South Africa. Rebekka highlights the contrasts:

> Although I'm not ignorant of the fact that people still live like this (and in far worse conditions) in many parts of the world I still feel haunted by the complex mixture of emotions (shame/guilt/gratitude/anger doesn't really begin to capture it) . . . . The contrasts may be unsettling and I have been constantly reminded of how incredibly privileged I am, but South Africa's beauty is undeniable. I've also been struck by how friendly and warm people are here.

Empathy, Sympathy and the Self

In this kind of response there was a concern for the well being of the people with whom the travellers had come into contact. The responses were at times empathic in that travellers thought about what it would be like to live in the ways they were witnessing. At other times the responses were sympathetic, where a simple external concern for the assessed plight of the local people was to the fore. This group of responses sometimes co-existed with a commentary about one's own good fortune but was distinguished from that category since a much more explicit awareness and recording of the plight of others was highlighted both in contemplating the locals' present lives and future prospects. There were invariably emotional reactions here such as concern, sadness and pity. Some of these travel blogs speculated on the future health and socio-economic circumstances of individuals or communities. The conceptualisation of the viewed communities has moved from viewing them as scenery to a concern with them as people. Often individual cases are cited. The reactions here are a close parallel to the observations of Uriely et al. (2009) describing successful Israeli–Arab interaction in the Sinai. Once similarities among the interacting parties are established and names of people are used, the sense of a common humanity reduces stereotyping and promotes engagement. The process though is not always easy to communicate. An example is provided by a Scottish tourist James who wrote:

This is hard stuff to write about. Everywhere there are smiling kids but they are living in the most barren and I suspect disease breeding villages. At a rest stop with our truck on a side road our driver and three of us kicked our soccer ball around with two young boys and traded smiles and laughter. Later I found out the parents of many children in that village had died from AIDS. This is a heartbreaking country. We felt good and then very sad within the hour. We became very aware that we do not want to exploit people for our little bit of happiness and pleasure.

Corrective Actions

Blog contributors sometimes suggested sources of action and stated that in the future they would act to provide assistance to help alleviate perceived poverty and generally benefit others. The calls to action included expressed desires to undertake volunteer work, avoid destructive socio-cultural behaviours, think about their purchasing patterns, donate money or put readers of the travel blog in touch with charities and aid organisations. There was a diverse array of emotional reactions here but they included anger and determination.

Kim reports on her feelings after visiting Soweto:

I walked around this 'middle class' home and thought how much excess I have ... Is life easier and better with all of our trappings, of course, does this mean I will get rid of all my excess things when I go home of course not. By maybe just maybe when I walk in Target and drop those unnecessary things into the cart, I will think about all of those whose basic needs are not covered maybe I will think harder about buying that extra pair of jeans which I don't really need and think that could provide 4 years worth of schooling for a child ... I hope I will anyway.

Other travellers attempt to communicate their sense of shock and horror at what they have seen and encourage others to donate to charities, to get involved or simply react as Charles, a young North American tourist, suggests:

I do not expect you will automatically understand but I believe my sharing this with you will indeed spark some anger some pity, some feeling that is not positive but it is necessary to create something positive.

A persistent concern of this volume is to specify what kinds of tourists we are considering before embarking on any broader consideration of the implications of study results. In the present research case a fundamental

consideration is exactly who is writing these stories. Two thirds of the internet travel story writers, at least as sampled in the study are women. It appears
from their photos and commentary that they are predominantly international travellers from Europe, North America and Australia. They are often
less than 30 years old (as assessed by images and story content) and quite
frequently they are involved in extended travels including volunteer tourism
experiences. In brief, the internet stories clearly under-represent affluent,
older and short-stay tourists. There are almost no domestic African or Asian
tourists providing these internet accounts. While the stories vary in length
they do have a high face validity or truthfulness – the styles often contain
spelling errors and untidy grammar but the expression is free flowing. It is
reasonable to conclude that most appear to have been written quickly and
without literary pretence or artifice. These observations support those made
by Schaad (2008) that the travel-based internet stories in general are honest,
unaffected and genuine.

A second consideration preceding any consideration of the implications
of these tourists' reactions lies in contemplating the unrecorded reactions to
poverty. There may be a lot more happening amongst all visitors than are
recorded in the blogs. This view needs to be advanced with caution and certainly requires the use of other data and a triangulation of sources to explore
its accuracy. At the very least, many structured group tour itineraries such as
those reported in many of the internet travel accounts provide travel experiences involving high levels of contact with local communities in varied economic conditions which one might assume evoke quite powerful even if
unreported reactions (cf. Guerba Experience Africa in Close-Up, 2009).

Despite these cautionary remarks, the study offers some hope for this
globally agreed-on concern to reduce poverty. Travellers whose internet stories were recorded in the categories empathy, sympathy and the self, and
action oriented, appear likely to do something as a consequence of their travels. Volunteering, donating money and agitating for others to be more concerned are mentioned quite frequently. These are powerful and potentially
influential outcomes. The total percentage of all the travellers who fit these
two categories is small; a conservative estimate here is less than 5% of tourists considered in the study. Importantly though, this figure is a small
percentage of a large number of people.

In the academic world of tourism research much has been written about
sustainability and the effects of travelling to places on environmental conservation attitudes. One possible implication of the present study is that it
begins to provide a foundation for more studies concentrating on the outcomes of travel, but on this occasion the issue of interest is the influence of
travel on attitudes to people and poverty. This line of work and thinking is
somewhat different to the dominant writing about tourism and poverty
alleviation which focuses more on tracking the power, politics and flow of
money from tourism industry expenditure (Chok et al., 2007; Scheyvens,

2007; Schilcher, 2007; UNDP, 1997). Such studies are important too, but programs providing more tourists with ways to convert their emotional reactions into useful behaviours to assist those they see and visit are potentially direct and powerful pathways for change. Possible, practical and preferred ways to effect this conversion of emotional responses into poverty alleviation behaviours could be a direction for tourism research in this field. Further studies of direct tourist involvement in poverty alleviation measures across different countries offer promise and a truly triple bottom line agenda for sustainable tourism and development research.

Volunteer Tourism

It can be quickly appreciated that volunteer tourists are a distinctive group. Jokes and humour about foolish tourists in general are plentiful and, as reported in Chapter 1, occasionally tourists deserve such treatment. Few people seem to ridicule volunteer tourists. Instead there is a measure of incredulity that individuals will pay quite handsomely for an experience where they have to work and contribute to the well-being of other people and the environment (Coghlan, 2005: 26–28). On some occasions there are positive comments boosting the value of volunteering to the host community and the sending society. The view is also expressed that the tourists gain character strengths and a new world view and the host society accesses, at least temporarily, some labour and expertise (Wearing, 2004: 210).

It can be noted quite readily that the source countries for volunteer tourists are from affluent western countries. That is, mostly the volunteer tourists are from Western Europe and North America and to a lesser extent from Australia and New Zealand (Galley & Clifton, 2004; McGehee, 2002; Wearing, 2001). A question to be asked here is why does this pattern of source countries seem to prevail amongst volunteers no matter where studies are conducted? To pose this question differently why are there not many more volunteer tourists from Asia and the Middle East where there are at least parallel and conspicuous pockets of affluence and skills?

A consideration of cultural differences in the values and attitudes of nationality groups appears to lie behind these differences. The same forces which have given rise to European-based or -derived societies and the pursuit of individual well being in such societies have had two other associated consequences. The first of these is described as alienation between humans and their environment, a Cartesian belief that men and women stand apart from nature and are able to use it for their well being (Gore, 2004; Nisbett, 2003). Yet paradoxically these same individualistic and exploitative traits also carry the seeds of ethical and moral responsibility – beliefs that individuals are responsible and have the capacity to change and correct mistakes. As Nisbett reports this Cartesian tradition is a different way of viewing responsibility and one's place in the world than the more integrated views of life which prevail in Muslim, Buddhist and Confucian societies (cf. Brown & Postel, 2004; McGehee, 2002). Volunteer tourists when viewed in this manner can be seen as an ethical, socio-cultural group with Western origins, remedying in a small way the historical exploitation and environmental mistakes on which their society has been built. This does not imply that every volunteer tourist is immediately conscious of or will report being a part of an environmental or social change group, but at this broad level of explanation there is some legitimacy to an overview of the activity as deriving from a collective ethical and remedial effort. There is a commonality in this explanation of the roots of volunteering and the concerns to be helpful noted amongst the tourists in the perceptions of poverty study.

In common with the other topics traversed in this volume the development of conceptual schemes and the application of ideas to interpret and understand the observed behaviours is central to our purpose. Two approaches stand out in considering volunteer tourism. First, the motivation of the volunteers can be examined closely using the same kinds of travel career pattern work advocated in earlier chapters. For volunteer tourists there is some evidence that it is the middle layer level of motives – the concern with exploring the host society and setting which are more prominent in their overall pattern of responses. This suggestion is built on some analyses of visitor behaviour explored empirically in the work of Coghlan (2005) and underpinned in part by Stebbins (2007) in his approach to the values and activities underlying serious leisure.

Interestingly, volunteer tourism might be seen as occupying an ambiguous position in Stebbins' catalogue of serious leisure perspectives or types. In his 2007 work, Stebbins suggests there is 'mainstream' serious leisure which is the systematic pursuit of a hobby or interest which often requires high levels of commitment and developing skills. He also identifies project-based leisure which is often a short term, one shot or infrequent activity requiring reasonably complicated and sometimes creative skills. Both of these types of leisure are distinguished from casual leisure which is immediate and commonplace and offers quick personal rewards. Volunteer tourism is perhaps best understood as project leisure with the possibility of becoming serious leisure. Researchers interested in investigating the way in which project leisure becomes serious leisure (especially in the context of volunteer tourism) could usefully work with the travel career pattern motives to track changes in tourists' views of their motives over time. Since previous chapters in this book have already highlighted the layers of the travel career pattern work, at this point the opportunity for further investigation of career development in volunteer tourism using the travel career pattern approach will be simply recommended. Attention will now be directed towards a second conceptual scheme to explore the specific rewards of volunteer tourism; the approach to be considered is termed equity theory.

The defining principle of equity theory is that a stable state in social relationships and exchanges can only exist if there is a perceived balance between costs and rewards or more specifically between perceived inputs and outputs (Kunkel, 1997). Such an approach has a strong emic component as it is the judgements of the participant not the outside observer which determines the relative worth of what they are giving and getting. This kind of sensitivity to the participants' views of their experiences is congruent with viewing the tourists from an emic perspective and giving credit to their active and engaged role in situations.

In the early writing on equity theory there was a consideration of philanthropist/recipient relationships. There are links too with the concept of altruism which has provided some explanations of pro-social behaviour in the literature on public helping actions (Smithson et al., 1983). Helping and philanthropic behaviour are arguably somewhat similar to volunteering, and hence there is an a priori case that the further use of equity theory may be of value in interpreting the tourism volunteering experience (Walster et al., 1978).

The identification of the inputs and the outputs as perceived and valued by the participant are consistent challenges when applying equity theory. If such inputs and perspectives can be measured, then equity theory proposes that any imbalance between inputs and outputs leads to distress and people in such situations will seek to restore equity. They can do this in one of two ways, elevate the value of the rewards they are receiving and work harder to get these rewards or decrease their own inputs and hence lower their costs. They cannot, according to equity theory, persist in a deeply inequitable relationship or exchange. The inputs and outputs may not be of the same kind, and often they are not, which is why a close examination of the value individuals place on the inputs and outputs is so central to equity analyses. Pearce and Coghlan (2008: 139) offer some specific ways in which researchers can measure and compare the equations which equity theory suggests are important in influencing the satisfaction of tourist volunteers.

It is particularly apparent from the travel blogs reported by volunteer tourists that their experiences are highly engaging and evoke strong emotional rewards. Three samples drawn from travel blogs are illustrative of the power of committing to both social and environmental volunteering tasks. Eric, a 28 year old travelled to Ghana, West Africa, for one month. He used his skills and experience gained while studying for a law degree to help work with an NGO called the Commonwealth Human Rights Initiative (CHRI). He reports:

Overall, I had an incredible experience in Ghana and I could not have asked for more from Projects Abroad and Commonwealth Human Rights Initiative. I was made to feel safe and welcome from the time I stepped off the plane until the time I made my heart-wrenching farewells. As I reflect on my time in Ghana, I believe the people and the indelible images associated with my experiences at CHRI will forever serve to remind me of the amazing personal growth that volunteering abroad fostered in me. It was a meaningful and worthwhile opportunity that I would recommend unreservedly to anyone who has a passion for the universal and unalienable nature of human rights and aspires to be part of the realization of such a promise. http://www.projects-abroad-pro.org/case-studies/?content=human-rights/eric-mcadamis/.

Hannah a 23-year-old German volunteer reports her enthusiasm for volunteering as a tourist: 'From mid-February to mid-May 2010 I worked as a volunteer in Cabo Blanco, Costa Rica, and it was the most fun, rewarding and exciting experience I could have wished for. Trying to take a break from the stressful study-routine at home this was the perfect place to recover my balance and still do something productive. The park needs the help of the volunteers to maintain it and keep it open for tourists, and everyone who is motivated to give something back to nature, get to know awesome people from all over the world and meet all kinds of wild animals along the way should give it a shot.' http://www.caboblanco-volunteering.com/Volunteer-Stories.htm?PHPSESSID=021b191d1c49c3164063d9a9378e5fcb.

A third account closely parallels the enthusiasm of these two volunteers but again in a different context. John working in Kenya provides a vivid account of involvement:

The volunteers I met were of a varied age, each individual bringing their own talents and personalities. Every person I met brought something different. I have got a brilliant relationship with all the volunteers I met out there. The lives that this project has saved, together with the help of the volunteers from all over the world is incredible and something to be proud of and something that Real Gap should be proud of being a part of also! I witnessed so many people who benefited from the volunteers' help in my time there, too many to note! ... the programme has got a place in my mind and heart forever! I never really experienced any problems and I enjoyed every moment of my time!' http://www.realgap.co.uk/John-s-Volunteer-Experience.

Such enthusiastic endorsements for volunteer experiences are matched by cautious remarks from other travellers about overly commercial operations which are seen as exploiting volunteer good will. The resulting internet debates neatly capture the applicability of the equity theory perspectives on volunteering and the needs for balanced appraisals of the inputs and rewards. The reports from the volunteer tourists raise another possible research study which could extend the learning outcomes research already reviewed in Chapter 5. Clearly some of the volunteers believe they have gained insights and developed personal qualities and character strengths from their experience. As yet there appear to be no studies directly appraising the volunteers perceived character strength changes nor are there analyses of what friends and relatives see as changes in the skills and strengths of the returning volunteers. The new characterisation of values in the positive psychology literature might be a starting point for such appraisals.

Humour

One of these understudied topics in tourism which has the potential to connect people to others is that of humour. Many authors have struggled with the definition of humour but some principles or commonalities have emerged in these discussions (Martin, 2007). Humour can be understood by recognising that it involves both the production and perception of a communication or act which induces an emotional state of mirth or mild excitement (cf. Ruch, 1993). Research attention to the role of humour in tourism is surprisingly infrequent (Wall, 2000). The opportunities to provide conceptual insights as well as to generate information from specific cases are rich and multifaceted (Pearce, 2009). The existing work can be divided into work concerning humour to attract tourists and tourists' experiences of on-site humour. There are other wider perspectives on tourism and humour including humour about tourists and humour created by tourists but the present interests lie in how humour facilitates the tourists' contact with others.

Having a good sense of humour is widely regarded as a positive trait. In the list of character strengths developed by positive psychologists, humour is identified as a virtue which helps individuals forge connections to the others and provide them with meaning (Park et al., 2005). In contemporary psychology studies there is now widespread agreement that a sense of humour is not a unitary trait or characteristic (Martin, 2007). At least two dominant meanings have emerged in a long running series of psychometric and factor analytic studies. Kohler and Ruch (1996) suggest that there is an ability to comprehend humorous situations and a different and independent ability to produce humour.

Martin (2007) subdivides the perception of humour by identifying habitual behaviour (such as people who laugh easily), temperament differences (such as ongoing cheerfulness), cognitive abilities (being able to comprehend subtleties and incongruities), select attitudes (a positive view of humour) and a world view which embraces a non-serious outlook on life. By way of contrast, the production of humour is dependent on individuals being good self-monitors (i.e. sensing how others are reacting to them) as well as having the memory, creativity and divergent thinking skills to spot the comic components of situations (Feingold & Mazzella, 1991; Kohler & Ruch, 1996). For tourists, having a good sense of humour may be a means of not simply reacting to provided jokes but being able to create a better experience by identifying the odd, the unusual and the humorous elements of travel with others.

The fine-grained studies of the links between personality types and humour appreciation have revealed a number of enduring and consistent relationships (Martin, 2007: 200–202; Ruch, 1994). In order to understand these studies two preliminary perspectives are required. Factor analytic studies suggest that most of the variation in humour appreciation is accounted for not so much by content but by the structure of the humour. The dominant categories involved in humour appreciation are firstly incongruity, and secondly, nonsense or zany humour. The third consistent category which appears in the factor analytic studies of jokes and humour types is the one content-based dimension which recurs across studies: it is humour built on sexual themes (Ruch, 1993). In assessing the links between personality and these types of humorous material, researchers in this field use two measures of humour.

There is an obvious first dimension concerned with the extent to which the material is amusing or funny. The second dimension is one of how unpleasant or aversive the humour is seen to be. Typical studies by Hehl and Ruch (1990), Ruch (1994) and Ruch and Hehl (1998) have produced an array of findings which broadly indicate that extroverts enjoy all kinds of humour a little more, that perceived aversiveness is weakly correlated with neuroticism, that religious fundamentalism is negatively correlated with seeing jokes as funny, that sensation seekers enjoy all humour types more, that conservative and authoritarian personalities appreciate the incongruity jokes much more than the bizarre or zany jokes and that those known as tough-minded, that is low on empathy, appreciate the sexual humour more. These kinds of individual differences are broadly useful for interpreting humour receptiveness and production at the individual and personality level of analysis. Nevertheless, a wider view is also required to understand how humour might function in tourism contexts and how tourism audiences including those coming from different countries might respond to the types of humour.

One way to understand humour, and it is an approach with a long history, is to see humour as effectively establishing superiority by one party over another individual, group of people or location. In particular Gruner (1997) views humour as playful aggression where one party wins compared to the other. For example, there is a global trade in jokes which depict the superiority of one social group over others, or perhaps more accurately demeans one labelled group compared to the joke teller and listener. These superiority informed jokes are of the type *What happens when English tourists come to Australia? The IQ of both countries is raised.* There is a ready substitution of groups and labels in these jokes but they are linked by the commonality of making the listener feel comfortable and superior both in easily recognising the joke and, provided they are not a member of the targeted group, not being personally implicated in its disparaging effect. A more subtle version of the assertion of superiority is evident in the following lines where the initial quest for superiority is challenged: *Local: Where are you from? Tourist: I am from somewhere where we do not end our sentences with a preposition. Local: Where are you from smart-arse?* Given the long history of somewhat disparaging remarks about tourists and tourism, of which perhaps Boorstin's 1962 analysis is the most widely familiar statement, it can be expected that much tourist humour tourist also fits this superiority format. This kind of aggressive, superiority drive humour is of course not very conducive to the theme of this chapter – the ways in which tourists can link to others.

A superiority explanation is only one way to understand humour about tourist local interaction and tourism places. Other theoretical perspectives offer the prospect of more positive links among interacting parties. For everyday settings and for many work environments involving elements of danger or stress, the foundation work of Goffman (1969) which emphasises the tension reduction and the social integration function of humour has been pivotal (Joyce, 1989; Mitchell, 1996; Scott, 2007; Young, 1995). Goffman's original approach stressed the way humour was used to bind members of a team when they are producing a performance. In his early work, the gentle mock role playing of the other group members' foibles as well as mild derisory comments about them were noted (see Goffman, 1969: 168–173). As a link to this approach, the work of both Sweet (1989) and Evans-Pritchard (1989) suggests that in tourism-oriented cultural performances and social interactions, ethnic groups may use humour in some positive ways. In her analyses of North American Pueblo Indians and their dance performance, Sweet observes that tourists and performers join together to laugh at the Pueblo dance routines which mimic tourist behaviour and stereotypes. Evans Pritchard also studied North American Indian and white American interaction. Her case studies revealed that a number of Indians played with the stereotypes visitors held and confounded the tourists by such actions as dressing in a formal suit, parodying the sullen Indian image depicted in films and pretending not to understand English. It might be argued that the humour here is less about superiority and more about mutual engagement in the parody.

Goffman (1974) also identified how humour can act as mechanism to help interacting parties define or indeed redefine more clearly the nature of the frame or situation in which their meeting was taking place. In this view humour can be a tool which helps participants switch frames and readjust expectations. This approach allows for a positive, integrative and constructive use of humour. The jokes and amusing stories may be capable of binding together participants who are in ambiguous situations. There is a close compatibility between Goffman's approach and the work in psychology on the cognitive approaches to understanding humour. The idea of frames is somewhat analogous to the coexistence of two schema (Wyer & Collins, 1992). These researchers propose that that humour involves the activation of two different schema to understand a situation or interaction. One schema is then dropped or shown to be redundant as the other takes over. In their view humour results only when the less serious or more trivial schema takes over. The integrative approach to understanding and interpreting humour is also aligned with three of Martin's four dimensions of humour styles (Martin,

2007: 211). In particular, a link can be drawn between the Goffmanesque approach and what Martin has termed (1) the affiliative humour, (2) self-defeating or self-disparaging humour and (3) self-enhancing or coping humour. Martin's fourth humour style, aggressive humour, which he regards as used for criticizing or manipulating others is clearly aligned with superiority theory.

In a study of the use of humour by guides and presenters at three tourist attractions, Pearce (2009) identified some initial views of the special role of tourism humour. Individuals who presented humorous scripts and perfor-mances in a Disney Jungle tour setting, at the Polynesian cultural centre and at an adventure tourism site were described as effective in promoting visitor comfort levels and assisting visitor concentration. The humour provided to tourists was also seen as establishing social connections as well as providing a commentary on the role of being a tourist. Examples from the study reveal how those entertaining the tourist audience provide commentary at a basic level about easily comprehensible themes. For example, at a simple level the Samoan presenter jokes about his age and the contrast between his appear-ance and that of the audience. 'Now I'm going to show you how to open a coconut. Get a coconut. Look for the ripe ones. This one is ripe. You can tell by its colour. It turns brown like me when it is ripe, which tells me that some of you are not ripe yet.' At a more subtle level, in the Samoan presentation traditional practices are not just presented as specific skills of Samoan society but are related to the presenter's abilities. In presenting the task of collecting coconuts the presenter plays with the audience's expectations that he will be the tree climber, but then effectively changing roles and becoming the over-awed sophisticate when confronted with the difficulty of the task. In this process the audience and the presenter merge as one in admiring the skill of another performer when the actual tree climbing takes place. Balme (1998) refers to this playing with reflexivity as 'strategies of resistance against the tourist gaze' (Balme, 1998: 58). In the Jungle Cruise the presenter comments; 'And just ahead you'll notice an alligator playing with an elephant. That's something you don't see everyday (Long pause) but I do', and similarly; 'I had such a good time – I'm going to go again! (in a low voice) and again and again and again.' The stress on such performative labour of the presenters works to provide humour linking the audience in a common light-hearted enjoy-ment of the experience with no cost to other targets (cf. Bryman, 2004).

There is also now sound physical evidence that enjoying humour is healthy (Lefcourt, 2005; Wiseman, 2007). Summarising the work by Rotton (1992), Wiseman comments:

> According to this work people who spontaneously use humour to cope with stress (*which might include the stress of travel*) have especially healthy immune systems, are 40% less likely to suffer a heart attack and strokes,

experience less pain during dental surgery and live 4.5 years longer than most. (Wiseman, 2007: 208)

Jan Morris suggests that those who particularly appreciate humour represent a transnational cohort of like-minded people. She suggests:

there are people everywhere who form a fourth world, or a diaspora of their own ... They share with each other, across all the nations, common values of humour and understanding. When you are among them you know you will not be mocked or resented because they will not care about your race, your faith, your sex or your nationality and they suffer fools if not gladly, at least sympathetically. They laugh easily. They are never mean ... they form a mighty nation if only they knew it. (in Shapiro, 2004: 365)

Directions

Humour may well be a key mechanism in the development of the learning opportunities and the personal skills noted earlier in this chapter. It also may be important in providing a degree of personal management amongst travellers when they encounter stressful circumstances. In the experiential terms which guide this volume, humour is intimately linked to cognitive skills and is defined by particular types of affective reactions – mirth and a level of excitement – not to mention that when the humour is successful there are the very visible behavioural components of broad smiles and outright laughter. Nevertheless, the detailed tourism studies of humour remain limited in terms of the empirical analysis of actual behaviour and tourist experiences. As a new and contemporary topic in tourist behaviour it appears that the further study of humour both due to its widespread use and its benefits should be on the agenda of more researchers in the coming decade.

7   Additional Perspectives

Introduction

In this chapter we will consider some further lightly explored areas of interest in tourist behaviour and experience. Some topics which researchers might investigate in the next decade will also be considered and the ways that future academic excursions might be conducted will be highlighted. As a final contribution to the continuing study of tourists' behaviour and experiences, a figure depicting key issues and contexts will be employed to provide an organising mental map and souvenir of the journeys undertaken. This figure will also outline the larger terrain in which all the topics we have considered are located.

Slow Tourism

An emerging approach to a range of experiences including tourism experiences is expressed by the concept of slowness. Honore (2004), a journalist and a key organiser of the ideas in this interest area, suggests that in modern and postmodern cultures speed and fast-paced living are very common. The standard view is that to do things quickly is to be efficient. Further, doing as much as possible in the finite time lines of one's life is seen as using time well and makes for an energised and engaged existence. Honore argues that there are multiple reasons to question this prevailing view and that the antonym of the fast and efficient life is selective slowness. The argument here is that there are many activities which are better appreciated and more richly fulfilling if undertaken in a leisurely and low key manner. The origins of the term slowness are Italian and the concept was initially used to refer specifically to food and an appreciation of its cultivation, production and consumption. In the first applications of the term, the sensual qualities of the food experience were clearly highlighted. As slowness has been applied to daily life, leisure and entertainment it has also acquired sensuous overtones, even including notions of slow sex. In whatever areas of life the term has been used it is seen as a contrast to tightly defined allocations of time which juxtapose many activities and tasks into a crowded life style.

The concepts of slow travel and slow tourism are rich in providing distinctive types of tourist experiences. Slow travel is a type of travel where tourists experience a deeper understanding of a place by moving at a deliberate and controlled pace through landscapes. Walking, bicycle tourism and some forms of train and car travel may qualify as slow travel particularly when seen as a contrast to the rapid transit across continents and countries now commonly available through international flights. Typically such travellers stay in one place for an extended period of time. Additionally, slow tourists tend to avoid long day trips. For example, this type of travel may involve remaining in a vacation rental for a week and attempting to live simply. Molz suggests that those participating in slow tourism seek to live like locals '... establishing local routines, indulging in local cuisines, and becoming connoisseurs of the local culture' (Molz, 2009: 280). The activities enjoyed are simple and can include shopping at local stores, going to the same places each day or taking the time to see attractions that are in the vicinity of the vacation home (Dickinson, 2007; Slow Travel website, 2008). Findings from Dickinson's research suggest that these travellers typically engage more deeply with places and people and that slow travel experiences can be rewarding and relaxing. Dickinson and Lumsdon (2010) note that slow tourism activities involve contemplation of one's type of transport with desirably low emission forms preferred over airplanes, cruise ships and cars (Figure 7.1).

A related but still rather minor style of slow travel, that involving Willing Workers on Organic Farms (WWOOF), is being investigated by Lipman and Murphy (in press). Their study deals with the responses of travellers in eastern Australia. They observe that a unique feature of this program which separates it from volunteer tourism is the lack of money exchanged between hosts and guests. Travellers, or 'WWOOFers', exchange 4–6 h of labour for meals and a place to stay at a host's property. These properties are not all remote or large properties; some are even in urban areas. All hosts are involved in organic forms of production including cropping, vegetable, fruit and flower production and animal husbandry. The type of work WWOOFers undertake covers a wide range, but invariably is outdoors. Tending to animals, weeding, harvesting and property maintenance are common tasks. It is of particular interest to the present discussion that this form of work and the living arrangements created for WWOOFers enables a high level of information sharing in general about global issues and specifically, because of the farming context, environmental management. Early results from this program of work encourage the researchers to suggest there is value in approaching slow tourism with a different mindset:

Slowness can provide much more fulfilling and rich experiences that involve full participation and immersion in the local communities. Even if slow tourism remains a niche, fully embraced by only a small portion of tourists, it is absolutely essential that some elements of this concept have widespread adoption. This is necessary in order to avoid serious,

Figure 7.1 Slow tourism
The photograph of a guide explaining the function and history of a small light-house on Kangaroo Island, South Australia to a modest number of visitors represents the kind of low key but detailed exploration of an area implicit in the concept of slow tourism. In this style of travel tourists make the most of resources and stories in a relatively confined area. Businesses in a region can benefit from slow tourism by providing local food products and offering accommodation options suitable for longer stays and community contact

irreparable harm to the earth and its inhabitants through global warming. (Lipman & Murphy 9)

The experiential agenda for slow tourism is powerful in sensory and behavioural terms. Individuals who become WWOOFers are physically involved in the landscape, exposed to the smells of farms, interaction with animals and the earth and have to deal with the weather and the stress of completing novel tasks. Equally the experience is accompanied by much conversation about the food production, the process of food distribution and the state of the planet, all topics which can be the basis for learning as well as pivotal points for arguments. Lipman and Murphy suggest that mostly these encounters are amicable.

These remarks reiterate the interdependence of some of the major themes explored in this volume. Through the comments of Lipman and Murphy it can be seen that an interest in volunteer tourism and slow tourism provides experiences linking to sustainability issues particularly in the form of climate change concerns. It is a small reminder of course that setting out ideas and concepts in any kind of linear book format provides an orderly approach to social issues and the concerns of tourists. In the experiential world of the tourist there is much more of the chaotic interpretation of the curriculum noted by de Botton (2002) and the buzzing, blooming confusion of a multitude of information and experiential inputs once noted by William James as defining social life (Boring, 1950). The WWOOFers experience as well as that of slow tourists is a clear reminder that there is an orchestra of influences operating in these tourism or tourism-linked settings and while we may emphasise some components in research efforts all factors – emotions, cognitive processes, behaviours, relationships and sensory inputs – are simultaneously in action. The value of the slow tourism perspective resides in a reassessment of how much importance we place on this array of inputs and particularly how we view the time in and of our lives.

Spending Behaviour

Another emerging topic which has not been specifically considered is the spending behaviour and experiences of tourists. Clearly, the overall income from tourists and tourism is of major importance to the theme of sustainability. The economic returns from tourism are at the root of most agendas for tourism growth and development (Jenkins, 2008; Sharpley, 2009). Many researchers and many papers have documented tourism's economic impacts (World Tourism Organisation, 1999). Tourists' spending together with business expenditure is a part of that overall effect. Dwyer *et al.* (2004) provide a review of techniques to undertake large-scale economic appraisals and conclude that computable general equilibrium (CGE) models are more thorough in determining overall contributions of tourism than input–output models and satellite accounts. Stoeckl (2008) points out that these CGE models require many resources for their development and for smaller rural areas estimates of tourism multipliers and benefits may be exaggerated. For our present interest in tourists' behaviour these larger economic discussions and systems of calculating overall economic influences represent a separate kind of inquiry to our compass of interests. It is possible however to propose some research approaches specifically focusing on the tourist behaviour of spending money which can supplement some of the tourism economics literature (Figure 7.2).

The concern of much of the tourism economics agenda is with how much is spent and where that expenditure is directed and sourced. In a forthright appraisal of economic research in tourism, Archer and Cooper (1998: 68) recommended that economists work closely with other specialists to avoid merely replicating existing techniques. Certainly there are many economic and marketing studies which categorise tourist expenditure by demographic and psychographic variables (cf. Morrison, 2010). There is less attention to

Figure 7.2 Spending behaviour
In less affluent communities, tourists represent a potentially important source of direct income through their spending at small stores and shops. In the photograph a street of vendors greets tourists arriving at the Terracotta Warriors' site outside Xi'an, China. These kinds of vendors are not permitted inside the tourist attraction. Local opportunists cluster hopefully at the entrance to maximise their chance of encouraging tourists to spend on their regional produce and art work. Products are often repeated and bargaining is common

the judgement processes, heuristics, evaluations and justifications that tourists enact when spending money. The research attention then may be depicted as focused on how much tourists spend rather than the experience of spending. Using the same rubric of inquiry pursued elsewhere in this volume (a consideration of motives and emotions, cognitive processes, behaviours, relationships and sensory inputs) several facets of the experience of spending money will be identified to advance the research effort to understand these transactions.

Shopping, Bargaining and Tipping

Some topics which might be explored in some novel ways include gift shopping, bargaining, paying fees and tipping. It is not the case that these items have gone unobserved by previous researchers but it can be argued that a joint attack by economists and those specifically interested in tourist behaviour has been limited. Elkington (1997) has identified these kinds of overlapping topics as 'shear' or conjoint zones of the triple bottom line; in this case the intersection between sociocultural factors and economic factors. For the topic of shopping for example, economists are typically interested in the actual amount generated by a transaction. A tourist behaviour and experience researcher is equally concerned with the way a tourist enters a shopping environment and then in turn reviews that setting, categorises what is available, identifies personal options, specifies a particular object for further consideration, judges that potential purchase, validates the selected item with socially relevant others, undertakes the transaction, justifies that choice in a post-purchase environment, and then assesses the purchase in the psychological review of the success of the whole process. Additionally, the present focus of the research interests of even micro-economists is not on the costs and benefits of the processes which preceded the direct financial transaction. And yet there are costs in each of these phases of tourist behaviour which are subtle and potentially able to be calculated. An example from one kind of tourist shopping setting can provide an illustration of the possibilities (Figure 7.3).

In an extended study of tourist shopping villages, Murphy *et al.* (2011) discuss many of the supporting ambient factors which make for a tourist successful shopping village. This work provides a detailed appraisal of the social and environmental factors influencing tourist village shopping behaviour. The work notes the establishment costs and the maintenance budgets which support the transaction. There are costs in streetscaping and in road maintenance, in providing the village toilets, parking and information centres. There are individual business costs in setting up the layout of the store and its merchandising arrangements as well as in staff employment and training. All of these inputs shape the tourist decision-making processes and affect the phases of choosing to enter a business, the time spent in that environment and the evaluation of the distinctiveness of the product. The sensory qualities of the setting, the rules of thumb purchasers use to buy items and the relationships they have with those who accompany all represent forces shaping their spending experience. While these remarks are only indicative of the possibilities in this area it can be suggested that some of the future efforts in the tourist shopping realm could usefully be approached by integrating the research worlds of experience, behaviour and expenditure in tighter ways.

The topics of bargaining, tipping and the payment of user fees are further topics which are candidates for studies linking tourist experience appraisals and economic perspectives. For bargaining there is much tourist guide book and local advice but the ways in which the very existence of this economic behaviour affects the willingness of tourists to engage in certain types of purchases remains understudied. So too the diverse global practices surrounding tipping and its acceptability as well as its impact on employees warrants further combined economic and tourist behaviour analysis (Barkan *et al.*, 2004). In a study of user fees, Lee and Pearce (2002) established that the

Figure 7.3 Specialist shopping settings
This photograph was taken on a rainy summer's day in Innsbruck, Austria. The
hardy tourists, mostly German and Japanese were content to brave the weather
in search of high-quality Svorovski ware and other relatively expensive Austrian
souvenirs. Special shopping streets in most big cities as well as tourist shopping villages in rural and picturesque locations provide some of the tourist
expenditure most likely to stay in the region and not suffer external leakage to
large companies and international firms and chains. Such shopping can be an
effortful experience and documenting the psychological heuristics in persisting
with the activity and its rewards arguably still awaits further studies

issue of the public acceptability of the fees in Australia was shown to vary
considerably according to the setting not just the level of the charge. It is a
small demonstration that economic management measures are subject to
interpretations form the tourists' and users' social representations of what is
appropriate in certain cultures and places. Researching economic instruments and their perceived effects would seem to be a natural area for liaison
between tourist behaviour and economic analysts (Figure 7.4).

Themed Tourist Behaviour

Other topics which have received minimal attention in this volume may
be classified under a common heading of themed tourist behaviour.
In essence, this nomenclature identifies those research efforts which
tackle what people do in such contexts as viewing wildlife, scuba diving, bird

Figure 7.4 Bargaining
This image from Kenya illustrates the process of individuals from different cultures negotiating the price of goods. It was originally supplied to the *Journal of Tourism Studies* by Dr Peter Dieke. Some tourists enjoy the process and quickly learn skills; others more used to set prices find it socially difficult and seek to avoid it. Bargaining etiquette varies and may influence the tourists' trust in the goods and their willingness to spend mutually agreed on amounts of money

watching, long-distance driving, attending concerts, wine tasting, museum visiting, sailing, hiking and sundry and other entertainments. Similarly there has not been explicit attention to the many demographic tourist markets such as seniors, generation Y or X, female travellers, children as tourist or the very wealthy. The perspective adopted in this volume is that undoubtedly there are some distinctive behavioural and experiential outcomes associated with each of these activities and markets. Nevertheless it is too easy to believe that a separate behavioural and experiential account should be derived for each of these kinds of tourists and their activity involvement.

A separatist research path is likely to produce repetition and redundancy in the overall research effort. Instead, the preferred approach is to use a set of conceptual schemes which offer flexibility and which can be adapted at their periphery to accommodate special concerns. Importantly the use of common underlying mini-theories provides connections and affords insights through comparisons and analogies. Such useful exploratory processes cannot be undertaken if every one of the tourist interest areas is investigated by unique mechanisms for understanding the experience. It is wryly amusing to note that many authors who write about these specific topics often claim that they are addressing one of if not the fastest growing sector of tourism. Setting aside basic statistical errors about growth rates and percentages built on low initial figures, it is perhaps instructive to observe that one kind of themed tourism which is not given this accolade is sex tourism. It appears on occasions that researchers may simply be boosting the significance of their study themes, a process which works best if the theme is more socially acceptable.

Final Souvenirs

It is well recognised in studies of communication that maps, diagrams and images, when compared to material which is presented simply as text, facilitate the reader's storage and recall of information (Lynch, 1960). Two visual souvenirs will now be used to draw together much of the previous discussion in this volume. The approaches suggest how the reader can create both an enduring schematic and symbolic summary of this volume.

In Figure 7.5, topics in tourist behaviour and experience are outlined. Three phases are identified; pre-travel factors which occur prior to departure, on-site experiences and post-travel outcomes. In the figure, the three phases are divided by dotted and curved lines which represent the elastic boundaries of influence created in part by the new technologies of communication. Being at home and being away, we have argued, are not as distinct as they once were for the tourist in the contemporary world.

In the pre-travel phase both the characteristics of tourists and the features of destinations are represented. These influences are seen as coming together in the study of tourist behaviour through the common mechanism of activities. Specifically, it is the activities tourists seek to fulfil their motives and the perceived activities available in a destination which lie at the heart of destination choice models and the decision-making processes. It is consistent with the themes and research explored in Chapters 2 and 4 of this volume that it is both tourists' social representations of other places as well as information about destinations derived from new Web 2.0 communication routes which influence the way contemporary tourists not only choose but report on and learn from the locations they visit.

The on-site experiences of tourists embrace a diversity of processes and contacts. Several of the emphases discussed in this volume are depicted in Figure 7.5. Some of these key on-site processes include orienting to new settings, being in queues and crowds, and dealing with one's safety. It is suggested following the text presented in Chapter 5 that throughout these experiences tourists are influenced by their ongoing relationships and the needs of others. The direct contacts tourists have with environmental sites, as discussed in Chapter 3, as well as their cultural and social encounters may be influenced by interpretation efforts and humour. Such experiences can be

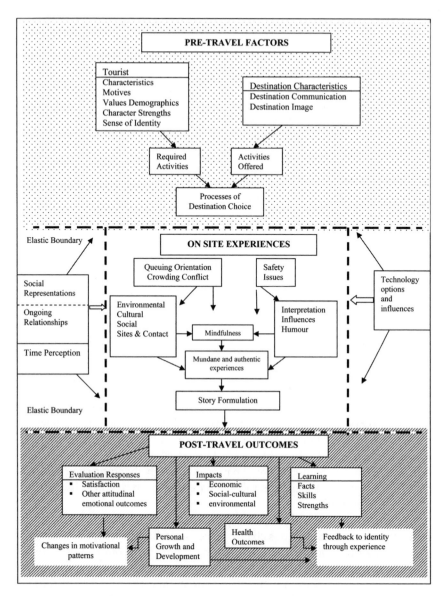

Figure 7.5 Contemporary tourist behaviour and experiences; phases, components and influences

cast as resulting in an array of mundane and existential tourist moments which form in turn the bases of travel stories. Technology and social representations matter throughout the on-site phases of the tourist experience because technologies may assist orientation and interpretation as well as the delivery of services while social representations structure tourists' views in terms of their constellation of attitudes, interests and explanations for what they are both seeing and avoiding.

The post-travel outcomes discussed in this volume represent both common and lightly researched travel consequences. The commonly reported topic of impacts is one standard issue. In particular, the impacts of tourists themselves, not just tourism and its business and government arms, are recognised as significant, particularly in terms of expenditure, social influences and environmental effects. All of these influences may be positive or negative though it is notable that the term impacts has tended to become a pejorative one and outcomes might be a more useful term to preserve the good that can arise from tourist contact. The notion that tourists' experiences can be evaluated with a greater range of terms and processes was pursued in Chapter 6 of this book with attention being placed on emotional reactions as well as the kinds of loyalty to experiences which may be of interest to business concerns.

Other outcomes of the tourists' trek through strange and even familiar holiday destinations were recorded with an emphasis on key aspects of learning both as facts and skills as considered in Chapter 5. Health outcomes which involve stress reduction were highlighted in Chapter 3 and while the associated field of travel medicine is awash with the dire health consequences of tourist mobility, there is mounting evidence that a good life can often involve periods of travel. The personal growth and development outcomes of tourism were noted and while they should not be overstated, an opportunity to research these experience-derived benefits is not trivial for individual and community well-being, particularly as revealed in this volume in terms of attitudes to one's environmental footprint and remedial actions to poverty. All of these travel outcomes feedback to the individual's world view as manifested in their social representations. The travel experiences tourists have influence their future motivational patterns through changing their personal patterns of needs and social capital. The interplay of these forces is captured, in part, in Figure 7.5.

As a final mental souvenir to crystallise our view of the tourist in the contemporary world it is possible to select an animal totem or image. For those who write about tourism changing and tourists becoming post-tourists the implications would seem to suggest that a possible symbolic species for tourists is that of a dodo. In this view tourism and the presence of tourists in many places will tend to fade in the coming years not only because of international responses to the threats of global warming and rising fuel prices but also because technology will provide more substantial entertainments to occupy leisure. It is necessary though to quibble about the use of this once plentiful but now extinct species as the right image. In a curious twist of tourism-generated fame, tourism businesses on the southern Indian Ocean island of Mauritius, the home of the dodo, utilise the dodo imagery in a vast array of contemporary memorabilia. Undoubtedly the dodo is now more famous than it ever would have been if it had survived the Dutch explorers slaughtering. The dodo then does not seem quite the right emblematic species, because while technology and the explorer's behaviour may have doomed its actual existence, it lives on in odd and bizarre forms.

We might select a more powerful species such as a dominant carnivore, especially one which is higher in the food chain. Such images would however overemphasise the exploitative nature of tourists and their behaviour and while perhaps partially appropriate, fail to reflect the emerging imperatives of those seeking to act responsibly and with good will towards others. Instead we will opt for the symbol of the chameleon; a species which has many variants, some of which have the powerful ability to blend into new surroundings and quickly change with contexts and threats. The diversity of tourists and the multiple ways they are changing as they fit into the new contexts created by technology, moral imperatives and global circumstances demand just such a final symbol of adaptability. It is the ongoing task of tourist researchers and the informed managers who use their work to predict and further understand the changing behaviours and experiences of our chameleon tourist species.

References

Ahmed, Z.U. (1992) Islamic pilgrimage (Hajj) to Ka'aba in Makkah (Saudi Arabia): An important international tourist activity. *Journal of Tourism Studies* 3, 35–43.

Albers, P.C. and James, W.R. (1988) Travel photography: A methodological approach. *Annals of Tourism Research* 15, 134–158.

Ambinder, E. (1992) Urban violence raises safety fears. *Corporate Travel* 9, 10.

Aramberri, J. (2010) The real scissors crisis in tourism research. In D.G. Pearce and R. Butler (eds) *Tourism Research: A 20-20 Vision* (pp. 15–27). Oxford: Goodfellow.

Archer, B. and Cooper, C. (1998) The positive and negative impacts of tourism. In W.M. Theobald (ed.) *Global Tourism* (pp. 63–81). Oxford: Butterworth-Heinemann.

Argyle, M., Furnham, A. and Graham, J.A. (1981) *Social Situations*. Cambridge: Cambridge University Press.

Argyle, M. and Henderson, M. (1985) *The Anatomy of Relationships*. Harmondsworth, Middlesex: Penguin.

Armstrong, J. (2003) Conditions of love. In *The Philosophy of Intimacy*. London: Penguin.

Arntzen, J., Pearce, P.L. and Cottrell, S. (2008) Tourism as a shared income earner. *Botswana Notes and Record* 39, 1–14.

Ashcroft, F. (2000) *Life at the Extremes: The Science of Survival*. London: Flamingo.

Baerenholdt, J., Haldrup, M., Larsen, J. and Urry, J. (2004) *Performing Tourist Places*. Aldershot: Ashgate.

Bains, G. (1983) Explanations and the need for control. In M. Hewstone (ed.) *Attribution Theory* (pp. 126–143). Oxford: Basil Blackwell.

Bales, R.F. (1950) *Interaction Process Analysis*. Cambridge, MA: Addison-Wesley.

Ball, P. (2004) *Critical Mass How One Thing Leads to Another*. London: Arrow.

Ballantyne, R. (1998) Problems and prospects for heritage and environmental interpretation in the new millennium. In D. Uzzell and R. Ballantyne (eds) *Contemporary Issues in Heritage and Environmental Interpretation: Problems and Prospects*. London: The Stationery Office.

Balme, C.B. (1998) Staging the Pacific: Framing authenticity in performances for tourists in the Polynesian Cultural Centre. *Theatre Journal* 50, 53–70.

Bandyopadhyay, R. (2009) The perennial Western tourism representations. *India Tourism* 57, 23–36.

Barkan, R., Erev, I., Zinger, E. and Tzach, M. (2004) Tip policy, visibility and quality of service in cafes. *Tourism Economics* 10, 449–462.

Bates, M., Nettle, D. and Roberts, G. (2006) Cues of being watched enhance cooperation in real world setting. *Biology Letters* 2, 412–414.

Batty, M., Desyllas, J. and Duxbury, E. (2003) Safety in numbers? Modelling crowds and designing control for the Notting Hill carnival. *Urban Studies* 40, 1573–1590.

Bauer, I. (2005) Educational issues and concerns in travel health advice: Is all the effort a waste of time? *Journal of Travel Medicine* 12, 45–52.

Bauer, I. (2007) Understanding sexual relationships between tourists and locals in Cuzco/ Peru. *Travel Medicine and Infectious Disease* 5, 287–294.

Becher, T. (1989) *Academic Tribes and Territories. Intellectual Enquiry and the Culture of Disciplines.* Milton Keynes: The Society for Research into Higher Education and the Open University Press.

Beirman, D. (2003) *Restoring Tourism Destinations in Crisis.* Crows Nest, Australia: Allen & Unwin.

Bellenger, D. and Korgaonkar, P. (1980) Profiling the recreational shopper. *Journal of Retailing* 56, 77–92.

Berger, H., Dittenbach, M., Merkl, D., Bogdanovych, A., Simoff, S. and Sierra, C. (2007) Opening new dimensions for e-tourism. *Virtual Reality* 11, 75–87.

Berridge, K.C. and Robinson, T.E. (2003) Parsing reward. *Trends in Neurosciences* 26, 507–513.

Berry, J.W. (1999) Emics and etics: A symbiotic conception. *Culture and Psychology* 5, 165–171.

Biggs, J.B. (2003) *Teaching for Quality Learning at University* (2nd edn). Phildelphia, PA: Society for Research into Higher Education.

Bitgood, S. (2003) Visitor orientation: When are museums similar to casinos? *Visitor Studies Today* 6, 10–12.

Bitgood, S. (2006) An analysis of visitor circulation: Movement patterns and the general value principle. *Curator: The Museum Journal* 49, 463–475.

Bitgood, S. and Cota, A. (1995) Principles of orientation and circulation within exhibitions. *Visitor Behavior* 10, 7–8.

Bitgood, S. and Dukes, S. (2006) Not another step! Economy of movement and pedestrian choice point behavior in shopping malls. *Environment and Behavior* 38, 394–405.

Bitgood, S. and Lankford, S. (1995) Museum orientation and circulation. *Visitor Behavior* 10, 4–6.

Blainey, G. (2004) *A Very Short History of the World.* London: Penguin.

Boakye, K.A. (2010) Studying tourists' suitability as crime targets. *Annals of Tourism Research* 37, 727–743.

Boring, E. (1950) *A History of Experimental Psychology* (2nd edn). New York: Appleton-Century-Crofts.

Boud, D., Keogh, R. and Walker, D. (1985) *Reflection: Turning Experience into Learning.* London: Kogan Page Ltd.

Bowen, D. and Clarke, J. (2009) *Contemporary Tourist Behaviour: Yourself and Others as Tourists.* Wallingford: CABI.

Bowlby, J. (1972) *Attachment and Loss* (Vol. 1). *Attachment.* New York: Basic Books.

Bramwell, B. and Lane, B. (1993) Sustainable tourism: An evolving global approach. *Journal of Sustainable Tourism* 1, 1–5.

Braun, K., Ellis, R. and Loftus, E. (2002) Make my memory: How advertising can change our memories of the past. *Psychology and Marketing* 19, 1–23.

Brown, L.F. and Postel, S. (2004) A vision of a sustainable world. In L.P. Polman (ed.) *Environmental Ethics. Readings in Theory and Application* (4th edn, pp. 670–678). Belmont, CA: Wadsworth Thomson.

Brown, M.B., Muchira, R. and Gottlieb, U. (2007) Privacy concerns and the purchasing of travel services online. *Information Technology & Tourism* 9, 15–25.

Bryman, A. (2004) *The Disneyization of Society.* London: Sage.

Buhalis, D. and Law, R. (2008) Progress in information technology and tourism management: 20 years on and 10 years after the Internet – The state of eTourism research. *Tourism Management* 29, 609–623.

Buhalis, D. and O'Connor, P. (2006) Information communication technology- revolutionizing tourism. In D. Buhalis and C. Costa (eds) *Tourism Management Dynamics* (pp. 196–209). Amsterdam: Elsevier.

Casalo, L.V., Flavian, C. and Guinaliu, M. (2010) Determinants of the intention to participate in firm-hosted online travel communities and effects on consumer behavioural intentions. *Tourism Management* 31, 898–911.

Chalfen, R.M. (1979) Photograph's role in tourism: Some unexplored relationships. *Annals of Tourism Research* 6, 435–447.

Chesney-Lind, M. and Lind, I. (1986) Visitors as victims: Crimes against tourists in Hawaii. *Annals of Tourism Research* 13, 167–192.

Chok, S., MacBeth, J. and Warren, C. (2007) Tourism as a tool for poverty alleviation: A critical analysis of 'pro-poor tourism' and implications for sustainability. *Current Issues in Tourism* 10, 144–165.

Cialdini, R. (2001) *Influence: Science and Practice*. Boston: Allyn and Bacon.

Cleermans, A. (1993) *Mechanisms of Implicit Learning*. Cambridge, MA: MIT Press.

Coghlan, A. (2005) Towards an understanding of the volunteer tourism experience. PhD thesis, James Cook University, Townsville.

Coghlan, A. and Pearce, P.L. (2010) Tracking affective components of satisfaction. *Tourism and Hospitality Research* 10, 42–58.

Cohen, E. (1974) Who is a tourist? A conceptual clarification. *The Sociological Review* 22, 527–555.

Cohen, E. (1979) Rethinking the sociology of tourism. *Annals of Tourism Research* 6, 18–35.

Cohen, E. (1984) The sociology of tourism: Approaches, issues and findings. *Annual Review of Sociology* 10, 373–392.

Cohen, E. (1993) The study of touristic images of native people: Migrating the stereotype of a stereotype. In D.G. Pearce and R.W. Butler (eds) *Tourism Research: Critiques and Challenges* (pp. 36–69). London: Routledge.

Cohen, E. (1996) Touting tourists in Thailand: Tourist-oriented crime and social structure. In A. Pizam and J. Mansfeld (eds) *Tourism, Crime and International Security Issues* (pp. 77–90). New York: Wiley.

Cohen, E. (2007) Authenticity in tourism studies: après la lutte. *Tourism Recreation Research* 32, 75–82.

Cohen, E., Nir, Y. and Almagor, U. (1992) Stranger–local interaction in photography. *Annals of Tourism Research* 19, 213–233.

Cohen, S. and Janicki-Deverts, D. (2009) Can we improve physical health by altering our social networks? *Perspectives on Psychological Science* 4, 375–378.

Cohen, S.A. (2010) Personal identity (de) formation among lifestyle travellers: A double-edged sword. *Leisure Studies* 29, 289–301.

Cooley, B. (2005) Navigation systems: Why they're lame, what we need – On WWW at: http://www.cnet.com.au?navigation-systems-why-they-re-lame-what-they-need-240058686.htm. Accessed 20.10.10.

Cooper, C.P. (1981) Spatial and temporal patterns of tourist behaviour. *Regional Studies* 15, 359–371.

Cooper, C.P. (2006) Knowledge management and tourism. *Annals of Tourism Research* 33, 45–58.

Cooper, C.P. and Sheldon, P. (2010) Knowledge management in tourism: From databases to learning destinations. In D.G. Pearce and R. Butler (eds) *Tourism Research: A 20-20 Vision* (pp. 215–228). Oxford: Goodfellow.

Crang, P. (1997) Performing the tourist product. In C. Rojek and J. Urry (eds) *Touring Cultures* (pp. 137–154). London: Routledge.

Crompton, J.L. (1979) Motivations for pleasure vacation. *Annals of Tourism Research* 6, 408–424.

Crompton, J.L. (2005) Issues related to sustaining a long-term research interest in tourism. *The Journal of Tourism Studies* 16, 34–43.

Cronen, V.E. and Shuter, R. (1983) Forming intercultural bonds. In W.B. Gudykunst (ed.) *Intercultural Communication Theory: Current Perspectives* (pp. 89–118). Sage: Beverley Hills.

Crotts, C. (1996) Theoretical perspectives on tourist criminal victimisation. *Journal of Tourism Studies 7*, 2–9.

Crotts, J. (2011) Serendipitous gleanings. In P.L. Pearce (ed.) *The Study of Tourism Foundations from Psychology* (pp. 230–254). Bingley: Emerald.

Csikszentmihalyi, M. (1990) *Flow: The Psychology of Optimal Experience*. New York: Harper Perennial.

Cutler, S.Q. and Carmichael, B.A. (2010) The dimensions of the tourist experience. In M. Morgan, P. Lugosi and J.R. Brent Ritchie (eds) *The Tourism and Leisure Experience* (pp. 3–26). Bristol: Channel View Publications.

Dahlsgaard, K., Petersen, C. and Seligman, M. (2005) Shared virtue: The convergence of valued human strengths across culture and history. *Review of General Psychology 9*, 203–213.

Dawkins, R. (2009) *The Greatest Show on Earth: The Evidence for Evolution*. London: Bantam Press.

De Albuquerque, K. and McElroy, J. (1999) Tourism and crime in the Caribbean. *Annals of Tourism Research 26*, 968–984.

de Botton, A. (2002) *The Art of Travel*. London: Penguin.

de Botton, A. (2004) *Status Anxiety*. London: Penguin.

de Botton, A. (2009) *A Week at the Airport: A Heathrow Diary*. London: Profile.

De Lauretis, T. (1991) Queer theory: Lesbian and gay sexualities. An introduction. *Differences 3*, 1–10.

De Spindler, A., Norrie, M.C. and Grossniklaus, M. (2008) Recommendation based on opportunistic information sharing between tourists. *Information Technology & Tourism 10*, 297–311.

Desforges, L. (2000) Traveling the world: Identity and travel biography. *Annals of Tourism Research 27*, 926–945.

Diamond, J. (2005) *Collapse: How Societies Choose to Fail or Succeed*. New York: Penguin Group.

Dickinson, J.E. (2007) 'Travelling slowly': Slow forms of travel as holiday experiences. In Extraordinary Experiences Conference: Managing the consumer experience in hospitality, leisure, sport, tourism, retail and events, 3–4 September 2007, Bournemouth University, England.

Dickinson, J.E. and Lumsdon, L. (2010) *Slow Travel and Tourism*. London: Earthscan.

Diener, E. and Biswas-Diener, R. (2008) *Happiness: Unlocking the Mysteries of Psychological Wealth*. Oxford: Blackwell.

Donnelly, M., Vaske, J., Whittaker, D. and Shelby, B. (2000) Toward an understanding of norm prevalence: A comparative analysis of 20 years of research. *Environmental Management 25*, 403–414.

Driver, B., Brown, P.J. and Peterson, G. (1991) *Benefits of Leisure*. Pennsylvania: Venture Publishing Inc.

du Cros, H. and Johnstone, C. (2002) Tourism tracks and sacred places: Pashupatinath and Uluru. Case studies from Nepal and Australia. *Historic Environment 16*, 38–42.

Dwyer, L., Forsyth, P. and Spurr, R. (2004) Evaluating tourism's economic effects: New and old approaches. *Tourism Management 25*, 307–317.

Earth Times (2009) 'On your left poverty' – Tourists flock to Kenyan slums. On WWW at: http//www.earthtimes.org/articles/show/96039.html. Accessed 05.06.09.

Edensor, T. (2000) Walking in the British countryside: Reflexivity, embodied practices and ways to escape. *Body & Society 6*, 81–106.

Elkington, J. (1997) *Cannibals with Forks. The Triple Bottom Line of 21st Century Business*. Oxford: Capstone.

Epstein, A.D. and Kheimets, N.G. (2001) Looking for Pontius Pilate's footprints near the western wall: Russian Jewish tourists in Jerusalem. *Tourism, Culture & Communication 3*, 37–56.

European Travel Commission (2009) New media trend watch. On WWW at http://www. newmedia trend watch.com/world-overview/34-world-usage-patterns-and-demographics. Accessed 03.06.10.

Evans-Pritchard, D. (1989) How 'they' see 'us': Native American images of tourists. *Annals of Tourism Research* 16, 89–105.

Eyles, J. (1988) Interpreting the geographical world: Qualitative approaches in geographical research. In J. Eyles and D.M. Smith (eds) *Qualitative Methods in Human Geography* (pp. 1–16). Cambridge: Polity Press.

Fagence, M. (1983) The Lynch 'images' formula – An experiment in small town analysis. Proceedings of the Conference on People and Physical Environment Research. Wellington, New Zealand.

Falco-Mammone, F. (2005) Beach images: Meaning, measurement and management. Unpublished PhD thesis, James Cook University, Townsville, Australia.

Falk, J. (1993) Assessing the impact of exhibit arrangement on visitor behaviour and learning. *Curator: The Museum Journal* 36, 133–146.

Falk, J.H. and Dierking, L.D. (2000) *Learning from Museums: Visitor Experiences and the Making of Meaning*. Walnut Creek, CA: AltaMira.

Falk, J.H. and Storksdieck, M. (2005) Using the contextual model of learning to understand visitor learning from a science centre exhibition. *Science Education* 89, 744–778.

Farsides, T. and Woodfield, R. (2003) Individual differences and undergraduate academic success; The roles of personality, intelligence and application. *Personality and Individual Differences* 34, 1225–1243.

Feingold, A. and Mazzella, R. (1991) Psychometric intelligence and verbal humor ability. *Personality and Individual Differences* 12, 427–435.

Feleppa, R. (1986) Emics, etics, and social objectivity. *Current Anthropology* 27, 243–255.

Ferreira, S.L.A. (1999) Crime: A threat to tourism in South Africa. *Tourism Geographies* 1, 313–324.

Fielding, K., Pearce, P.L. and Hughes, K. (1992) Climbing Ayers Rock: Relating motivation, time perception and enjoyment. *Journal of Tourism Studies* 3, 49–57.

Flaherty, J.A., Gaviria, M., Pathak, D., Mitchell, T., Winterbob, R. and Richman, J.A. (1988) Developing instruments for cross cultural psychiatric research. *The Journal of Nervous and Mental Disease* 176, 257–263.

Fleishman, L., Feitelson, E. and Salomon, I. (2004) The role of cultural and demographic diversity in crowding perception: Evidence from nature reserves in Israel. *Tourism Analysis* 9, 23–40.

Flyvbjerg, B. (2001) *Making Social Science Matter*. Cambridge: Cambridge University Press.

Foley, G. (2000) *Understanding Adult Education and Training* (2nd edn). St. Leonards, NSW: Allen & Unwin.

Foo, J., McGuiggan, R. and Yiannakis, A. (2004) Roles tourists play: An Australian perspective. *Annals of Tourism Research* 31, 408–427.

Foth, M. (ed.) (2009) *Handbook of Research on Urban Informatics: The Practice and the Promise of the Real-Time City*. Hershey, PA: Information Science Reference.

Fraisse, P. (1963) *The Psychology of Time*. New York: Greenwood Press.

Francescato, D. and Mebane, W. (1973) How citizens view two great cities: Milan and Rome. In R.M. Downs and D. Stea (eds) *Image and Environment – Cognitive Mapping and Spatial Behaviour* (pp. 131–147). Chicago: Aldine Publishing.

Fredrickson, B.L. (2001) The role of positive emotions in positive psychology – The broaden-and-build theory of positive emotions. *American Psychologist* 56, 218–226.

Friedman, J.L., Levy, A.S., Buchanan, R.W. and Price, J. (1972) Crowding and human aggressiveness. *Journal of Experimental and Social Psychology* 8, 528–548.

Fuchs, S. (1992) *The Professional Question for Truth: A Social Theory of Science and Knowledge*. Albany, NY: State University of New York.

Furnham, A. (2008) *50 Psychology Ideas You Really Need to Know*. London: Quercus.

Galley, G. and Clifton, J. (2004) The motivational and demographic characteristics of research ecotourists: Operation Wallacea volunteers in South East Sulawesi. *Journal of Ecotourism* 3, 69–82.

Galtung, J. (1981) Structure, culture, and intellectual style: An essay comparing Saxonic, Teutonic, Gallic and Nipponic approaches. *Social Science Information* 20, 817–856.

Garland, A. (1997) *The Beach*. London: Penguin.

Garrod, B. (2009) Understanding the relationship between tourism destination imagery and tourist photography. *Journal of Travel Research* 47, 346–358.

Gartner, W. (1993) Image formation process. *Journal of Travel and Tourism Marketing* 2, 191–216.

George, R. (2003) Tourists' perceptions of safety and security while visiting Cape Town. *Tourism Management* 24, 575–585.

George, R. (2010) Visitor perceptions of crime-safety and attitudes towards risk: The case of Table Mountain National Park, Cape Town. *Tourism Management* 31, 806–815.

Gergen, K.J. (1997) The place of the psyche in a constructed world. *Theory and Psychology* 7, 723–746.

Ghiglieri, M.P. and Myers, T.M. (2001) *Over the Edge: Death in the Grand Canyon*. Flagstaff: Puma Press.

Ghimire, K.B. (2001) *The Native Tourist*. London: Earthscan.

Gibbs, D. and Ritchie, C. (2010) Theatre in restaurants: Constructing the experience. In M. Morgan, P. Lugosi and J.R. Brent Ritchie (eds) *The Tourism and Leisure Experience: Consumer and Managerial Perspectives* (pp. 182–201). Bristol: Channel View Publications.

Gibson, H. and Yiannakis, A. (2002) Tourist roles – Needs and the life course. *Annals of Tourism Research* 29, 358–383.

Gillis, A.R., Richard, M.A. and Hagan, J. (1989) Ethnic susceptibility to crowding: An empirical analysis. *Environment and Behavior* 18, 683–706.

Giroux, H. (1999) *The Mouse that Roared: Disney and the End of Innocence*. Lanham, MD: Rowman and Littlefield.

Gmelch, G. (1997) Crossing cultures: Student travel and personal development. *International Journal of Intercultural Relations* 21, 475–490.

Gnoth, J. (1997) Tourism motivation and expectation formation. *Annals of Tourism Research* 24, 283–304.

Goffman, E. (1969) *The Presentation of Self in Everyday Life*. London: Penguin.

Goffman, E. (1974) *Frame Analysis*. Cambridge, MA: Harvard University Press.

Gold, B. (2002) Epistemology among the lumpers and splitters. *The Human Nature Review* 2, 135–143.

Goleman, D. (2009) *Ecological Intelligence*. London: Allen Lane.

Gore, A. (2004) Dysfunctional society. In L.P. Polman (ed.) *Environmental Ethics: Readings in Theory and Application* (4th edn, pp. 614–623). Belmont: Wadsworth Thomson.

Gössling, S. (2002) Global environmental consequences of tourism. *Global Environmental Change* 12, 283–302.

Gössling, S., Borgstrom Hansson, C., Horstmeier, O. and Saggel, S. (2002) Ecological footprint analysis as a tool to assess tourism sustainability. *Ecological Economics* 43, 199–211.

Gould, S.J. (2004) *The Hedgehog, the Fox and the Magister's Pox: Mending and Minding the Misconceived Gap between Science and the Humanities*. London: Vintage.

Graburn, N.H. (1989) Tourism: The sacred journey. In V. Smith (ed.) *Hosts and Guests: The Anthropology of Tourism* (2nd edn, pp. 21–36). Philadelphia: University of Pennsylvania Press.

Grandin, T. and Johnson, C. (2009) *Making Animals Happy*. London: Bloomsbury.

Grayling, A.C. (2005) *The Heart of Things*. London: Phoenix.

Greenfield, A. (2006) *Everyware the Dawning Age of Ubiquitous Computing*. Berkeley, CA: New Riders.

Greenfield, S. (2000) *The Private Life of the Brain*. London: Penguin.

Gruner, C.R. (1997) *The Game of Humor: A Comprehensive Theory of Why We Laugh*. New Brunswick, NJ: Transaction Publishers.

Guerba Experience Africa in Close-Up (2009) *African Wildlife Safaris*. Melbourne, VIC: African Wildlife safaris.

Gulick, J. (1963) Images of an Arab city. *Journal of the American Institute of Planners* 29, 179–197.

Gunn, C. (1972) *Vacationscape: Designing Tourist Regions*. Austin, TX: University of Texas.

Gunn, C. (1994) A perspective on the purpose and nature of tourism research methods. In J.R.B. Ritchie and C.R. Goeldner (eds) *Travel, Tourism, and Hospitality Research* (2nd edn, pp. 3–11). New York: John Wiley & Sons.

Gunn, C.A. (2004) *Western Tourism Can paradise be reclaimed?* New York: Cognizant Communication Corporation.

Guy, B.S., Curtis, W.W. and Crotts, J.C. (1990) Environmental learning of first time travellers. *Annals of Tourism Research* 17, 419–431.

Habermas, J. (1987) *Knowledge and Human Interests*. Cambridge: Polity Press.

Hall, C.M. (2005) *Tourism: Re-thinking the Social Science of Mobility*. Harlow: Prentice-Hall.

Hall, C.M., Timothy, D.J. and Duval, D.T. (eds) (2003) *Safety and Security in Tourism*. New York: Haworth Hospitality Press.

Hammitt, W. and Rutlin, W. (1995) Use encounter standards and curves for achieved privacy in wilderness. *Leisure Sciences* 17, 245–262.

Hansel, B. (1998) Developing an international perspective in youth through exchange programs. *Education and Urban Society* 20, 177–195.

Harre, R. (1979) *Social Being*. Oxford: Blackwell.

Harris, D. (2005) *Key Concepts in Leisure Studies*. London: Sage.

Harris, N. (2004) The rising cost of shuffleboard and buffets. Retrieved 24 July 2011, From http://online.wsj.com/article/SB107758561580937309.html

Harrison, D. (2010) Tourism and development: Looking back and looking forward – more of the same? In D.G. Pearce and R.W. Butler (eds) *Tourism Research A 20-20 Vision* (pp. 40–52). Oxford: Goodfellow.

Harvey, J.H., Turnquist, D. and Agostinelli, G. (1988) Identifying attributions in written and oral explanations. In C. Antaki (ed.) *Analysing Everyday Explanations* (pp. 32–42). London: Sage.

Hayduk, L.A. (1983) Personal space: Where we now stand? *Psychological Bulletin* 94, 293–335.

Heberlein, T.A. (1992) Reducing hunter perception of crowding through information. *Wildlife Society Bulletin* 20, 372–374.

Heggie, T.W. (2009) Geotourism and volcanoes: Health hazards facing tourists at volcanic and geothermal destinations. *Travel Medicine and Infectious Diseases* 7, 257–261.

Heggie, T.W. (2010) Swimming with death: *Naegleria fowleri* infections in recreational waters. *Travel Medicine and Infectious Disease* 8, 201–206.

Heggie, T.W. and Amundson, M.E. (2009) Dead men walking: Search and rescue in U.S. national parks. *Wilderness and Environmental Medicine* 20, 244–249.

Hehl, F-J. and Ruch, W. (1990) Conservatism as a predictor of responses to humour: III. The prediction of appreciation of incongruity resolution based humour by content saturated attitude scales in five samples. *Personality & Individual Differences* 11, 439–445.

Helbing, D., Molnár, P., Farkas, I.J. and Bolay, K. (2001) Self-organizing pedestrian movement. *Environment and Planning B: Planning and Design* 28, 361–383.

Hennig-Thurau, T., Gwinner, K.P., Walsh, G. and Gremler, D.D. (2004) Electronic word-of-mouth via consumer opinion platforms: What motivates consumers to articulate themselves on the internet? *Journal of Interactive Marketing* 18, 38–52.

Hewstone, M. (1983) Attribution theory and common-sense explanations an introductory overview. In M. Hewstone (ed.) *Attribution Theory* (pp. 1–24). Oxford: Basil Blackwell.

Hibbert, C. (1969) *The Grand Tour.* London: Weidenfeld and Nicolson.

Hicks, A. (2004) *Thai Girl.* Bangkok: TYS Books.

Higham, J. and Kearsley, G. (1994) *Wilderness Perception and Its Implications for the Management of the Impacts of International Tourism on Natural Areas in New Zealand.* Paper presented at the 'Tourism Down Under' Conference. Palmerston North: Massey University.

Hillery, M., Nancarrow, B., Griffin, G. and Syme, G. (2001) Tourist perception of environmental impact. *Annals of Tourism Research* 28, 853–867.

Hofstede, G. (1995) Multilevel research of human systems: Flowers, bouquets and gardens. *Human Systems Management* 14, 207–217.

Hogg, M.A., Terry, D.J. and White, K. (1995) A tale of two theories: A critical comparison of identity theory with social identity theory. *Social Psychology Quarterly* 58, 255–269.

Honore, C. (2004) *In Praise of Slow.* London: Orion.

Horne, D. (1992) *The Intelligent Tourist.* McMahons Point, NSW: Margaret Gee.

Hottola, P. (2004) Culture confusions: Intercultural adaptation in tourism. *Annals of Tourism Research* 31, 447–466.

Howard, R.W. (2009) Risky business? Asking tourists what hazards they actually encountered in Thailand. *Tourism Management* 30, 359–365.

Howarth, C. (2005) How social representations of attitudes have informed attitude theories: The consensual and the reified. *Theory & Psychology* 16, 691–714.

Hsu, C.H.C. and Huang, S. (2008) Travel motivation: A critical review of the concept's development. In A. Woodside and D. Martin (eds) *Tourism Management Analysis, Behaviour and Strategy* (pp. 14–27). Wallingford, Oxon: CABI.

Hueneke, H. and Baker, R. (2009) Tourist behaviour, local values, and interpretation at Uluru: 'The sacred deed at Australia's mighty heart'. *GeoJournal* 74, 477–490.

Hui, M.K. and Bateson, J.E.G. (1991) Perceived control and the effects of crowding and consumer choice on the service experience. *Journal of Consumer Research* 18, 174–184.

Hunt, J.B. (2000) Travel experience in the formation of leadership: John Quincy Adams, Frederick Douglass & Jane Addams. *Journal of Leadership Studies* 7, 92–106.

Hunter, C. (2002) Sustainable tourism and the touristic ecological footprint. *Environment, Development and Sustainability* 4, 7–20.

Hunter, C. and Shaw, J. (2007) The ecological footprint as a key indicator of sustainable tourism. *Tourism Management* 28, 46–57.

Huxley, A. (1925) *Along the Road.* London: Chatto & Windus.

Huxtable, A.L. (1997, March 30) Living with the fake and liking it. *New York Times* 1, 40.

Hyun, M.Y., Lee, S. and Hu, C. (2008) Mobile-mediated virtual experience in tourism: Concept, typology and applications. *Journal of Vacation Marketing* 15, 149–164.

Iso-Ahola, S. (2011) Tourism as leisure behaviour. In P.L. Pearce (ed.) *The Study of Tourism: Foundations from Psychology* (pp. 91–96). Bingley: Emerald.

Jackson, M.S., White, G.N. and Schmiere, C.L. (1996) Tourism experience within an attributional framework. *Annals of Tourism Research* 23, 798–810.

Jafari, J. (2005) Bridging out, nesting afield: Powering a new platform. *The Journal of Tourism Studies* 16, 1–5.

Jain, U. (1992) Concomitants of population density in India. *Journal of Social Psychology* 133, 331–336.

Jaspars, J. and Fraser, C. (1984) Attitudes and social representations. In R.M. Farrand and S. Moscovici (eds) *Social Representation* (pp. 101–123). Cambridge: Cambridge University Press.

Jenkins, C.L. (2008) Tourism and welfare: A good idea and a pious hope! *Tourism Recreation Research* 32, 225–226.

Jennings, G. (2010) Research processes for evaluating quality experiences: Reflections from the 'Experiences' field(s). In M. Morgan, P. Lugosi and J.R. Brent Ritchie (eds) *The Tourism and Leisure Experience: Consumer and Managerial Perspectives* (pp. 81–98). Bristol: Channel View Publications.

Jin, Q. and Pearce, P.L. (2009) A model of tourism crowding management at cultural sites in China. In Role of hospitality and tourism in globalization Proceedings of the 8th Asia Pacific Forum for Graduate Students' Research in Tourism, Seoul, Korea, 8–10 July 2009.

Jones, M.E., Walker, E., Chiodini, P.L., Angus, B., Boyne, L. and Grieve, A. (2009) Travel medicine has come of age and a new examination marks the 21st century. *Travel Medicine and Infectious Disease* 7, 179–180.

Jones, R.A. (1974) *Emile Durkheim*. Newbury Park, CA: Sage.

Joyce, D. (1989) Why do police officers laugh at death? *The Psychologist* September, 379–381.

Kah, J.A., Vogt, C. and MacKay, K. (2008) Online travel information search and purchasing by internet use experience. *Information Technology & Tourism* 10, 227–243.

Kelley, H. (1967) Attribution theory in social psychology. In D. Levine (ed.) *Nebraska Symposium on Motivation* (Vol. 15, pp. 192–238). Lincoln: University of Nebraska Press.

Kim, Y.J. (Edward), Pearce, P.L., Morrison, A.M. and O'Leary, J.T. (1996) Mature vs. youth travelers: The Korean market. *Asia Pacific Journal of Tourism Research* 1, 102–112.

Klenosky, D.B. (2002) The 'Pull' of tourism destinations: A means – Ends investigation. *Journal of Travel Research* 40, 385–395.

Kohlberg, L. (1986) *The Philosophy of Moral Development*. San Francisco: Harper & Row.

Kohler, G. and Ruch, W. (1996) Sources of variance in current sense of humor inventories: How much substance, how much method variance? *Humor: International Journal of Humor Research* 9, 363–397.

Kozak, M. (2001) A critical review of approaches to measure satisfaction with tourist destinations. In J.A. Mazanec, G. Crouch, J.R. Brent Ritchie and A. Woodside (eds) *Consumer Psychology of Tourism Hospitality and Leisure* (Vol.2, pp. 303–320). Wallingford, Oxon: CABI Publishing.

Kozak, M. and Decrop, A. (eds) (2009) *Handbook of Tourist Behaviour: Theory and Practice*. London: Routledge.

Kramer, R., Modsching, M., ten Hagen, K. and Gretzel, U. (2007) Behavioural impacts of mobile tour guides. In M. Sigala, L. Mich and J. Murphy (eds) *Information and Communication Technologies in Tourism* (pp. 109–118). Vienna, Austria: Springer Computer Science.

Krueger, R. and Casey, M. (2000) *Focus Groups – A Practical Guide for Applied Research* (3rd edn). London: Sage Publications Inc.

Kuh, G.D. (1995) The other curriculum: Out-of-class experiences associated with student learning and personal development. *The Journal of Higher Education* 66, 123–155.

Kuhn, T.S. (1962) *The Structure of Scientific Revolutions*. Chicago: University of Chicago Press.

Kunkel, J.H. (1997) The analysis of rule-governed behaviour in social psychology. *The Psychological Record* 47, 699–716.

Langer, E.J. (1989) *Mindfulness*. Reading, MA: Addison-Wesley.

Langer, E.J. (2009) *Counterclockwise: Mindful Health and the Power of Possibility*. New York: Ballantine Books.

Lau, G. and McKercher, B. (2007) Understanding tourist movement patterns in a destination; A GIS approach. *Tourism and Hospitality Research* 7, 39–49.

Law, R., Bai, B. and Leung, B. (2008) Travel website use and cultural influence: A comparison between American and Chinese travellers. *Information Technology & Tourism* 10, 215–225.

Law, R., Qi, S. and Buhalis, D. (2010) Progress in tourism management: A review of website evaluation in tourism research. *Tourism Management* 31, 297–313.

Lee, D. and Pearce, P.L. (2002) Community attitudes to the acceptability of user fees in natural settings. *Tourism and Hospitality Research* 4, 158–173.

Lee, J., Soutar, G. and Daly, T. (2007) Tourists' search for different types of information: A cross national study. *Information Technology & Tourism* 9, 165–176.

Lefcourt, H.M. (2005) Humour. In C.R. Snyder and S.J. Lopez (eds) *Handbook of Positive Psychology* (pp. 619–631) Oxford: Oxford University Press.

Lincoln, S.R. (2009) *Mastering Web 2.0: Transforming your Business Using Key Website and Social Media Tools*. London: Kogan Page.

Lipman, M. and Murphy, L. (in press) 'Make haste slowly': Environmental sustainability and willing workers on organic farms. In S. Fullagar, K. Markwell and E. Wilson (eds) *Slow Mobilities: Experiencing Slow Travel and Tourism*. Bristol: Channel View Publications.

Loftus, E. (1997) Creating false memories. *Scientific American* 277, 7–75.

Loomis, R. (1987) *Museum Visitor Evaluation*. Nashville, TN: American Association for the State and Local History.

Lue, C., Crompton, J. and Fesenmaier, D. (1993) Conceptualization of multi-destination pleasure trips. *Annals of Tourism Research* 20, 289–301.

Lynch, K. (1960) *The Image of the City*. Cambridge, MA: MIT Press.

MacCannell, D. (1973) Staged authenticity: Arrangements of social space in tourist settings. *The American Journal of Sociology* 79, 589–603.

MacCannell, D. (1976) *The Tourist: A New Theory of the Leisure Class*. New York: Schocken Books.

MacLaurin, T.L. (2003) The importance of food safety in travel planning and destination selection. In C.M. Hall, D.J. Timothy and D.T. Duval (eds) *Safety and Security in Tourism* (pp. 233–258). New York: Haworth Hospitality Press.

Mannell, R. and Iso-Ahola, S. (1987) Psychological nature of leisure and tourism experience. *Annals of Tourism Research* 14, 314–331.

Manning, R.E. (1997) Social carrying capacity of parks and outdoor recreation areas. *Parks and Recreation* 32, 32–38.

Manning, R.E. (1999) *Crowding in Outdoor Recreation: Use Level, Perceived Crowding and Satisfaction*. Corvallis, OR: Oregon State University Press.

Manning, R.E., Lime, D., Hof, M. and Freimund, W. (1995) The visitor experience and resource protection (VERP) process: The application of carrying capacity to Arches National Park. *The George Wright Forum* 12, 41–55.

Manning, R.E., Valliere, W., Wang, B. and Jacobi, C. (1999) Crowding norms: Alternative measurement approaches. *Leisure Sciences* 21, 219–229.

Mansfeld, Y. (1992) From motivation to actual travel. *Annals of Tourism Research* 19, 399–419.

Maoz, D. (2005) Young adult Israeli backpackers in India. In C. Noyand and E. Cohen (eds) *Israeli Backpackers: From Tourism to Rite of Passage* (pp. 159–188). New York: State University of New York Press.

Maoz, D. and Bekerman, Z. (2010) Searching for Jewish answers in Indian resorts: The postmodern traveler. *Annals of Tourism Research* 37, 423–439.

Markwell, K.W. (2000) Photo-documentation and analyses as research strategies in human geography. *Australian Geographical Studies* 38, 91–98.

Martin, G.N., Carlson, N.R. and Buskist, W. (2007). *Psychology* (3rd edn). Harlow: Pearson.

Martin, R.A. (2007) *The Psychology of Humor: An Integrative Approach.* Burlington, MA: Elsevier Academic Press.

Masberg, B.A. (1998) Defining the tourist: Is it possible? A view from the convention and visitors bureau. *Journal of Travel Research* 37, 67–70.

Mazanec, J.A. (2011) Marketing science perspectives of tourism. In P.L. Pearce (ed.) *The Study of Tourism: Foundations from Psychology* (pp. 79–92). Bingley: Emerald.

McCabe, S. (2009) Who is a tourist? Conceptual and theoretical developments. In J. Tribe (ed.) *Philosophical Issues in Tourism* (pp. 25–42). Bristol: Channel View Publications.

McCarthur, S. (2000) Beyond carrying capacity: Introducing a model to monitor and manage visitor activity in forests. In X. Font and J. Tribe (eds) *Forest Tourism and Recreation: Case Studies in Environmental Management* (pp. 259–278). Wallingford: CABI Publishing.

McElroy, J.L., Tarlow, P. and Carlisle, K. (2008) Tourist harassment and responses. In A. Woodside and D. Martin (eds) *Tourism Management Analysis, Behaviour and Strategy* (pp. 94–106). Wallingford, Oxon: CABI.

McGehee, N. (2002) Alternative tourism and social movements. *Annals of Tourism Research* 29, 124–143.

McMullan, R., Edwards, P.J., Kelly, M.J., Millar, B.C., Rooney, P.J. and Moore, J.E. (2007) Food-poisoning and commercial air travel. *Travel Medicine and Infectious Disease* 5, 276–286.

McNulty, A.M., Egan, C., Wand, H. and Donovan, B. (2010) The behaviour and sexual health of young international travellers (backpackers) in Australia. *Sexually Transmitted Infections* 86, 247–250.

McTaggart, R. (1991) *Action Research: A Short Modern History.* Geelong, Victoria: Deakin University.

Melton, A.W. (1972) Visitor behavior in museums: Some early research in environmental design. *Human Factors* 14, 393–403.

Michalko, G. (2003) Tourism eclipsed by crime: The vulnerability of foreign tourists in Hungary. In C.M. Hall, D.J. Timothy and D.T. Duval (eds) *Safety and Security in Tourism* (pp. 159–172). New York: Haworth Hospitality Press.

Mitchell, M. (1996) Police coping with death: Assumptions and rhetoric. In G. Howarth and P.C. Jupp (eds) *Contemporary Issues in the Sociology of Death, Dying and Disposal* (pp. 137–148). London: MacMillan.

Modsching, M., Kramer, R., ten Hagen, K. and Gretzel, U. (2007) Effectiveness of mobile recommender systems for tourist destinations: A user evaluation. *Intelligent Data Acquisition and Advanced Computing Systems: Technology and Applications*, IDAACS, 4th IEEE Workshop.

Mohsin, A. and Christie, M.F. (2000) *Alternative forms of learning and contemporary trends in hospitality and tourism training.* Online document: http://www.pedu.chalmers.se/inst/pdf/alternative.pdf. Accessed 12.02.07.

Molz, J.G. (2009) Representing place in tourism mobilities: Staycations, slow travel and the amazing race. *Journal of Tourism and Cultural Change 7*, 270–286.

Morgan, M., Lugosi, P. and Brent Ritchie, J.R. (eds) (2010) *The Tourism and Leisure Experience: Consumer and Managerial Perspectives*. Bristol: Channel View Publications.

Morrison, A. (2010) *Hospitality and Travel Marketing* (4th edn). New York: Delmar.

Moscardo, G. (1999) *Making Visitors Mindful: Principles for Creating Quality Sustainable Visitor Experiences through Effective Communication*. Champaign, IL: Sagamore Publishing.

Moscardo, G. (ed.) (2008) *Building Community Capacity for Tourism Development*. Wallingford, Oxon: CABI.

Moscardo, G. (2010a) The shaping of tourist experience: The importance of stories and themes. In M. Morgan, P. Lugosi and J.R. Brent Ritchie (eds) *The Tourism and Leisure Experience* (pp. 43–58). Bristol: Channel View Publications.

Moscardo, G. (2010b) Tourism research ethics: Current considerations and future options. In D.G. Pearce and R. Butler (eds) *Tourism Research: A 20-20 Vision* (pp. 203–214). Oxford: Goodfellow.

Moscardo, G., Ballantyne, R. and Hughes, K. (2008) *Designing Interpretive Signs*. Golden, Colorado: Fulcrum.

Moscardo, G. and Pearce, P.L. (2003) Presenting destinations: Marketing host communities. In S. Singh, D. Timothy and R.K. Dowling (eds) *Tourism in Destination Communities* (pp. 253–272). New York: CAB International.

Moscardo, G. and Pearce, P.L. (2007). The rhetorix and reality of structured tourism work experiences: A social representational analysis. *Tourism Recreation Research 32*, 21–28.

Moscardo, G., Pearce, P.L., Morrison, A., Green, D. and O'Leary, J.T. (2000) Developing a typology for understanding visiting friends and relatives markets. *Journal of Travel Research 38*, 251–259.

Moscovici, S. (1984) The phenomenon of social representations. In R.M. Farr and S. Moscovici (eds) *Social Representations* (pp. 3–70). Cambridge: Cambridge University Press.

Moscovici, S. (1988) Notes towards a description of social representations. *European Journal of Social Psychology 18*, 211–250.

Moscovici, S. and Hewstone, M. (1983) Social representaions and social expalanations: From the naïve to the amateur scientist. In M. Hewstone (ed.) *Attribution Theory* (pp. 98–124). Oxford: Basil Blackwell.

Moss Kanter, R. (1989) *When Giants Learn to Dance*. New York: Simon & Schuster.

Murphy, L.E. (2001) Exploring social interactions of backpackers. *Annals of Tourism Research 28*, 50–67.

Murphy, L.E., Moscardo, G., Benckendorff, P. and Pearce, P.L. (2011) *Tourist Shopping Villages: Forms and Functions*. New York: Routledge.

Murphy, P. and Murphy, A. (2004) *Strategic Management for Tourism Communities: Bridging the Gaps*. Clevedon: Channel View Publications.

Nawijn, J. (2010) The holiday happiness curve: A preliminary investigation into mood during a holiday abroad. *International Journal of Tourism Research 12*, 281–290.

Newman, O. (1972) *Defensible Space: Crime Prevention through Urban Design*. New York: MacMillan.

Newman, O. (1995) Defensible space: A new physical planning tool for urban revitalization. *Journal of the American Planning Association 61*, 149–155.

Niblo, D.M. and Jackson, M.S. (2004) Model for combining the qualitative emic approach with the quantitative derived etic approach. *Australian Psychologist 39*, 127–133.

Nisbett, R.E. (2003) *The Geography of Thought*. Nicholas Brearley: London.

Noy, C. (2004) This trip really changed me: Backpackers' narratives of self-change. *Annals of Tourism Research* 31, 78–102.

Noy, C. (2005) Israeli backpackers: Narrative, interpersonal communication, and social construction. In C. Noy and E. Cohen (eds) *Israeli Backpackers* (pp. 111–152). New York: State University of New York.

O'Leary, J.T. (2011) Finding tourism. In P.L. Pearce (ed.) *The Study of Tourism: Foundations from Psychology* (pp. 99–114). Bingley: Emerald.

Oddou, G., Mendenhall, M.E. and Ritchie, J.B. (2000) Leveraging travel as a tool for global leadership development. *Human Resource Management* 39, 159–172.

Oldham, G.R. (1988) Effects of changes in workspace partitions and spatial density on employee reactions: A quasi-experiment. *Journal of Applied Psychology* 73, 253–258.

Olds, J. (1977) *Drives and Reinforcement: Behavioral Studies of Hypothalamic Functions.* New York: Raven Press.

Oliver, T. (2001) The consumption of tour routes in cultural landscapes. In J.A. Mazanec, G.I. Crouch, J.R. Brent Ritchie and A.G. Woodside (eds) *Consumer Psychology of Tourism, Hospitality and Leisure* (Vol. 2, pp. 273–284). Wallingford, Oxon: CABI.

Olsen, K. (2007) Staged authenticity: A grand idée? *Tourism Recreation Research* 32, 83–85.

Ormiston, D., Gilbert, A. and Manning, R. (1997) Indicators and standards of quality for ski resort management. *Journal of Travel Research* 36, 35–42.

Outhwaite, W. (2000) The philosophy of social science. In B.S. Turner (ed.) *The Blackwell Companion to Social Theory* (2nd edn, pp. 47–70). Oxford: Blackwell.

Paganelli, F. and Giuli, D. (2008) Context-aware information services to support tourist communities. *Information Technology & Tourism* 10, 313–327.

Panksepp, J. (1992) A critical role for affective neuroscience resolving what is basic about basic emotions. *Psychological Review* 99, 554–560.

Panksepp, J. (1998) *Affective Neuroscience: The Foundations of Human and Animal Emotions.* London: Oxford University Press.

Panksepp, J. (2005) Affective consciousness: Core emotional feelings in animals and humans. *Consciousness and Cognition* 14, 30–80.

Panksepp, J. and Biven, L. (2010) *The Archaeology of the Mind.* New York: W.W. Norton.

Park, N., Peterson, C. and Seligman, M. (2005) *Character Strengths in Forty Nations and Fifty States.* Unpublished manuscript, University of Rhode Island.

Parolin, B.P. (2001) Structure of day trips in the Illawarra Tourism region of New South Wales. *Journal of Tourism Studies* 12, 11–27.

Patterson, T.M., Niccolucci, V. and Bastianoni, S. (2006) Beyond 'more is better': Ecological footprint accounting for tourism and consumption in Val di Merse, Italy. *Ecological Economics* 62, 747–756.

Pearce, D.G. (1995) *Tourism Today: A Geographical Analysis* (2nd edn). Harlow: Longman.

Pearce, P.L. (1977) Mental Souvenirs: A study of tourist and their city maps. *Australian Journal of Psychology* 29, 203–210.

Pearce, P.L. (1981) Route maps: A study of travellers' perception of a section of countryside. *Journal of Environmental Psychology* 1, 141–155.

Pearce, P.L. (1982) *The Social Psychology of Tourist Behaviour.* Oxford: Pergamon.

Pearce, P.L. (1989) Towards the better management of tourist queues. *Tourism Management* 10, 279–284.

Pearce, P.L. (1990) *The Backpacker Phenomenon.* Townsville, QLD: James Cook University.

Pearce, P.L. (1992) Fundamentals of tourist motivation. In D. Pearce and R. Butler (eds) *Tourism Research: Critiques and Challenges* (pp. 85–105). London: Routledge and Kegan Paul.

Pearce, P.L. (1999) Touring for pleasure: Studies of the senior self-drive travel market. *Tourism Recreation Research* 24, 35–42.

Pearce, P.L. (2004) Theoretical innovation in Asia Pacific tourism research. *Asia Pacific Journal of Tourism Research* 9, 57–70.

Pearce, P.L. (2005) *Tourist Behaviour: Themes and Conceptual Schemes.* Clevedon: Channel View Publications.

Pearce, P.L. (2007) Persisting with authenticity. *Tourism Recreation Research* 32, 86–90.

Pearce, P.L. (2009) Now that is funny humour in tourism settings. *Annals of Tourism Research* 36, 627–644.

Pearce, P.L. (2010) New directions for considering tourists' attitudes towards others. *Tourism Recreation Research* 35, 251–258.

Pearce, P.L. (in press a) Travel motivation, benefits and constraints to destinations. In R. Wang and A. Pizam (eds) *Destination Marketing and Management.* Wallingford, Oxon: CABI.

Pearce, P.L. (in press b) Tourists' written reactions to poverty in Southern Africa. *Journal of Travel Research.*

Pearce, P.L. and Coghlan, A. (2008) The dynamics behind volunteer tourism. In S. Wearing and K. Lyons (eds) *Journeys of Discovery: International Case Studies in Volunteer Tourism* (pp. 130–143). Wallingford, Oxon: CABI.

Pearce, P.L. and Fenton, M. (1994) Multidimensional scaling and tourism research. In J.R. Brent Richie and C.R. Goeldner (eds) *Travel, Tourism, and Hospitality Research: A Handbook for Managers and Researchers* (pp. 523–532). New York: John Wiley & Sons, Inc.

Pearce, P.L., Focken, K., Kanlayanasukho, V., Smith, S. and Semone, P. (2009) Tourist scams in Thailand. Unpublished manuscript, Assumption University of Thailand and James Cook University, Australia.

Pearce, P.L. and Foster, F. (2007) A 'University of Travel': Backpacker learning. *Tourism Management* 28, 1285–1298.

Pearce, P.L. and Lee, U. (2005) Developing the travel career approach to tourist motivation. *Journal of Travel Research* 43, 226–237.

Pearce, P.L. and Maoz, D. (2008) Novel insights into the identity changes among backpackers. *Tourism Culture and Communication* 8, 27–43.

Pearce, P.L. and Panchal, J. (2010) The integration of health as a travel motive in the travel career pattern (TCP) model. Asia Pacific Tourism Research Association Conference, Macau (pp. 37–40).

Pearce, P.L. and Thomas, M. (2010) Mapping the road; Developing the cognitive mapping methodology for accessing road trip memories. In B. Prideaux and D. Carson (eds) *Drive Tourism – Trends and Emerging Markets* (pp. 263–277). London: Routledge.

Pearce, P.L., Morrison, A. and Rutledge, J. (1998) *Tourism: Bridges across Continents.* Sydney, Australia: McGraw-Hill.

Pearce, P.L., Moscardo, G. and Ross, G. (1996) *Tourism Community Relationships.* Oxford: Elsevier Science Ltd.

Pearce, P.L., Murphy, L. and Brymer, E. (2009) *Evolution of the Backpacker Market and the Potential for Australian Tourism.* Brisbane: CRC Sustainable Tourism.

Pearce, P.L., Son, A. and Wu, Y. (2008) Developing a framework for assessing visitors' responses to Chinese cities. *China Tourism Research* 4, 22–44.

Pennington-Gray, L., Lane, C.W. and Holdnak, A. (2003) Developing a typology for understanding VFR as a primary purpose vs. VFR as a type of accommodation. In R. Schuster, comp. (ed.) *Proceedings of the 2002 Northeastern Recreation Research Symposium. Gen. Tech. Rep. NE-302* (pp. 190–193). Newtown Square, PA: U.S. Department of Agriculture, Forest Service, Northeastern Research Station.

Peters, T. (2005) *Essentials Design.* London: DK.

Peterson, C. and Seligman, M.E.P. (2004) *Character Strengths and Virtues: A Handbook and Classification*. Washington, DC: American Psychological Association.

Pike, K.L. (1966) *Language in Relation to a Unified Theory of the Structure of Human Behavior*. The Hague: Mouton.

Pine, B.J. and Gilmore, J.H. (1999) *The Experience Economy: Work is Theatre and Every Business a Stage*. Boston: Harvard Business School Press.

Pizam, A. (2011) This I believe. In P.L. Pearce (ed.) *The Study of Tourism: Foundations from Psychology* (pp. 63–78). Bingley: Emerald.

Pizam, A. and Mansfeld, J. (eds) (1996) *Tourism, Crime and International Security Issues*. New York: Wiley.

Pizam, A. and Mansfeld, J. (eds) (2006) *Tourism Security and Safety: From Theory to Practice*. New York: John Wiley.

Pizam, A. and Mansfield, Y. (2000) *Consumer Behaviour in Travel and Tourism*. New York: The Haworth Hospitality Press.

Pizam, A., Tarlow, P. and Bloom, J. (1997) Making tourists feel safe: Whose responsibility is it? *Journal of Travel Research* 36, 23–29.

Plog, S.J. (2011) Tourism research: A pragmatist's perspective. In P.L. Pearce (ed.) *The Study of Tourism Foundations from Psychology* (pp. 43–60). Bingley: Emerald.

Prentice, R. (2003) Revisiting 'heritage: A key sector of the (then) 'New' tourism': Out with the 'new' and out with 'heritage'? In C. Cooper (ed.) *Classic Reviews in Tourism* (pp. 164–191). Clevedon: Channel View Publications.

Priskin, J. (2003) Tourist perceptions of degradation caused by coastal nature-based recreation. *Environmental Management* 32, 189–204.

Pritchard, M. and Havitz, M.E. (2006) Destination appraisal: An analysis of critical incidents. *Annals of Tourism Research* 33, 25–46.

Quenza, C.J.P. (2005) On the structural approach to social representations. *Theory & Psychology* 15, 77–100.

Ramey, J. and Boren, T. (2001) *Keep Them Thinking Aloud: Two Ways to Conduct a Verbal Protocol and Why it Matters*. Las Vegas, NV: Usability Professional Association, 2001 Conference.

Rees, W.E. (2000) Eco-footprint analysis: Merits and brickbats. *Ecological Economics* 32, 371–374.

Ritzer, G. (2004) *The Globalization of Nothing*. Thousand Oaks, CA: Pine Forge Pr.

Robinson, E.S. (1928) The behaviour of the museum visitor. Cited in P. Bell, J. Fisher and R. Loomis (eds) (1978) *Environmental Psychology*. Philadelphia: W.B. Saunders.

Rogers, E. (2003) *Diffusion of Innovations* (5th edn). New York: Free Press.

Roggenbuck, J.W., Loomis, R.J. and Dagostino, J.V. (1991) The learning benefits of leisure. In B.L. Driver, P.J. Brown and G.L. Peterson (eds) *Benefits of Leisure* (pp. 195–214). State College, Pennsylvania: Venture Publishing Inc.

Rogstad, K. (2004) Sex, sun, sea, and STIs: Sexually transmitted infections acquired on holiday. *British Medical Journal* 329, 214–217.

Ross, A. (1999) *The Celebration Chronicles: Life Liberty and the Pursuit of Property Values in Disney's New Town*. New York: Ballantine.

Ross, M.B., Erickson, L.B. and Schopler, J. (1973) Affect, facial regard and reactions to crowding. *Journal of Personality and Social Psychology* 28, 69–76.

Rotton, J. (1992) Trait humour and longevity: Do comics have the last laugh? *Health Psychology* 11, 262–266.

Rounds, J. (2004) Strategies for the curiosity-driven museum visitor. *Curator: The Museum Journal* 47, 389–411.

Rouphael, A.B. and Hanafy, M. (2007) An alternative management framework to limit the impact of SCUBA divers on coral assemblages. *Journal of Sustainable Tourism* 15, 91–103.

Ruch, W. (1993) Exhilaration and humour. In M. Lewis and J.M. Haviland (eds) *Handbook of Emotions* (pp. 605–616). New York, NY: Guilford.

Ruch, W. (1994) Temperament, Eysenck's PEN system and humor related traits. *Humor. International Journal of Humor Research* 7, 209–244.

Ruch, W. and Hehl, F.J. (1998) A two mode model of humour appreciation: Its relation to aesthetic appreciation and simplicity-complexity of personality. In W. Ruch (ed.) *The Sense of Humour* (pp. 109–142). Berlin: Mouton de Gruyter.

Rustemli, A. (1992) Crowding effects of density and interpersonal distance. *The Journal of Social Psychology* 132, 51–58.

Ryan, C. (1993) Crime, violence, terrorism and tourism an accidental or intrinsic relationship? *Tourism Management* 14, 173–183.

Ryan, C. (1995) *Researching Tourist Satisfaction: Issues, Concepts, Problems*. London: Routledge.

Ryan, C. (1997) *The Tourist Experience: A New Introduction*. New York: Cassell.

Ryan, C. and Collins, A. (2008) Entertaining international visitors – The hybrid nature of tourism shows. *Tourism Recreation Research* 33, 143–149.

Ryan, C. and Kinder, R. (1996) The deviant tourist and the crimogenic place-the case of the tourist and the New Zealand prostitutue. In A. Pizam and J. Mansfeld (eds) *Tourism, Crime and International Security Issues* (pp. 37–49). New York: Wiley.

Sax, J.L. (1980) *Mountains without Handrails*. Ann Arbor, MI: The University of Michigan Press.

Scales, R.H. (2009) The past and present as prologue: Future warfare through the lens of contemporary conflicts. The future of the U.S. military series. Center for a New American Security.

Schaad, E. (2008) Perceptions of Scandinavia and the rhetoric of touristic stereotypes in internet travel accounts. *Scandinavian Studies* 80, 201–239.

Schellinck, D.A. (1982) Cue choice as a function of time pressure and perceived risk. In *Advances in Consumer Research* (pp. 470–475). Ann Arbor, MI: Association for Consumer Research.

Scheyvens, R. (2001) Poverty tourism. *Development Bulletin* 55, 18–21.

Scheyvens, R. (2007) Exploring the tourism–poverty nexus. *Current Issues in Tourism* 10, 231–254.

Schilcher, D. (2007) Growth versus equity: The continuum of pro-poor tourism and neoliberal governance. *Current Issues in Tourism* 10, 166–193.

Schmitt, B.H. (2003) *Customer Experience Management*. Hoboken, NJ: John Wiley & Sons.

Scott, T. (2007) Expression of humour by emergency personnel involved in sudden death. *Mortality* 12, 350–363.

Seidman, S. (ed.) (1996) *Queer Theory/Sociology*. Cambridge, MA: Blackwell.

Seligman, M.E.P. (2000) The positive perspective. *The Gallup Perspective* 3, 2–7.

Selwyn, T. (ed.) (1996) *The Tourist Image: Myths and Myth Making in Tourism*. West Sussex: Wiley.

Sen, A. (2000) A decade of human development. *Journal of Human Development* 1, 17–23.

Serrell, B. (1997) Paying attention: The duration and allocation of visitors' time in museum exhibitions. *Curator: The Museum Journal* 40, 108–125.

Shapiro, M. (2004) *A Sense of Place. Great Travel Writers Talk About their Craft, Lives and Inspiration*. San Francisco: Travelers' Guides.

Sharpley, R. (2009) *Tourism Development and the Environment; Beyond Sustainability?* London: Earthscan.

Shaw, M. (2009) Consumers relying on in-car navigation and voice. Online document: http://hothardware.com/News/Consumers-Relying-on-InCar-Navigation-More/. Accessed 20.10.10.

Shaw, M.T.M. and Leggat, P.A. (2009) Illness and injury to travellers on a premium seniors' tour to Indo-China. *Travel Medicine and Infectious Disease* 7, 367–370.

Shelby, B. and Heberlein, T. (1984) A conceptual framework for carrying capacity deter-mination. *Leisure Sciences* 6, 433–451.

Shelby, B., Vaske, J.J. and Donnelly, M.P. (1996) Norms, standards, and natural resources. *Leisure Sciences* 18, 103–123.

Shelby, B., Vaske, J.J. and Harris, R. (1988) User standards for ecological impacts at wilder-ness campsites. *Journal of Leisure Research* 20, 245–256.

Sheldon, P. (1997) *Tourism Information Technology*. Oxford: CAB.

Siegel, J. and Shaughnessy, M.F. (1996) An interview with Bernard Weiner. *Educational Psychology Review* 8, 165–174.

Sigala, M., Mich, L. and Murphy, J. (eds) (2007) *Information and Communication Technologies in Tourism*. Vienna, Austria: Springer Computer Science.

Simmel, G. (1950) *The Sociology of Georg Simmel* (H. Woolf, trans.). New York: Free Press of Glencoe.

Simmel, G. (1971) *Individuality and Social Forms*. Chicago: University of Chicago Press.

Slow Travel Website. (2008) Available: http://www.slowtrav.com/.

Smith, S. and Lee, H. (2010) A typology of 'theory' in tourism. In D.G. Pearce and R. Butler (eds) *Tourism Research: A 20-20 Vision* (pp. 28–39). Oxford: Goodfellow.

Smith, S.L.J. (1989) *Tourism Analysis: A Handbook*. New York: John Wiley & Sons.

Smithson, M., Amato, P. and Pearce, P.L. (1983) *Dimensions of Helping Behaviour*. Oxford: Pergamon Press.

Smithson, M. and Verkuilen, J. (2006) *Fuzzy Set Theory Applications in the Social Sciences*. Thousand Oaks, CA: Sage Publications.

Snow, C.P. (1960) *The Two Cultures*. Cambridge: Cambridge University Press.

Solomon, J. (1996) Humour and aging well: A laughing matter or a matter of laughing. *American Behavioral Scientist* 39, 249–271.

Sonak, S. (2004) Ecological footprint of production: A tool to assess environmental impacts of tourist activity. *Journal of Tourism Studies* 15, 2–12.

Sontag, S. (1979) *On Photography*. London: Penguin.

Stajano, F. and Wilson, P. (2009) Understanding scam victims: Seven principles for sys-tems security. Technical report UCAM-CL-TR-754, University of Cambridge Computer Laboratory, Sep. 2009 (Computing). On WWW at http://www.cl.cam.ac.uk/techreports/UCAM-CL-TR-754.pdf.

Stankey, G.H. and Lime, D.W. (1973) *Recreational Carrying Capacity: An Annotated Bibliography*. Ogden, UT: USDA Forest Service Intermountain Forest and Range Experiment Station.

Stebbins, R. (2007) *Serious Leisure a Perspective for Our Time*. New Brunswick, NJ: Transaction Publishers.

Stoeckl, N. (2008) Enhancing local economic benefits of tourism. In G. Moscardo (ed.) *Building Community Capacity for Tourism Development* (pp. 16–28). Wallingford, Oxon: CABI.

Stryker, S. (1987) Identity theory: Developments and extensions. In K. Yardley and T. Honess (eds) *Self and Identity* (pp. 89–104). New York: Wiley.

Sulaiman, S., Mohamed, H., Arshad, M.R.M., Rashid, N.A.A. and Yusof, U.K. (2009) Hajj-QAES: A knowledge-based expert system to support hajj pilgrims in decision making. *Computer Technology and Development ICCTD* 2009, 442–446.

Swain, M.M. and Momsen, J.H. (eds) (2002) *Gender/Tourism/Fun?* New York: Cognizant Communication.

Swarbrooke, J. (1999) *Sustainable Tourism Management*. Wallingford, Oxon: CABI Publishing.

Sweet, J.D. (1989) Burlesquing 'The other' in Pueblo performance. *Annals of Tourism Research* 16, 62–75.

SWOV (2009) Safety effects of navigation systems – Online document: http://www.swov.nl/rapport/Factsheets/UK/FS_Navigation_systems.pdf. Accessed 24.7.11.

Tajfel, H. (ed.) (1982) *Social Identity and Intergroup Relations.* Cambridge: Cambridge University Press.

Tajfel, H. and Turner, J.C. (1979) An integrative theory of intergroup conflict. In W. Austin and S. Worchel (eds) *The Social Psychology of Intergroup Relations* (pp. 33–47). Monterey: Brooks-Cole.

Tan, E.M., Foo, S., Goh, D.H. and Theng, Y. (2009) TILES: Classifying contextual information for mobile tourism applications. *Aslib Proceedings: New Information Perspectives* 61, 565–586.

Tao, T.C.H. (2006) Tourism as a livelihood strategy in indigenous communities: Case studies from Taiwan. Unpublished PhD, University of Waterloo, Ontario.

Tarlow, P.E. (2000) Creating safe and secure communities in economically challenging times. *Tourism Economics* 6, 139–149.

Tarlow, P.E. (2006) A social theory of terrorism and tourism. In A. Pizam and J. Mansfeld (eds) *Tourism Security and Safety: From Theory to Practice* (pp. 33–48). New York: John Wiley.

Tenner, E. (1997) *Why Things Bite Back: New Technology and the Revenge Effect.* London: Fourth Estate.

Thomas, R., Pigozzi, B.W. and Sambrook, R.A. (2005) Tourist carrying capacity measures: Crowding syndrome in the Caribbean. *The Professional Geographer* 57, 13–20.

Timothy, D. (2006) Safety and security issues in tourism. In D. Buhalis and C. Costa (eds) *Tourism Management Dynamics* (pp. 19–27). Oxford: Elsevier.

TOMTOM. (2008) *Independent Research Proves the Positive Influence of Satellite Navigation Devices on Driving and Traffic Safety.* TOMTOM, The Netherlands: TOMTOM.

Townsend, A. (2009) Foreword. In M. Foth (ed.) *Handbook of Research on Urban Informatics: The Practice and the Promise of the Real-Time City* (pp. xxiii–xxvi). Hershey, PA: Information Science Reference.

Tribe, J. (2004) Knowing about tourism: Epistemological issues. In J. Phillimore and L. Goodson (eds) *Qualitative Research in Tourism* (pp. 46–62). London: Routledge.

Tribe, J. (2008) Tourism: A critical business. *Journal of Travel Research* 46, 245–255.

Tribe, J. (2009) Philosophical issues in tourism. In J. Tribe (ed.) *Philosophical Issues in Tourism* (pp. 3–22). Bristol: Channel View Publications.

Tse, T.S.M. (2006) Crisis management in tourism. In D. Buhalis and C. Costa (eds) *Tourism Management Dynamics* (pp. 28–38). Oxford: Elsevier.

Tulving, E. (1983) *Elements of Episodic Memory.* Oxford: Clarendon Press.

Turner, J.C. (1991) *Social Influence.* Milton Keynes: Open University Press.

Turner, R.H. (1978) The role and the person. *American Journal of Sociology* 84, 1–23.

Turner, U. and Turner, E. (1978) *Image and Pilgrimage in Christian Culture.* New York: Columbia University Press.

Tussyadiah, I.P. and Fesenmaier, D.R. (2009) Mediating tourist experiences access to places via shared videos. *Annals of Tourism Research* 36, 24–40.

Twain, M. (1864) *The Innocents Abroad.* Reprinted Clinton, MA: Airmont Classic.

Ubiquitous Computing (2009) Technology to enhance Tokyo 2016 visitor experience – online document: http://www.sports-city.org/news_details.php?news_id=7085&idCategory=11. Accessed 11.02.09.

UNDP (1997) *Human Development Report 1997: Human Development to Eradicate Poverty.* New York: Oxford University Press.

United Nations (2000) *Millennium Summit Goals.* New York: United Nations.

United Nations World Tourism Organisation (UNWTO) (2004) *Management of World Heritage Areas.* Madrid: UNWTO.

University of Exeter (2009) The psychology of scams: Provoking and committing errors of judgement. Prepared for the Office of Fair Trading by the University of Exeter School of Psychology, May 2009.

Uriely, N. (2005) The tourist experience – Conceptual developments. *Annals of Tourism Research* 32, 199–216.

Uriely, N., Maoz, D. and Reichel, A. (2009) Israeli guests and Egyptian hosts in Sinai: A bubble of serenity. *Journal of Travel Research* 47, 508–522.

Urry, J. (1990) *The Tourist Gaze: Leisure and Travel in Contemporary Societies*. London: Sage.

Urry, J. (2000) *Sociology beyond Societies: Mobilities for the Twenty-First Century*. London: Routledge.

Urry, J. (2002) *The Tourist Gaze* (2nd edn). London: Sage.

van Egmond, T. (2007) *Understanding Western Tourists in Developing Countries*. Wallingford, Oxon: CABI.

Van Egmond, T. (2011) A career of wonder. In P.L. Pearce (ed.) *The Study of Tourism Foundations from Psychology* (pp. 115–132). Bingley: Emerald.

Vaske, J.J. and Donnelly, M.P. (2002) Generalizing the encounter–norm–crowding relationship. *Leisure Sciences* 24, 255–269.

Vaske, J.J., Graefe, A.R., Shelby, B. and Heberlein, T.A. (1986) Backcountry encounter norms – Theory, method and empirical-evidence. *Journal of Leisure Research* 18, 137–153.

Veal, A.J. (2005) *Business Research Methods – A Managerial Approach*. Frenchs Forest, NSW: Pearson Education Australia.

Venedig, G. (1997) Tourism and disability – Advances in holiday mainstreaming. *Rehabilitation* 36, 121–125.

Venetoulis, J., Chazan, D. and Gaudet, C. (2004) *Ecological Footprint of Nations*. Oakland: Redefining Progress.

Volkow, N.D., Fowler, J.S. and Wang, G.J. (2002) Role of dopamine in drug reinforcement and addiction in humans, results from imaging studies. *Behavioural Pharmacology* 13, 355–366.

Vonk, T., van Rooijen, T., Hogema, J. and Feenstra, P. (2007) *Do Navigation Systems Improve Traffic Safety?* Report TNO 2007-D-R0048/B. Soesterberg, The Netherlands: TNO Mobility and Logistics.

Wackernagel, M. (1999) An evaluation of the ecological footprint. *Ecological Economics* 31, 317–318.

Wackernagel, M. and Yount, J.D. (2000) Footprints for sustainability: The next steps. *Environment, Development and Sustainability* 2, 21–42.

Wainwrights, A. (1969) *Pennine Way Companion*. Kendal: Westmorland Gazette.

Waitt, G. and Markwell, K. (2006) *Gay Tourism Culture and Context*. New York: Haworth Hospitality Press.

Wall, G. (2000) Humour in tourism. In J. Jafari (ed.) *Encyclopedia of Tourism* (p. 291). London: Routledge.

Walle, A.H. (1997) Quantitative versus qualitative tourism research. *Annals of Tourism Research* 24, 524–536.

Walmsley, D.J. and Jenkins, J.M. (1991) Mental maps, locus of control, and activity: A study of business tourists in Coffs Harbour. *Journal of Tourism Studies* 2, 36–42.

Walmsley, D.J. and Jenkins, J.M. (1992) Tourism cognitive mapping of unfamiliar environments. *Annals of Tourism Research* 19, 268–286.

Walster, E., Berscheid, E. and Walster, G.W. (1973) New directions in equity research. *Journal of Personality and Social Psychology* 25, 151–176.

Walster, E., Walster, C.W. and Berscheid, E. (1978) *Equity: Theory and Research*. Boston, MA: Allyn & Bacon.

Wang, D., Fesenmaier, D., Werthner, H. and Wober, K. (2010) The journal of information technology and tourism: A content analysis of the past ten years. *Information Technology and Tourism* 12, 3–16.

Wang, Y. and Fesenmaier, D. (2003) Assessing motivation of contribution in online communities; An empirical investigation of an online travel community. *Electronic Markets* 13, 33–45.

Wang, Y. and Fesenmaier, D. (2004) Towards understanding members' general participation in and active contribution to an online travel community. *Tourism Management* 25, 709–722.

Warner, R. (1999) The emics and etics of quality of life assessment. *Social Psychiatry and Psychiatric Epidemiology* 34, 117–121.

Watson, A. (1995) Opportunities for solitude in the boundary waters canoe area wilderness. *Northern Journal of Applied Forestry* 12, 12–18.

Watts, J. (2010) *When a billion Chinese jump.* London: Faber & Faber.

Waugh, A. (1999) *Time.* London: Headline Book Publishing.

Wearing, S. (2001) *Volunteer Tourism: Experiences that Make a Difference.* New York: CABI.

Wearing, S. (2004) Examining best practice in volunteer tourism. In R.A. Stebbins and M. Graham (eds) *Volunteering as Leisure/Leisure as Volunteering: An International Assessment* (pp. 209–224). Wallingford, Oxon: CABI.

Weiner, B. (2000) Attributional thoughts about consumer behaviour. *The Journal of Consumer Research* 27, 382–387.

Weiner, B. (2008) Reflections on the history of attribution theory and research. *Social Psychology* 39, 151–156.

Weiner, B. (2010) The development of an attribution-based theory of motivation: A history of ideas. *Educational Psychologist* 45, 28–36.

Weiner, B., Russell, D. and Lerman, D. (1978) Affective consequences of causal ascriptions. In J.H. Harvey, W.J. Ickes and R. Kidd (eds) *New Directions in Attribution Research* (pp. 59–88). Hillsdale, NJ: Erlbaum.

Weiner, B., Russell, D. and Lerman, D. (1979) The cognition–emotion process in achievement related contexts. *Journal of Personality and Social Psychology* 37, 1211–1220.

Weiss, R. and Boutourline, S. (1963) The communication value of exhibits. *Museum News* 42, 23–27.

Westphal, M. and Waibal, A. (1999) *Towards Spontaneous Speech Recognition for On-Board Car Navigation and Information Systems.* University of Karlsruhe, Germany: Interactive Systems Laboratories.

White, N.R. and White, P.B. (2007) Home and away: Tourists in a connected world. *Annals of Tourism Research* 34, 88–104.

Wickens, E. (2002) The sacred and the profane. *Annals of Tourism Research* 29, 834–851.

Wilks, J., Watson, B. and Hansen, J. (2000) International drivers and road safety in Queensland, Australia. *Journal of Tourism Studies* 11, 36–43.

Wiseman, R. (2007) *Quirkology: The Curious Science of Everyday Lives.* London: Pan.

Wong, M., Chan, R. and Koh, D. (2007) HIV prevention among travelers: Why do men not use condoms when they engage in commercial sex overseas? *Sexually Transmitted Diseases* 34, 237–244.

Woodside A.G. and Ahn, I. (2008) Culture's consequences on experiencing international tourism services and products: Quantitative and qualitative fuzzy-set testing of an integrative theory of national culture applied to the consumption of behaviours of Asian, European and North American consumers. In A.G. Woodside and D. Martin (eds) *Tourism Management: Analysis, Behaviour and Strategy* (pp. 28–61). Wallingford: CABI.

Woodside, A.G., Cruickshank, B.F. and Dehuang, N. (2007) Stories visitors tell about Italian cities as destination icons. *Tourism Management* 28, 162–174.

World Tourism Organization (WTO) (1999) *International Tourism: A Global Perspective.* Madrid, Spain: WTO.

Wyer, R.S., and Collins, J.E. (1992) A theory of humour elicitation. *Psychological Review* 99, 663–688.

Xia, J., Evans, F.H., Spilsbury, K., Ciesielski, V., Arrowsmith, C. and Wright, G. (2010) Market segments based on the dominant movement patterns of tourists. *Tourism Management* 31, 464–469.

Yagi, C. and Pearce, P.L. (2007) The influence of appearance and the number of people viewed on tourists' preferences for seeing other tourists. *Journal of Sustainable Tourism* 15, 28–43.

Yeung, S., Wong, J. and Ko, E. (2004) Preferred shopping destination: Hong Kong vs. Singapore. *International Journal of Tourism Research* 6, 85–96.

Yiannakis, A. and Gibson, H. (1992) Roles tourists play. *Annals of Tourism Research* 19, 287–303.

Yoo, K.H. and Gretzel, U. (2008) What motivates consumers to write online travel reviews? *Information Technology & Tourism* 10, 283–295.

Young, J.M., Williams, D.R. and Roggenbuck, J.W. (1991) *The Role of Involvement in Identifying Users' Preference for Social Standards in the Cohutta Wilderness* (Vol. 12). Athens, GA: USDA Forest Service, Southeastern Forest Experiment Station.

Young, M. (1995) Black humour: Making light of death. *Policing and Society* 5, 151–167.

Young, M. (1999) Cognitive maps of nature based tourists. *Annals of Tourism Research* 26, 817–839.

Zadeh, L. (1998) Some reflections on the anniversary of fuzzy sets and systems. *Fuzzy Sets and Systems* 100, 5–7.

Zhang, G. (2003) Tourism research in China. In A.A. Lew, L. Yu, J. Ap and G. Zhang (eds) *Tourism in China* (pp. 67–81). New York: Haworth Hospitality Press.

Zhang, L., Pan, B., Smith, W. and Li, X. (2008) An exploratory study of travellers' use of online reviews and recommendations. *Information Technology & Tourism* 11, 157–167.

Zimbardo, P. and Boyd, J. (2008) *The Time Paradox.* London: Rider.

Zimbardo, P.G. and Boyd, J.N. (1999) Putting time in perspective; A valid reliable individual difference metric. *Journal of Personality and Social Psychology* 77, 271–288.

Zuckerman, J.N. (2009) Grass roots growing into travel medicine. *Travel Medicine and Infectious Disease* 7, 1.

Zukin, S. (1991) *Landscapes of Power: From Detroit to Disney World.* CA: The University of California Press.

Index

Author

Subject

attribution theory, 63
anomie, 73
Australia, 46
Australian tourists, 71, 72
Appalachian way (USA), 88
autobiographical, 120

Baedeker guides, 34
Bangladesh, 103
behaviour, 2, 3
benefits, 59
Botswana, 136, 137

Cabo Blanco, Costa Rica, 144
carrying capacity, 97
Chinese tourists, 32, 33
congestion, 94, 100
constant crowding, 98
constructivist, 17, 18
Cooktown, 121
crime, 71
crimogenic, 72
critical theory, 18, 19, 49, 56

deep processing, 119
Disneyfization, 50-51
domestic tourists, 5, 7

ecological footprints, 102-103
El Camino de Santiago
   (Spain) 88
emic approach, 10, 11
episodic memory, 120
epistemology, 5
equity theory, 143
evaluative dimensions, 98
expectations, 59
experience, 2-3

Facebook, 49
Flickr, 39
fluctuating crowding, 99
footprints, 83

generic skills, 123
German tourists, 71, 72
Germany, 46, 48
Ghana, 73, 143
Grand Canyon, 78, 79

hajj, 84
Hong Kong, 32, 100
hot spot theory, 73
humour, 145
hybridization, 52

identity theory, 116
international tourists, 5
interpretive paradigm, 17
Israel, 85
Italy, 46

Jerusalem, 43, 84, 86

Ka'aba, 84
Kenya, 144
knowledge management, 14, 15
knowledge transfer, 14
Kokoda trail (Papua New Guinea),
   88, 89

learning, 119
Libya, 46
limits to acceptable change
   approaches, 97
Lonely Planet, 34
lumpers, 6

Mecca, 84
micro-sociological approach, 116
Milan, 116
Milford track (New Zealand), 88
mindfulness, 92, 119
mindlessness, 92
mobilities approach, 6
Mozambique, 136, 137
mundane authenticity, 133

Nagasaki, 52
Namibia, 136
normative theory, 97

paradigm, 16
perceived crowding, 94-95, 98
personal identities, 115
Photobucket, 39
Picasa, 39
positivism, 17
post-positivism, 17, 56
poverty tourism, 135–136
project leisure, 142